Chemistry of Natural Products

Chemistry of Natural Products

A Laboratory Handbook

SECOND EDITION

N R Krishnaswamy

Former Professor and Head, Department of Chemistry
Sri Sathya Sai University
Prasanthi Nilayam

Universities Press

CRC Press
Taylor & Francis Group
Boca Raton London New York

CRC is an imprint of the Taylor & Francis Group,
an informa business

CHEMISTRY OF NATURAL PRODUCTS:
A LABORATORY HANDBOOK, Second Edition

UNIVERSITIES PRESS (INDIA) PRIVATE LIMITED

Registered Office
3-6-747/1/A & 3-6-754/1, Himayatnagar, Hyderabad 500 029, Telangana, India
info@universitiespress.com; www.universitiespress.com

Distributed by
Orient Blackswan Private Limited

Registered Office
3-6-752 Himayatnagar, Hyderabad 500 029, Telangana, India

Other Offices
Bengaluru, Bhopal, Chennai, Guwahati, Hyderabad, Jaipur, Kolkata, Lucknow, Mumbai, New Delhi, Noida, Patna, Vijayawada

First published 2003
Second edition 2012
Reprinted 2018

501470

Cover and book design

ISBN 978 81 7371 757 4

Typeset in CG Times 10.6/13.2 *by*
OSDATA, Hyderabad 500 029

Printed in India by
Navya Printers, Hyderabad 500 013

Published by
Universities Press (India) Private Limited
3-6-747/1/A & 3-6-754/1, Himayatnagar, Hyderabad 500 029, Telangana, India

Preface to the First Edition

Nature is an inexhaustible source of secondary metabolites—different types of alkaloids, terpenoids, phenolics and other classes of organic compounds. In the process of isolation, purification and determination of the structures of these compounds, every type of experimental tool and strategy, known to and developed over the years by practicing organic chemists, is used. Thus, a comprehensive study of a few naturally occurring organic compounds can help a student gain experimental expertise which will enable him (or her) to tackle any organic chemical problem. It is necessary to understand and realise that a complete study of a natural product involves unequivocal characterisation of the compound based on as many chemical reactions as possible, as well as the extensive use and interpretation of spectral data. Every attempt should also be made to confirm the structure by synthetic studies. If the compound is new, there is an element of mystery till the very end, and the thrill one feels when the final structure emerges as a clear picture is something worthy of experience. However, the path from the isolation to the determination of the final structure may often cover some rough and difficult terrain. If one does not consider the efforts needed to overcome the problem as drudgery, it is not only possible to enjoy working at the bench but also to gain very valuable experience from the exercise.

In order to drive home the point that the chemistry of natural products has every aspect of organic chemistry in its make up, the experiments in this book are classified under isolation and characterisation, chemical transformations and synthesis. The procedures described have been tested by the author and have been assigned as practical exercises to undergraduate and postgraduate students over a number of years. A few of the experiments require special equipment and instruments, but most of them can be carried out in any college laboratory. Some experimental areas of the subject bordering biology like chemical ecology, biosynthesis, chemotaxonomy and biological testing have been left out. Several more experiments could have been added under the topics covered, but for the constraints of size and cost. Suggestions for improvement are welcome.

In the preparation of this book, Dr Malladi Srinivas has rendered very valuable help and I wish to express my sincere thanks to him. The lessons that I have learnt from my teachers, colleagues and students are many and that experience has been used in the selection of the experimental procedures. I would like to tell my teacher, Prof. VVS Murti, that I have always remembered his admonition, ‘‘Never take a shortcut!’’.

However, I must admit that I have taken shortcuts through fields and waste grounds to collect plant materials. Years ago in a lecture given in Delhi, Prof. LH Briggs of New Zealand mentioned that he carried a pen knife, a pair of scissors and a few polythene bags while going for walks so that he could collect any interesting plant specimen seen on the road side. Perhaps, one could even think of rigging up a small kit for doing a few preliminary experiments as field trials while on a plant collection tour. The kit could have a spirit lamp, a few test tubes (small and large), prepared thin layer chromatographic plates, chromatographic paper, a pair of Petri dishes, a sprayer and a few bottles containing solvents and a few reagents. The list could be enlarged as long as the kit does not become too bulky.

I wish to thank everyone at Universities Press for their kind cooperation in bringing out this book. I must also add that I had to be prodded from time to time to get on with the book. I must thank my wife, Usha, for providing that stimulus.

Preface to the Second Edition

The objectives and scope of this book have been stated in the preface to the first edition. The emphasis is on experimental procedures and therefore the theory part is retained without any changes. However, additional references have been added under recommended additional reading at the end of Chapters 2 and 3 to make the students aware of some recent advances in methodology. On the other hand, additional experimental procedures have been added under Chapter 4, 5 and 6. It may be pointed out here that the theory part had been extensively revised and updated in the new edition of the companion volume, *Chemistry of Natural Products—A Unified Approach*.

In ths edition, two new chapters have been added. Chapter 7 describes experiments of a biochemical nature. Two of these are of relevance to drug metabolism. The substrates used are mangiferin, 7-hydroxy-4-phenylcoumarin and its methyl ether. Also included in this chapter is an experiment on the biochemical transformation of a natural product, namely bakuchiol. Chapter 8 lists ten suggested projects which can be taken up by senior students under the supervision of a teacher. Sufficient details are given under each of these projects but the students should also feel free to introduce innovations. A couple of the projects are designed to motivate students to examine natural sources not only for new compounds but also to explore their applications as antifungal compounds or as chemotaxonomic markers. Thus, in addition to additional material in Chapters 4, 5 and 6, two new chapters have been added to enlarge the scope of the book to make it useful to not only students of organic chemistry but also of biochemistry. Additional notes have been added on the collection and identification of plant materials. An appendix lists the preparation of more diagnostic chemical reagents used in the characterization of natural products. It is hoped that with these additions the book will serve better than before as a ready-to-reach laboratory handbook.

The author thanks Dr Perveen Sharma and Dr Vani Rao for some of the experimental procedures in Chapter 7.

Instructions for Students and Guidelines for Teachers

A chemical laboratory is a potential place for hazards. Safety measures have to be strictly and religiously followed inside a laboratory. Every laboratory should prominently display the precautions to be taken while handling chemicals and carrying out reactions, as well as the first aid measures to be taken in case of an accident. It is not possible to list here all the safety measures to be taken. However, a few important suggestions are mentioned, particularly with relevance to the experiments recommended in this book.

1. Students should never work alone in a laboratory. The presence of a teacher is absolutely essential. Students should strictly follow the instructions given by the supervising teacher.
2. It has been this author's experience that some students are allergic to some plants. Students who are susceptible to allergic complaints should avoid working with plants likely to cause allergy such as species of Parthenium, Eupatorium and pollen in general.
3. Most chemicals and solvents, if inhaled or improperly handled, particularly for prolonged periods of time, can prove to be toxic. For example, it is advisable to avoid the use of benzene which is carcinogenic, though it has been recommended in a few of the experiments in this book; it can be replaced by toluene. However, it can be used in small quantities, taking care that its vapours are not inhaled. Chemicals can also enter the body through the skin. Therefore, it is advisable to use a pair of gloves while working with them. Similarly, the use of pyridine should be minimal. Benzene is also volatile and highly inflammable. This fact should be kept in mind while removing the solvent from solutions made in benzene.
4. *o*-Methylation is an important reaction in the characterisation of phenols and sugars. The reagents used for this reaction,

namely diazomethane and dimethyl sulphate, are, however, toxic. Diazomethane should be generated only when needed inside a fume cupboard. In an undergraduate laboratory it is not advisable to distill it; it is better to use an ethereal solution of the reagent. Though a number of new diazomethane-generating reagents are now available, they are expensive. Nitrosomethylurea is a convenient source for the reagent but it is an explosive and should be prepared only when needed and immediately converted into diazomethane. However, acetyl methylurea from which nitrosomethylurea is obtained can be prepared and stored in a dry cold place. Its preparation and conversion into nitrosomethylurea are described in the appendix at the end of Chapter 3. Dimethyl sulphate is highly toxic and every care should be taken that it does not come into contact with the skin. Its purification, described in the appendix, should be done in the presence of the supervising teacher. Accidents have occurred due to careless handling of this chemical. Having said this, it should also be emphasised that it may not always be possible to avoid using toxic chemicals. What is imperative is to learn how to handle them. Besides an efficient fume cupboard, it is desirable to have close by an eye fountain and a shower. The laboratory should be very well ventilated.

5. Several liquid chemicals are sold in bottles with glass stoppers. Quite often, opening such a bottle may prove to be troublesome and the use of a little force may be necessary. When opening such a bottle, the mouth of the bottle should be kept as far away from the face and the body as possible. The bottle should be covered with a cloth and cooled in a container of ice cold water or an ice bath before opening it, as in the space above the surface of the liquid, there could be vapours which may escape forcibly when the stopper is removed. Further, it is necessary to cover one's nose and mouth and wear safety glasses while opening such bottles As a matter of fact, the last mentioned precautions may be taken while handling any volatile liquid or corrosive solid chemical.

A couple of guidelines for supervising teachers may not be out of place here.

1. As far as possible the teacher must perform an experiment which she or he wishes to prescribe before giving the instructions to the students. Almost all the experiments described in this book have been personally checked out by the author but a few have been taken from original research publications.
2. Personal continuous supervision of a student's bench work will greatly help a student improve her or his practical skills and techniques and will go a long way towards making the student a reliable experimentalist. This way it is possible to effectively impart whatever practical knowledge the teacher had learnt from his or her mentors.
3. It is imperative to insist and see to it that the students strictly adopt appropriate safety measures when doing an experiment.

A Note on the Collection and Identification of Plant Materials

It is desirable, whenever and wherever possible, to personally collect plant materials needed for one's work and get their identities confirmed with the help of a taxonomist. However, while doing so certain guidelines have to be followed. These have been clearly set out in the small monograph, *Guidelines on Good Agricultural and Collection Practices for Medicinal Plants*, brought out by the World Health Organisation (WHO), Geneva, in 2003. This book should serve as a ready reference guidebook for anyone working with medicinal plants. Some plants may be available in the neighbourhood, but care must be taken to see that the locations of collections are clean and free from contaminants such as animal waste, sewage water, industrial wastes, etc. Only healthy, disease-free plant specimens should be collected. If the collections are made from forests and other wild areas, it is better to take the help of the concerned forest officials/local guides who are familiar with the plant populations in the region. Local folklore and practitioners of indigenous systems of medicine can often give useful information regarding medicinally useful plants and how, where and when to collect them. Care should be taken not to indiscriminately collect rare and endangered species.

When going on a field trip for collection of plants, it is advisable to take along a few plastic mesh bags, some old sheets of newspaper, a pair of scissors, a pair of gloves and a notebook to write down the date and time of collection, location, vernacular names of plants and any other interesting information provided by the local people. You may need a spade and a knife (or a small machete) if you wish to collect underground parts such as roots or rhizomes. While collecting roots, care must be taken not to cut the main roots. The roots and rhizomes thus collected must be immediately cleaned to remove adhering soil matter, packed in a bag and labelled.

You may also need a knife if you want to scrape bark off a tree. While doing so care should be taken not to completely strip the tree of its bark cover. Longitudinal strips of bark from one side of a tree may be collected by careful cutting without harming the wood underneath. For the collection of heartwoods the help of a forest official has to be sought for. For example, in India, the divisional forest officers in different ranges in various parts of the country could provide the needed help. As a matter of fact, as far as possible, it is best to approach government agencies and institutions, such as the Forest Research Institute in Dehradun and its regional centre in Bengaluru, in order to avoid infringing laws covering preservation of forest wealth.

Tree parts can also be obtained from private and public gardens, whenever a tree is being pruned or cut, provided there is no doubt about the botanical identity of the tree. If it is a flowering tree, specimens of its flowers and leaves should also be collected for a firm identification by a botanist. Here, I wish to recall one incident. When I was doing research work for my doctorate degree in the University of Delhi under the supervision of Prof. TR Seshadri, more than fifty years ago, my laboratory mate was Dr RS Thakur who later became the Director, Central Institute of Medicinal Plants, Lucknow. One day, while he was coming from his home to the University in a bus, he saw a sisam tree (*Dalbegia sissoo*) being cut in one of the bungalows. He got down at the next bus stop, walked to the bungalow and requested the owner to give him a log of the wood, explaining that he needed it for his research. The owner was kind enough to oblige and my friend came to our laboratory with the wood and a few leaves and flowers for proper identification!

For medicinal and aromatic plants, such as, for example, the different cultivated varieties of lemon grass, the Central Institute of Medicinal Plants, Lucknow, and its regional centre in Bengaluru can be approached for help in collection. The National Botanical Gardens, Lucknow, the Lal Bagh Gardens, Bengaluru, the Department of Horticulture, Karnataka (this Department maintains well-kept gardens in other hill stations of the state), Ooty Botanical Gardens, Udhagamandalam in Tamil Nadu and the Departments of Horticulture in all the states of India can be approached for help. These as well as the Indian Institute of Horticultural Research in Bengaluru can provide flowers, particularly the different types of cultivars, chemotypes and phenotypes. The Lal Bagh gardens have an exotic collection of orchids. Plants used in agriculture, such as, species of Trifolium (for example seeds of *Trifolium alexandrinum*) can be obtained from the Indian Institute of Agricultural Research, New Delhi. In South India, the Western as well as the Eastern Ghats are rich sources of flora. There are reserved forests in these areas and one has to seek the permission of the concerned forest range officers for the collection of plant materials. The same applies to other hill regions in India such as those in Himachal Pradesh, Uttarakhand, the tribal areas of Chhattisgarh and other states.

Lichens can be collected from the Palani Hills in Tamil Nadu (in and around the hill station, Kodaikanal), the Nilagiri hills, also in Tamil Nadu, and other parts of the Western and Eastern Ghats. The Himalayan regions in Himachal Pradesh and Uttarakhand also have a number of different types of lichens. While field trips to these regions could be interesting, exciting and educative, it is better to get authentic specimens of lichens from a botanical garden such as the National Botanical Gardens in Lucknow. The Department of Botany, University of Lucknow, has specialised in lichen taxonomy. Ferns (pteridophytes) are seen in abundance in several parts of the Western Ghats in the South, and the Himalayan regions in the North. This author could collect silver fern from the forests surrounding the KR Hill station in Karnataka.

The marine algae mentioned under Project 5 in Chapter 8 can be obtained from the Regional Centre of the National Institute of Oceanography in Cochin. The Central Institute of Spices Research, Kozhikode, can be approached for procuring authentic specimens of different varieties of spices such as cinnamon, pepper, etc.

In some countries, such as the United States of America, collections of plant materials can be done only with permission from the concerned authorities such as the Department of Agriculture, the National Resources Conservation Service (NRCS) and the various National Parks. Ten years ago, during a visit, I could see a particularly good specimen of a Parmelia lichen sticking to a twig in the Yellowstone National Park; it was lying on the ground but could not be picked up as I had not obtained prior permission.

Such regulations are necessary to prevent indiscriminate removal of plants from their natural habitats.

In India and China, where medicinal plants are extensively used in the indigenous systems of medicine, there are a number of outlets, small and big, from where such plants can be procured. For example, *Eclipta alba* can be readily obtained from the local markets in Delhi. Similarly, *Wedelia calendulacea* is sold in shops dealing with herbal drugs in Chennai. However, the botanical identities of such plants obtained for research work should be unambiguously established. This also applies to personal collections. Voucher specimens should be preserved.

A phytochemist should have a library of various books dealing with the flora of the world as well as different countries and regions. The foremost among them, in this author's opinion, is *Makino's Flora of Japan*, as the illustrations therein are enough to enable even a layman identify a particular plant with a fair amount of certainty. The multivolume *Flora of British India* by JD Hooker and the *Flora of the Presdiency of Madras* by JS Gamble are extremely valuable to researchers in India. In his introduction to his flora, Gamble has recorded:

> *The Presidency of Madras presents, probably, a more varied flora than any other track of equal area in India, possibly in the World. This phenomenon is due to the combined effects of the geographical situation and its topography.*

This is not surprising, as the then Madras Presidency consisted of the present (entire) Tamil Nadu, the Malabar area of Kerala, the southern coastal belt of Karnataka, and a good chunk of the present day Andhra Pradesh (Rayalseema and the coastal districts). Several compendia of regional flora are also available. For example, *Vanaspathi Kosha—Plant Wealth of Sringeri, Karnataka* by Balkrishna Gowda is a useful guide to the plants of the Malnad area of Karnataka. The images in this book are useful for identification.

When field trips are made in forest areas, a first aid kit is an essential item to be taken. The rain forests in the Western Ghats are infested with leeches. It is also advisable to carry mosquito repellants.

Contents

CHAPTER 1

Introduction

The chemistry of natural products is a hybrid science combining in itself the theory of organic chemistry with experimentation. The term 'natural products' is used to describe secondary metabolites which are organic compounds of natural origin with molecular weight less than 1500 amu. The term thus excludes naturally occurring macromolecules such as proteins, nucleic acids and polysaccharides which are dealt with under biochemistry. The several groups of polyphenolic compounds, such as the anthocyanins, flavonoids, isoflavonoids, hydroxylated xanthones, quinones, cinnamic acids and coumarins, the different types of alkaloids, the large number of terpenoids (mono, sesqui, di, sester, tri and tetra) and related steroids, also qualify for the name 'natural products'.

For the successful elucidation of the structure of a naturally occurring organic compound, correct, reliable and reproducible experimental methods are as important as the scientific interpretation of the collected data. While there are a number of good source materials—textbooks, advanced texts and serial publications, apart from review articles in journals—providing a wealth of information on the theoretical aspects of the subject, there are very few books, directed towards undergraduate and postgraduate students, on the experimental methods pertaining to the different aspects of natural products. A few experiments such as the isolation of caffeine, nicotine, lycopene and a few other compounds are described in some laboratory manuals, which are otherwise largely devoted to analytical and preparative methods of organic chemistry. Therefore, the average student remains unexposed to the large amount of published experimental details of isolation, characterization and synthetic transformations of the wide variety of organic compounds occurring in nature, unless and until a research career in this area of chemistry is taken up.

An excellent book by Rosenthaler was available to the students of earlier generations, but it has been out of print for nearly seventy years. During this period, remarkable developments have taken place in the subject ranging from phytochemical studies to investigations of marine organisms and insect species. Two books which provide, to a certain extent, the vital link between the lecture hall and the laboratory are Harborne's *Phytochemical Methods* and Ikan's *Natural Products—A Laboratory Guide*. The latter has undergone two editions and is at present the only real guide available to students aspiring to experiment with compounds isolated from natural sources. Some of the earlier volumes of *Modern Methods of Plant Analysis* edited by Paech and Tracey also contain some useful procedural details; but these books are expensive and are not easily available to all students.

One of the reasons for the lack of 'recipe' books for natural products, comparable to 'organic synthesis', is the fact that experimentation in this field still retains the characteristics of an art and the skill is often handed down from a master to his students within a school specialising in one specific area of the subject. These groups have evolved their own approaches designed on the basis of their special interests. There is, thus, a degree of subjectivity in the selection of a procedure for the isolation and purification of a natural product which is usually dictated by the training obtained. On the other hand, with the advent of spectroscopic methods, characterisation techniques are now more or less standard for a particular type of compound. For example, for the characterisation of flavonoids, the technique of UV spectroscopy with the use of shift reagents occupies a prime place. For most other types of compounds, particularly the terpenoids, the different modes of NMR spectroscopy take precedence over other techniques.

In almost all cases, a certain amount of chemical data is essential for the complete and satisfactory understanding of the structure of a compound. For example, confirmation of the presence of a functional group by conversion into a suitable derivative will considerably strengthen the diagnosis obtained based on spectral data. This may be illustrated by taking the example of a compound containing one or more hydroxyl groups. In such a case, acylation and oxidation reactions will provide not only additional information but will also give more volatile and less polar derivatives amenable to easier spectroscopic studies. However, considering the fact that the majority of natural products are available only in milligram quantities, the present trend, understandably, is to rely heavily on spectroscopic methods.

Chemical methods are often cut down to the essential bare minimum unlike as in the past, when there was a large, if not exclusive, dependence on chemical methods. In the experimental section of this book, the accent is on a judicious combination of both types of data, so that the student can also experience the flavour of the past. Thus, after describing the isolation of a compound, its spectral characteristics and conversion into appropriate derivatives are also described. The focus is not on the individual compounds but on the methods. Therefore, the experiments are described under heads such as 'Isolation', 'Characterisation' and 'Synthetic transformations'.

The experimental section is preceded by a brief survey of the methods available for the extraction, fractionation of mixtures of different types of secondary metabolites of plant origin, and the isolation and preliminary characterisation of the individual compounds. This part of the book, though not exhaustive, will also be of use to students on the threshold of a research career in the chemistry of natural products. Since the main objective of the book is to provide students with procedural details for the successful isolation of different types of natural products, the first part of the book is kept as concise as possible. For more information, the books listed overleaf are recommended.

Recommended reading

1. Cannell RJP, (Ed.), *Natural Products Isolation*, Humana Press, New Jersey, 1998.
2. Harborne JB, *Phytochemical Methods*, 2nd Edition, Chapman & Hall, London, 1984.
3. Houghton PJ and Raman A, *Laboratory Handbook for the Fractionation of Natural Extracts*, Chapman & Hall, London, 1998.
4. Ikan R, *Natural Products—A Laboratory Guide*, 2nd Edition, Academic Press, London, 1991.
5. Paech K and Tracey MV, (Eds), *Modern Methods of Plant Analysis*, Vols 1–7, Springer–Verlag, Berlin, 1956–64.

CHAPTER 2

A Survey of the Methods of Extraction, Isolation and Fractionation of Naturally Occurring Organic Compounds

2.1 SELECTION OF THE MATERIAL

The first step in a phytochemical investigation is the selection and collection of the plant material. The choice of the plant is dictated by several factors such as any unique characteristic, for example, striking pigmentation, smell and, most importantly, known medicinal properties or other biological activities like toxicity towards animals or insects. Another factor could be a chemotaxonomic consideration. Several schools specialise in the chemistry of plants belonging to a particular family such as the Compositae, Guttiferae, Labiateae or subfamily like the Senecioideae of the Compositae or genera such as the Crotalaria of the Leguminoseae, Euphorbia of the Euphorbiaceae, etc. Groups specialising in a particular group of secondary metabolites, such as the flavonoids, select plants likely to contain such compounds based on the results of earlier studies. Well-established folklore often gives useful indications. For example, plants used as fish poisons by several native communities are likely to contain either rotenoids or saponins. Plants of the family Compositae often provide sesquiterpene lactones and polyacetylenes, besides other types of secondary metabolites. Flavonoid and anthocyanin pigments are widespread in plants of the Malvaceae. Indole alkaloids are often found in plants of the Apocyanaceae. The selection of a particular plant part is also governed by the factors mentioned above. For example, someone interested in the lower terpenes would like to examine plant parts which yield essential oils. Similarly, those specialising in the betanin pigments would select coloured parts (leaves, flowers or roots) of plants of the order Centrospermae; in this particular case, the considerations are colour and chemotaxonomy.

The collection of a plant material is best made with the help of a botanist, and it is essential to ensure the botanical identity of the species selected, before taking up detailed chemical studies. Herbarium specimens with details regarding the place, date and time of year of collection should be preserved. There are also certain well-established suppliers of plant materials who can be depended on for collecting and providing authentic plant specimens in large quantities needed for exhaustive studies.

It is preferable to use fresh materials, in which case the plant part, cut into small pieces, should be immersed in alcohol within a short time after collection. This is possible only if the collection site is close enough to the laboratory, which is often not the case. When the material has to be transported over a distance and kept for a period of time, it is advisable to dry the material in a current of air, in the shade, at the collection centre. If the transportation can be done quickly, the fresh plant material can also be loosely packed in polythene bags without crushing the material. These precautions are necessary, particularly with regard to aerial parts such as leaves and flowers.

Woody parts like bark, sapwood and heartwood, and also underground parts, are not as susceptible as leaves and flowers to decomposition during storage, particularly if the moisture content of the fresh material is not high. In the context of collection of plant material, another note of caution is needed. It is known that in leaves and fruits yielding essential oils, quantitative, if not qualitative, changes in the chemical composition of the oil may occur with time.

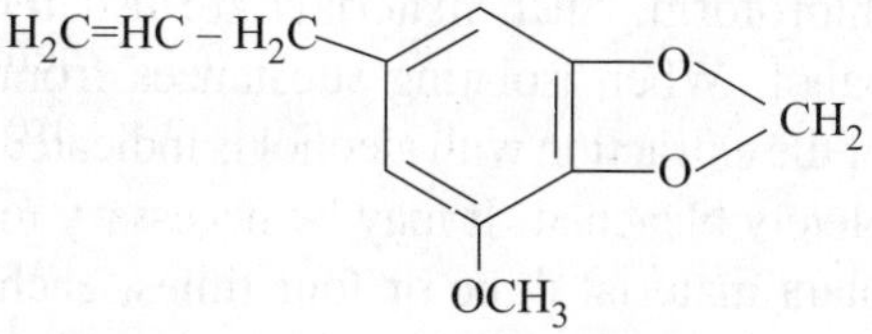

(2.1)

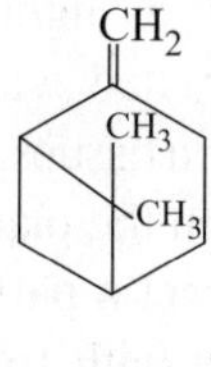

(2.2)

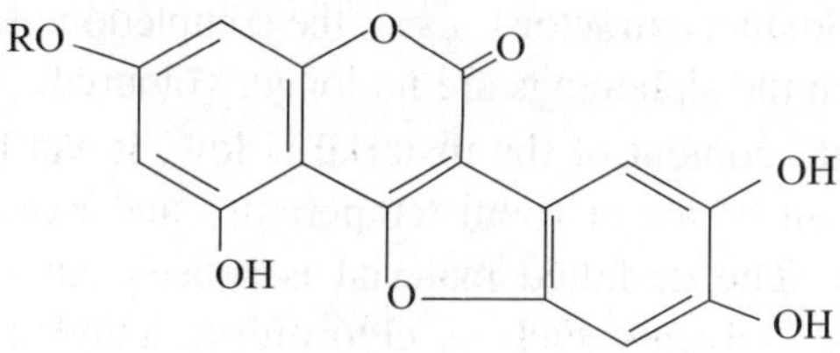

(2.3) : R = CH_3

(2.4) : R = H

For example, the myristicin (2.1) content of nutmeg, *Myristica fragrans* fruits, increases slowly on storage, while that of the more volatile β-pinene (2.2) decreases. Air-drying can also bring about decomposition of readily oxidisable polyphenolic compounds such as highly oxygenated flavonoids and related polyphenols. It is known that the coumestans, wedelolactone (2.3) and desmethylwedelolactone (2.4) present in *Wedelia calendulaceae* and *Eclipta alba* are lost when the plant material is crushed and dried. Incidentally, bruising a plant material could release enzymes which can change the chemical profile. One should also ensure that the plants used for extraction are free from disease. Plants affected by fungi and other microorganisms may contain compounds not present in the healthy specimens.

2.2 EXTRACTION

The method of extraction can vary depending on the texture and moisture content of the plant material being extracted and the type of substances to be isolated. Fresh plant parts such as leaves, flowers, stems and roots contain varying amounts of moisture and cannot be directly extracted with solvents which are immiscible with water, such as light petroleum or chloroform. Such materials are usually extracted with 90%–95% ethanol. When isolating substances from green tissues, the completion of the extraction with alcohol is indicated when the plant debris is completely bleached. It may be necessary to extract a particular batch of plant material three or four times, each time with fresh alcohol (alcohol recovered by distillation of earlier extracts of the same material can also be used), to ensure complete extraction. If a Soxhlet extractor is used, the completion of extraction is indicated when the siphonings are no longer coloured.

If the moisture content of the material is low, it can be quickly dried in a current of air at room temperature and extracted with light petroleum. The de-fatted material is subsequently extracted with more polar solvents such as chloroform, ethyl acetate and ethanol. This method has an advantage: A partial separation of the components based on their solubility characteristics is effected during the extraction stage itself, facilitating the subsequent fractionation processes.

The precautions necessary while extracting fresh green tissues become relatively unimportant in the case of woody tissues and materials rich in lipid content, such as most seeds and nuts. Barks and heartwoods are comparatively easy to extract; being dead tissues, they tend to accumulate considerable amounts of secondary metabolites. Occasionally, one finds deposits of secondary metabolites on the surfaces of leaves and nuts which can be gently scraped off and extracted with a suitable solvent, for example, the under parts of some ferns such as the silver fern and the white powdery deposit on the nuts of the mahogany tree; the latter consists of two complex, bitter terpenoids.

Large Soxhlet extractors are usually employed for the extraction of bulk quantities of plant materials. When solvents with high boiling points are used for extraction, the extracts get exposed to this high temperature over the period of time needed for the completion of the extraction. This could bring about some chemical changes in heat-sensitive compounds. A safe alternative method, though not as efficient as extraction with boiling solvents, is repeated percolation with cold solvents.

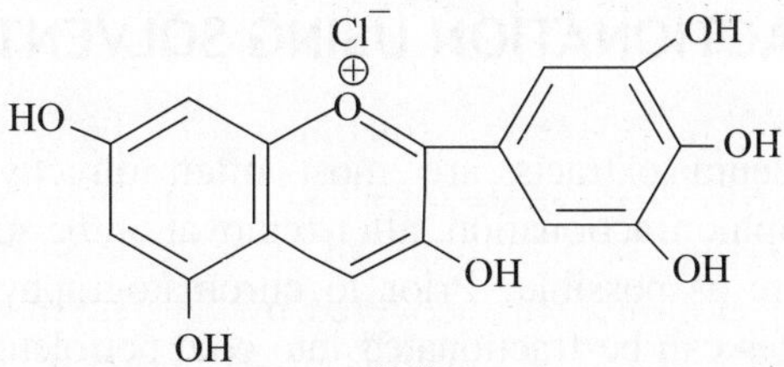

(2.5)

It should be remembered that a number of compounds such as anthocyanins and carotenoid pigments often occur in nature in the form of complexes, either with metals or proteins. The usual method of extraction of anthocyanin pigments using methanol-containing acids causes removal of the metal, and what is isolated is not the native pigment. An example is the blue pigment, which is a complex glycoside of delphinidin (2.5), present in the corn flower, *Commelina communis* (see Chapter 4). This point should also be kept in mind while trying to isolate the active principle(s) of a medicinal plant.

It is often true that the complete pharmacological profile of a crude plant drug is not due to any one pure compound, however powerful, but to a combination of two or more compounds. In this context, the procedure recommended by Dr JL Hartwell of the Drug Research and Development Laboratories of the NIH, USA, is worth mentioning. This procedure developed for getting extracts from plants likely to have anti-cancer activities, involves extraction of the finely ground material with light petroleum followed by 95% ethanol. The ethanolic extract is concentrated in vacuum and then extracted with chloroform. The chloroform solubles are examined for biological activity. However, for testing the whole range of pharmacological activities, no fraction should be neglected. A point worth noting is that while crushing a plant part prior to extraction, some enzymes may get released and these may act on certain secondary metabolites, such as glycosides, and bring about chemical changes. Therefore, it is advisable to extract the crushed material immediately with a hot solvent to deactivate the enzymes.

2.3 FRACTIONATION USING SOLVENTS

Light petroleum extracts are most often directly subjected to chromatographic fractionation, after removal of the solvent at as low a temperature as possible. Prior to chromatography, the total hot petrol solubles can be fractionated into cold petroleum solubles and insolubles. The former contain waxy substances which may include a mixture of esters of a variety of relatively non-polar alcohols with long-chain fatty acids. One way of dealing with mixtures which cannot be easily fractionated into individual pure compounds, is to subject the mixture to alkaline hydrolysis in the cold and in the absence of light and air (preferably under a nitrogen atmosphere). The neutral compounds thus liberated are extracted into diethyl ether. This is the standard procedure developed by Goodwin and his co-workers for the isolation of hydroxylated carotenoids, which usually occur in nature as esters with a mixture of long-chain fatty acids.

Alcoholic extracts, after filtering off any entrapped plant debris, are concentrated under reduced pressure, preferably with the help of a rotary evaporator. The concentrate is cooled and filtered. The residue in the case of leaf and floral extracts is usually a mixture of waxes and chlorophyll and is usually discarded. However, this may occasionally provide interesting secondary metabolites. The filtrate is then extracted, in a separatory funnel (if the volume is not too much; otherwise using a liquid–liquid extractor), in succession with diethyl ether, ethyl acetate and *n*-butanol, in that order, to bring about partial fractionation of the total extract. If the alcoholic extract contains flavonoids, this method helps to separate the compounds into aglycones which go into ether, monoglycosides which dissolve in ethyl acetate, and compounds containing more than one sugar unit which go into butanol.

The remaining aqueous alcoholic extract will contain more polar compounds such as polyglycosides, sulphate esters of polyphenols, free sugars and amino acids. The ether extract may also contain steroids or triterpenoid monoglycosides (saponins). The ether, ethyl acetate and butanol extracts may contain some amount of water carried over from the aqueous alcoholic concentrate These extracts, therefore, have to be dried preferably over anhydrous sodium sulphate or magnesium sulphate before further work-up. The extract is shaken with a small quantity of the drying agent when the extract becomes clear. It is then filtered, preferably through a fluted filter paper, and the residual sodium sulphate or magnesium sulphate is washed with a small quantity of the dry solvent. While using ether, sufficient care should be taken to ensure that the extract is well cooled.

Initially, the mixing of the two phases is done by swirling rather than by vigorous shaking. Occasionally, one may encounter the formation of emulsions which do not easily break down. In such cases, the separatory funnel may be gently rotated around a vertical axis and the layers allowed to separate. If this fails, the emulsion is transferred to a centrifuge, wherein under centrifugal force, the emulsion breaks up. While using butanol which has some affinity for the aqueous phase, addition of sodium chloride often helps to transfer moderately polar compounds like monoglycosides of phenols into the organic phase.

2.3.1 Specific extraction and fractionation procedures

Certain specific methods can be employed when the objective is to isolate a specific class of compounds such as alkaloids or flavonoids from a plant source. For example, for the extraction of alkaloids present as free bases, the plant material can be extracted with dilute acids or with ethanol-containing acetic acid (usually 2%). If the alkaloids are present as salts, the plant tissue is first soaked in dilute alkali to liberate the basic alkaloids, which are then extracted with an organic solvent, with or without the addition of acetic acid. To separate alkaloids from non-basic compounds present in an alcoholic or chloroform extract, the residue obtained after removal of the solvent is macerated with dilute hydrochloric acid and the acid extract neutralised with ammonia. The liberated alkaloids are once again extracted with chloroform. Svoboda has developed a pH gradient extraction method for the separation of alkaloids based on differences in their basicities.

Alkaloids can also be precipitated out from concentrated solutions with the help of reagents such as picric acid, potassium iodobismuthate (Dragendorff's reagent), potassium iodomercurate (Mayer's reagent) or ammonium reineckate. From these precipitates, the alkaloids can be regenerated either by treatment with aqueous alkali, as in the case of picrates, or by passing a solution of the precipitate in acetone–methanol–water (6:2:1) through a column of an anion-exchange resin.

Most of the monoterpenoids, and several sesquiterpenes, can be isolated from the essential oils obtained by steam distillation of plant materials possessing such compounds. These oils are invariably mixtures of compounds which can be separated from one another by efficient fractional distillation in vacuum or by chromatography. A few examples are given in the section on isolations.

Phenolic acids such as *p*-coumaric (2.6), caffeic (2.7), ferulic (2.8) and related cinnamic acid derivatives, which often accompany other polyphenolic compounds in a plant extract, can be separated by an aqueous, saturated sodium bicarbonate solution, provided they are present in the extracts as free acids; they may also occur as glycosides. It should be remembered that these compounds, being carboxylic acids, have a considerable affinity to water and hence the bulk of the aqueous solution should be kept as small as possible. Further, acidification of the bicarbonate extract should be done in the cold, with stirring and the help of cold concentrated hydrochloric acid added drop-wise.

Phenols can be extracted with aqueous sodium carbonate or dilute aqueous alkali of different strengths. Liberation of free phenols from the alkaline extracts is best brought about by bubbling carbon dioxide through the solution. These procedures were routinely employed in several laboratories till recently, but

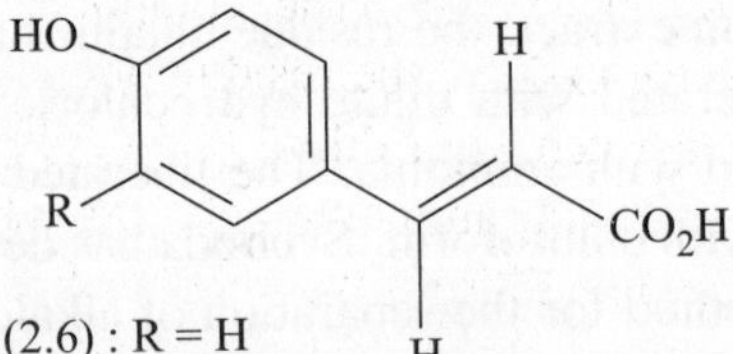

(2.6) : R = H
(2.7) : R = OH
(2.8) : R = CH_3

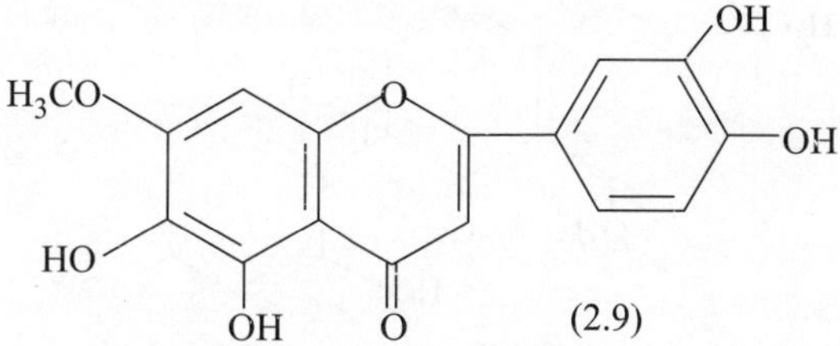

(2.9)

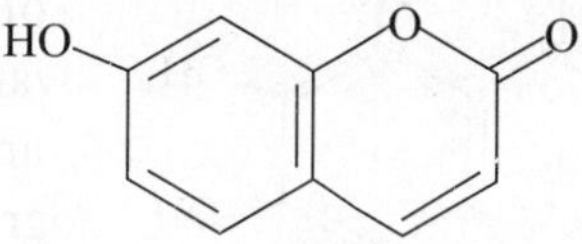

(2.10)

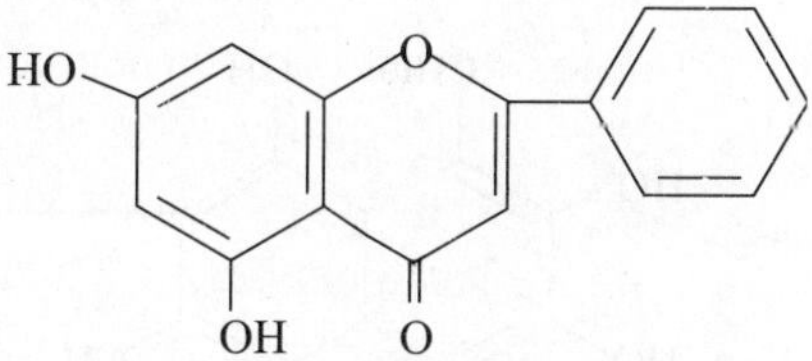

(2.11)

with the knowledge that several polyhydroxylated phenols are susceptible to oxidation in alkaline media, caution is now exercised in using such methods. Phenols susceptible to oxidation dissolve in alkaline solutions, often giving a play of colours, whereas phenols which are stable give solutions (often yellow) which retain their colour over a period of time. For example, pedalitin (2.9) and wedelolactone (2.3) dissolve in aqueous alkali to give green-coloured solutions which quickly fade in colour, ultimately turning brown; on the other hand, compounds like umbelliferone (7-hydroxycoumarin, 2.10) or chrysin (5,7-dihydroxyflavone, 2.11) can be safely extracted with aqueous alkali.

Polyphenols and their glycosides form insoluble lead salts. Extracts containing such compounds yield precipitates of lead salts on treatment with solutions of neutral or basic lead acetate. The free phenolic compounds can be obtained from these lead salts by treating an aqueous suspension of the latter with hydrogen sulphide, followed by extraction with an organic solvent. This procedure was widely used by AG Perkin and Robert Robinson and their co-workers during their early investigations on plant colouring matters. Decomposition of the lead salt can also be brought about by using sulphate or phosphate to avoid mechanical loss of the desired phenolic compounds due to the highly adsorptive nature of finely precipitated lead sulphide. The use of lead acetate for

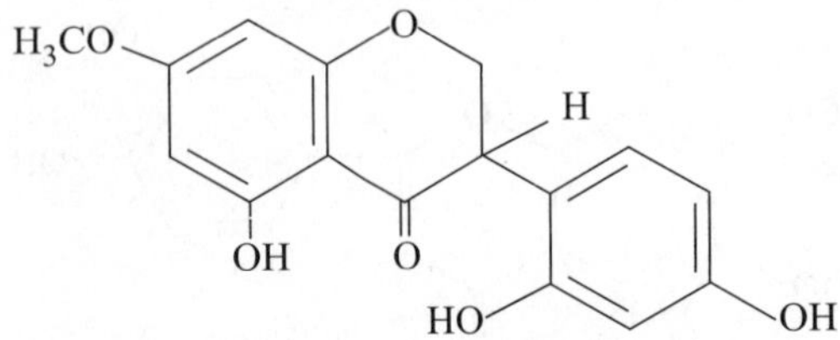

(2.12)

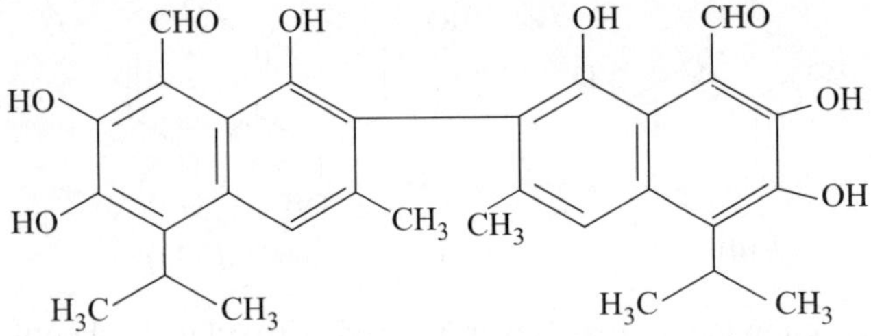

(2.13)

the isolation of polyphenols is rarely resorted to these days but occasionally, this method finds use when other methods fail. For instance, Seshadri and his co-workers employed this method for the isolation of ouegenin (2.12) and related isoflavonoids of the plant *Ouegenia dalbergioides*. Precipitation with lead acetate is also used to eliminate phenolic and glycosidic contaminants in the isolation of sesquiterpene lactones by some research groups.

Another structure-specific method for the isolation of polyhydric phenolic compounds possessing a catechol (1,2-dihydroxybenzene) unit is to extract the plant material directly with 0.2% aqueous borax solution. Seshadri and co-workers used this method to eliminate the toxic gossypol (2.13) from cotton seed oil. It has also been used to isolate wedelolactone (2.3) and desmethylwedelolactone (2.4) from *Eclipta alba*.

Chlorophyll and plant waxes may prove troublesome in the isolation of other compounds from leaf extracts. One effective method to remove traces of chlorophyll is to treat the crude alcoholic extract with charcoal powder. Sometimes, the desired compounds, particularly if they are heavily hydroxylated, such as flavonoid glycosides, may also get adsorbed along with the chlorophyll on charcoal. They can be recovered from charcoal by graded elution.

For example, the flavonoids from *Baptisia lecontei* were eluted from activated charcoal by washing successively with methanol, boiling water, 7% aqueous phenol and 15% methanolic phenol. The bulk of the flavonoid material appeared in the 7% phenol eluate. It was subsequently extracted with ether to obtain a phenol-free aqueous solution rich in flavonoid glycosides.

If the compounds to be isolated from a leaf extract are non-acidic and non-phenolic, the accompanying chlorophyll can be eliminated by subjecting the total extract to a mild hydrolytic treatment with alcoholic alkali, preferably in a nitrogen atmosphere. Chlorophyll and other esters undergo hydrolysis and the acidic compounds thus liberated dissolve in the alkaline solution. The solution is then diluted with water and extracted with diethyl ether or a similar solvent immiscible with water. After washing the organic extract free of alkali, the desired compounds are isolated by removal of the solvent. Besides hydroxylated carotenoids, hydroxylated steroids and triterpenes such as sitosterol (2.14), β-amyrin (2.15) and related compounds can be isolated in this manner.

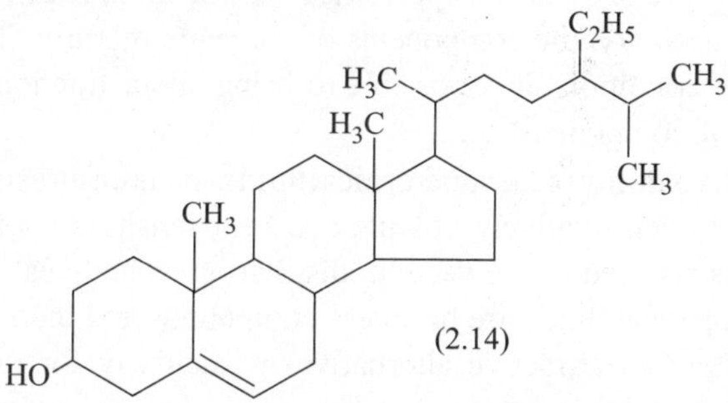

(2.14)

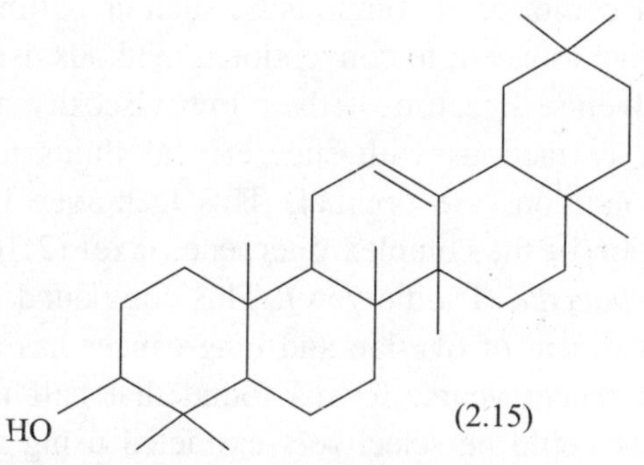

(2.15)

2.3.2 Supercritical fluid extraction

Extraction with a supercritical fluid, such as liquid carbon dioxide, is increasingly used for the isolation of sensitive compounds, such as the delicate odoriferous components of spices. Other gases used in liquid form for this purpose are nitrous oxide, ethylene, ethane, propane and dimethyl ether. The supercritical state of a gas refers to those conditions of temperature and pressure under which matter in a gaseous form can be compressed into a dense medium which approximates to a liquid. At temperatures above the critical point, a gas will remain in the gaseous state, even under high pressure, but its density will increase with increase in pressure. Under appropriate conditions of pressure and density, the gas turns into a supercritical state wherein it can dissolve considerable quantities of compounds which are otherwise sparingly soluble in the liquid or normal gaseous form of the solvent. For example, supercritical carbon dioxide at 60°C and 4350 psi pressure can extract all the compounds soluble in dichloromethane. At the same temperature, but at a pressure of 870 psi, supercritical carbon dioxide can dissolve all but the least volatile components of the same mixture. Thus, by varying the conditions it is possible to bring about fractionation of a mixture of compounds.

The high volatility of the supercritical fluid solvent ensures complete recovery of even relatively volatile and heat-sensitive compounds, and there is no need to use vacuum distillation techniques. Further, most supercritical fluids are harmless compounds and therefore this method offers an attractive alternative, particularly for the large-scale extraction of commercial compounds, such as caffeine from tea and nicotine from tobacco, to conventional methods using toxic and hazardous solvents. Because of their low viscosity and high ability to diffuse, extractions with supercritical fluids are rapid when solubility conditions are optimal. This technique has been used for the isolation of the complex diterpene, taxol (2.16), from the bark of *Taxus baccata* (Pacific yew). This compound which is effective in the treatment of ovarian and lung cancer has attracted much attention in recent years. It was found that half the taxol present in the plant could be selectively extracted using a carbon

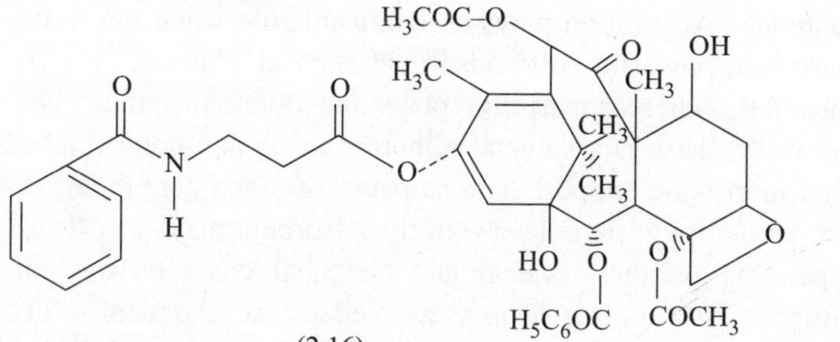

(2.16)

dioxide–ethanol mixture, which was twice as effective as using supercritical carbon dioxide alone.

2.3.3 Chromatographic methods

There is an old Dutch word for chemistry, 'Scheikunde', which means the art of separation. Indeed, separation is the key to the isolation of pure chemical compounds from any source, vegetable or otherwise, and therefore it is not surprising that the exciting structural studies on a new naturally occurring compound are preceded by often laborious and painstaking separation procedures. In this endeavour, chromatography, in its various forms, has played no mean role. The separation and isolation of individual pure compounds from a plant extract is achieved by resorting to one or more of the various chromatographic techniques which are now available. These include paper chromatography (PC), thin layer chromatography (TLC), column chromatography, flash chromatography, low-pressure liquid chromatography, high-pressure liquid chromatography (HPLC), gas–liquid chromatography (GC), centrifugal TLC, droplet counter-current chromatography and rotation locular counter-current chromatography. Among these, the most widely used methods are PC, TLC, GC, HPLC and column chromatography.

In all types of chromatography, two phases and two factors are involved, namely the stationary and mobile phases, and adsorption and partition factors. The relative contributions of adsorption and partition to the overall separation process varies from technique to technique. Adsorption plays a significant role when the stationary phase is a powerful solid adsorbent such as alumina or activated silica gel, whereas partition plays the dominant role when the stationary phase is a solvent, either polar or non-polar, embedded in an inert solid support such as paper or silica gel. In adsorption chromatography, particle size of the adsorbent plays a critical role. Depending on the physical and chemical characteristics of the stationary and mobile phases, as well as the chemical structures of the compounds being separated, each compound will have a characteristic distribution constant for a particular combination of stationary and mobile phases. This chromatographic parameter is known as the R_f value in paper and thin layer chromatography, and as *retention time* in the different types of column chromatography.

Paper and Thin Layer Chromatography

For preliminary studies of plant extracts, these two methods are the most widely used. Paper chromatography is particularly suitable for water-soluble compounds such as carbohydrates, amino acids, nucleic acid bases, phenols and phenolic acids. TLC is the method of choice for separating all lipid-soluble compounds, namely terpenoids, steroids, carotenoids and other compounds with comparable solubility characteristics. The basic characteristic of either of these techniques can be reversed by appropriate 'impregnation'. We shall revert to this aspect later.

The advantages of PC and TLC over other chromatographic methods include the ease of operation, low cost of equipment, speed with which chromatographic analysis can be completed and the considerable amount of valuable information that can be obtained from the analysis of a crude extract even prior to isolation of pure compounds. Extracts of different plants or different fractions of a particular extract can be simultaneously examined on the same paper or TLC plate, thus providing comparable data leading to useful inferences. A very small quantity of the extract is sufficient for a qualitative analysis. These methods are also useful as monitoring techniques for evaluating the progress of a particular fractionation procedure. By employing various spray reagents, a good amount of information regarding the nature of the functional groups present in the components of an extract can be obtained. The following examples help to illustrate some of the points noted above.

The coumestan, wedelolactone (2.3), was first isolated from the plants *Wedelia calendulaceae* and *Eclipta alba*. Subsequently, paper chromatographic examinations of the crude extracts showed the presence of another compound, with a lower R_f value than wedelolactone, but answering the same colour tests—green colour with alcoholic ferric chloride, blue fluorescence under ultraviolet light, and green colour with ammonia. These observations suggested that the new compound should be closely related to wedelolactone, but being more polar in character, as indicated by its lower R_f value, could have a hydroxyl group in place of the methoxyl of wedelolactone. Indeed, direct comparison with synthetically prepared desmethylwedelolactone (2.4) established the identity of the new compound.

Thiophene derivatives occur in several plants of the Compositae. One of these is α-terthienylmethanol (2.17), which is a chemical constituent of the leaves of *Eclipta alba*. In this plant it is accompanied by the corresponding aldehyde, 2-formylterthienyl (2.18). The identification of the latter was first made on TLC plates, wherein it appears as a pale yellow spot exhibiting a brilliant golden yellow fluorescence under UV light. The corresponding alcohol exhibits bright blue fluorescence and has a lower R_f value. The two compounds could be separated by preparative TLC and identified by direct comparison with synthetic samples. What was more interesting was the observation that pure terthienylmethanol undergoes oxidation on exposure to light and air to yield the aldehyde, the presence of which, even in traces, could be readily detected by TLC. Subsequently, the mechanism of the oxidation

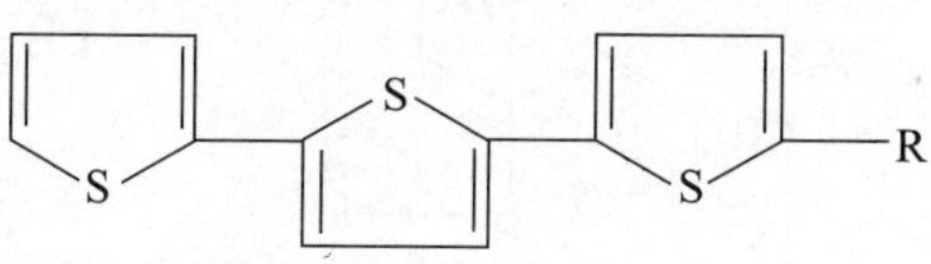

(2.17) : $R = CH_2OH$

(2.18) : $R = CHO$

was shown to involve singlet oxygen, with the terthienyl alcohol acting as a self-sensitiser.

During an examination of the light petroleum extracts of the aerial parts of the plant *Enhydra fluctuans*, a steroid fraction was obtained which appeared homogeneous on ordinary TLC plates. However, the acetate of the sterol resolved into three distinct spots on argentated silica gel. Two of the spots were identified as due to stigmasteryl acetate (2.19) and the acetate of 24-ethylcholesta-5,22,25-trienyl-3-β-ol (2.20), both of which had earlier been isolated from the same plant. The third spot had an R_f value between these two, indicating that it could be a diene, otherwise having the same skeletal structure. Indeed, it was identified as the acetate of 24-ethylcholesta-5, 25-dienyl-3-β-ol (2.21). The fact that separation of the three sterols occurs only after acetylation, suggests that the presence of the polar hydroxyl function in the free sterols obliterates the slight but distinct differences caused by the number and placement of the double bonds.

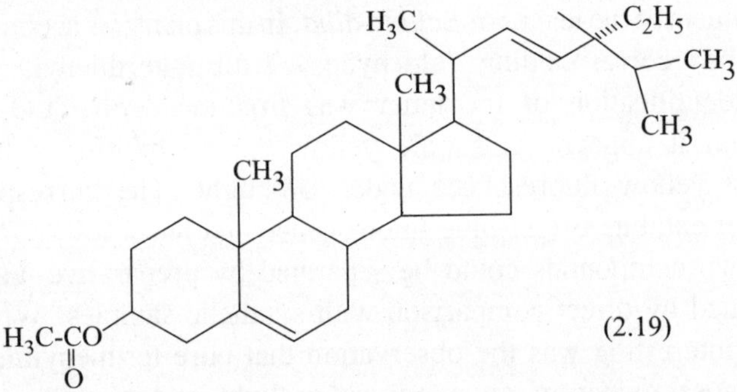

(2.19)

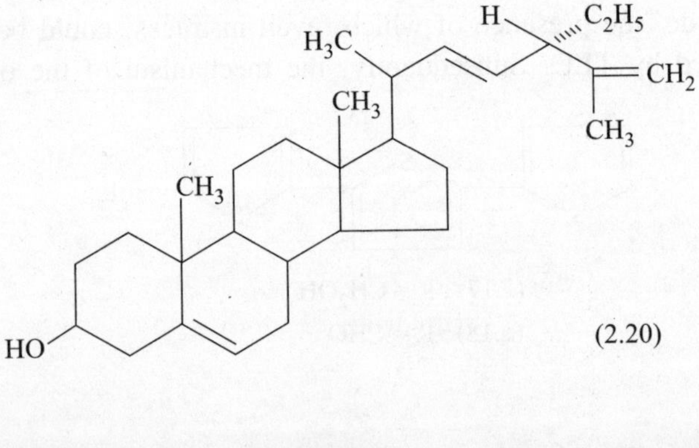

(2.20)

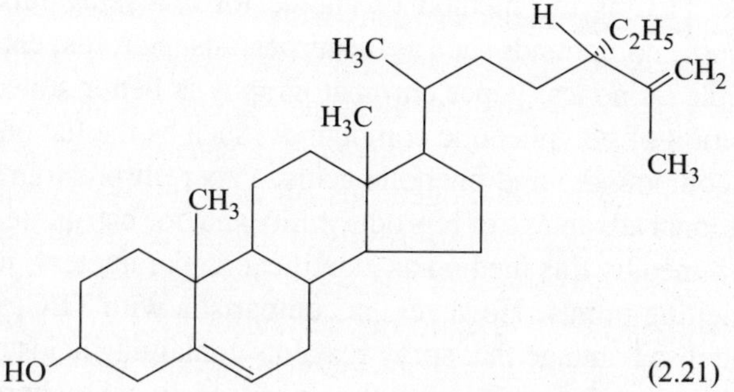

(2.21)

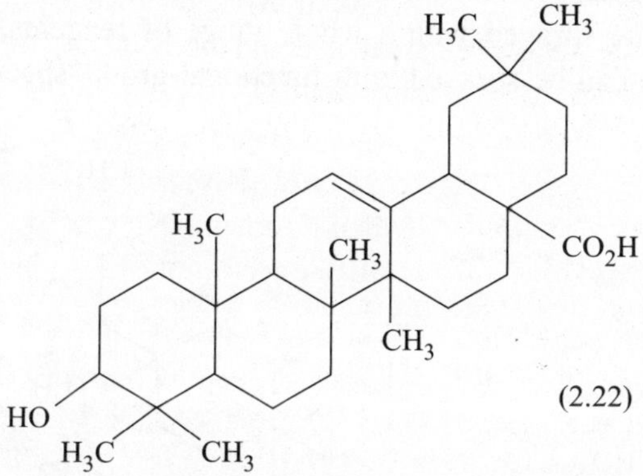

(2.22)

Another example, wherein conversion of an acidic functionality to a less polar derivative was necessary to highlight minor differences in structures of closely related compounds is given below.

A mixture of triterpene acids was isolated from the plant *Sesamum laciniatum*. One of them was identified as oleanolic acid (2.22). This was accompanied by four other compounds which could not be separated from each other by any of the conventional chromatographic methods. However, they could be relatively easily separated after acetylation and conversion into their methyl esters. Obviously, the presence of the polar carboxyl function effectively cancels out the smaller differences in polarity due to the differences in the degree of hydroxylation. These compounds were identified as the methyl ester acetates of 2α-hydroxyoleanolic acid (2.23), 2α, 23-dihydroxyoleanolic acid (2.24) , 2α, 24-dihydroxyoleanolic acid (2.25) and 1α, 2α, 23-trihydroxyoleanolic acid (2.26).

While TLC is the method of choice for analysing mixtures of lipid soluble compounds such as the terpenoids, steroids, carotenoids and simple quinones, paper chromatography is better suited for the examination of polyphenolic compounds, such as the flavonoids and related compounds, and phenolic acids. Paper chromatography has the additional advantage of reproducibility and one can quote R_f values as determined by this method as identification parameters, just as we quote melting points. However, in comparison with TLC, it suffers from the disadvantage that spray reagents containing acids or alkalis cannot be used for visualising the spots (or rings), whereas TLC plates can be sprayed with a whole range of reagents. Developed TLC plates can be sprayed with functional group–specific reagents

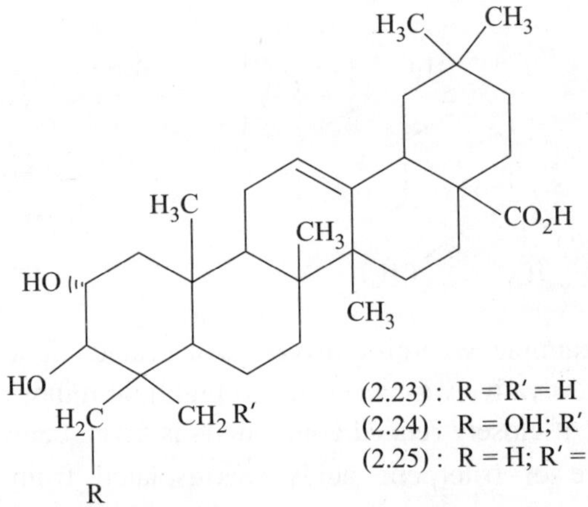

(2.23) : R = R′ = H
(2.24) : R = OH; R′ = H
(2.25) : R = H; R′ = OH

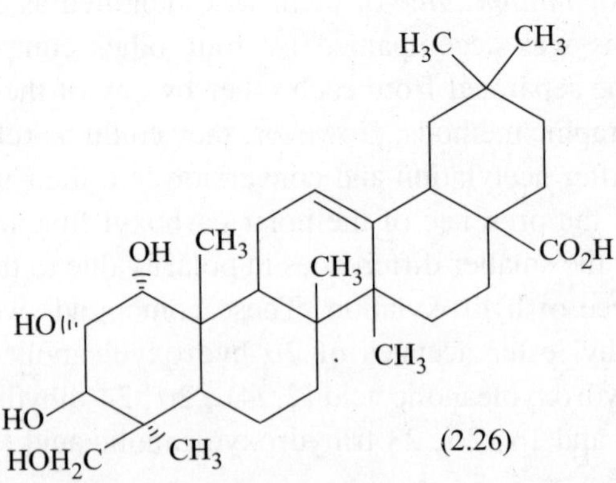

(2.26)

to obtain preliminary information useful in subsequent structural studies on the pure compound. Functional group transformations, such as acetylation of hydroxyl groups and esterification, using diazomethane of carboxyl groups, can also be brought about on TLC plates.

Separations on TLC plates are brought about by applying the mixture or extract under examination, dissolved in a suitable—preferably volatile—solvent as a spot or a thin line on the stationary phase (usually silica gel G), which is applied to a glass or plastic plate of appropriate dimension. For preliminary qualitative work, microscopic slides coated with the adsorbent are very convenient. The plate is then kept in a beaker or a cylinder containing the mobile phase which moves up the plate due to capillary action. This process is known as *development*. The R_f value of a compound is given by the equation:

$$R_f = \frac{\text{Distance of the spot from the origin}}{\text{Distance of the solvent from the origin}}$$

Generally, polar compounds, which have less affinity for the less polar mobile phase, will have lower R_f values than non-polar compounds, which tend to move with the mobile phase.

Reverse phase TLC

Ordinarily the support material used in TLC studies is silica gel G with water structurally associated with the material acting as the stationary phase. The polarity of the material can be changed from polar to non-polar by coating the activated silica gel plates with a solvent such as *n*-tetradecane or paraffin. The preparation of such plates is described in Chapter 4. The reverse phase TLC plates thus obtained can be developed with a more polar solvent such as propanone or acetonitrile serving as the mobile phase.

Argentated TLC

It is known that silver ions form complexes with pi-electrons of unsaturated centres, and that this complexation is reversible. This fact has been used, with advantage, to separate fatty acids differing in the degree of unsaturation on TLC plates using silica gel impregnated with silver nitrate. This method is also useful for separating sterols differing from each other in the number of double bonds present in them as described in an example quoted earlier.

Preparative TLC

Ordinarily, microgram quantities of mixtures of organic compounds are separated by analytical TLC. It is possible to scale-up the quantities to milligram amounts (10–50 mg) by using thicker layers (0.5–2.0 mm thickness) of the support material and by the use of larger plates (20 mm × 20 cm or 20 mm × 40 cm). Multiple developments also bring about better resolution. Since the amounts of a material being purified by preparative TLC (PTLC) are small, it is essential to ensure that the adsorbent and the developing solvents used are free from contaminants. It is customary to pre-wash the plate before applying the substance. Non-destructive methods are then used to visualise the developed spots or bands. If the compounds are coloured or fluorescent, the detection is easy. Otherwise, before spraying the developed plate is covered, except for a narrow strip which is exposed to a mild universal spotting agent such as iodine vapours. Having thus located the spots on the plate, the compounds can be recovered by scraping off the spots (or bands) and subsequently extracting them with a suitable solvent (methanol has to be avoided as it can carry over traces of the adsorbent). For visualising colourless compounds, plates coated with silica gel containing a fluorescent agent are also used. When such developed plates are viewed under UV light, the compounds will appear as dark spots against a luminous background. When such plates are used, it should be remembered that the extract of the desired substance may also contain some amount of the fluorescent indicator. Therefore, the material isolated by PTLC may have to be further purified by a conventional method such as crystallisation.

Centrifugal TLC

A centrifugal TLC instrument called the chromatotron has been successfully used in the separation of different types of mixtures of natural products. Using this device, mixtures are separated on a

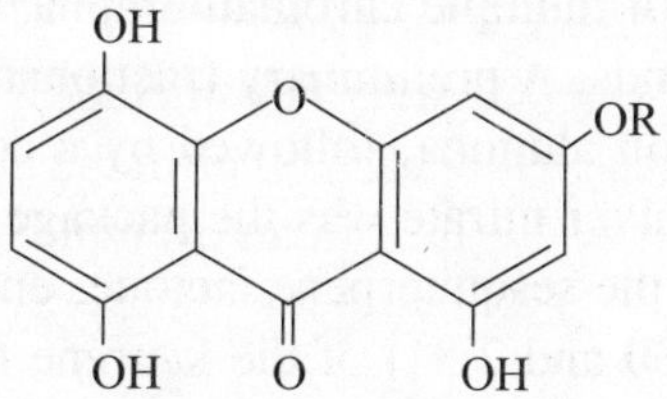

(2.27) : R = CH_3
(2.28) : R = H

spinning disc carrying a layer of the adsorbent (usually silica gel) of 1–4 mm thickness. Elution with a solvent gives concentric bands of the components which are spun off from the edge of the plate together with the solvent. A collection system brings the eluate to a single output tube. Using this technique, Hostettmann and his co-workers were able to isolate 55 mg of bellidifolin (7-methoxy-1,4,5-trihydroxyxanthone, 2.27) and 48 mg desmethylbellidifolin (1,4,5,7-tetrahydroxyanthone, 2.28) from a hydrolysed methanol extract of *Gentiana stictiflora* in less than half an hour. The advantages of this method over the conventional PTLC are rapid separations, low consumption of solvent, no scraping of bands, and higher recovery of purer samples.

Open Column Chromatography

For the isolation of gram quantities of compounds, chromatography over a column of a suitable adsorbent is the most convenient method. Apart from the various grades of alumina (the most well-known being Brockman alumina) and silica gel, silica gel impregnated with silver nitrate, cellulose powder, polyamide and sephadex are also used for the separation of mixtures of different types of secondary metabolites of natural origin. The recognition that a few chemical reactions, such as the opening of the epoxide group, may occur on the surface of alumina, imposes a limitation on the use of this material as a universal adsorbent—a status it occupied for many years. Silica gel is safer, though resolution on this material may not be as good as on alumina. Most plant extracts are complex enough to necessitate the use of multiple chromatographic resolution in order to get pure compounds. A preliminary fractionation on a column of silica gel, another on alumina, followed by a column of silica gel impregnated with silver nitrate was the package technique adopted for the isolation of the sesquiterpene lactone, enhydrin (2.29), two diterpene acids (2.30 and 2.31) of the kaurene family, a diterpene alcohol (2.32) of the same type, and three sterols from a petrol extract of the plant *Enhydra fluctuans*.

Although this technique is well suited for handling large amounts of samples, it suffers from the disadvantage that the time taken for one complete chromatographic operation can stretch from a few hours to a couple of days or more. As a consequence of the long exposure of the compounds adsorbed on the column material to light and dissolved air in the solvents used for elution, chemical changes may occur, if the compounds are light-sensitive and oxidisable. In recent years, improved methods have been adopted to bring about reduction in separation time. One of these is flash chromatography and another is vacuum liquid chromatography.

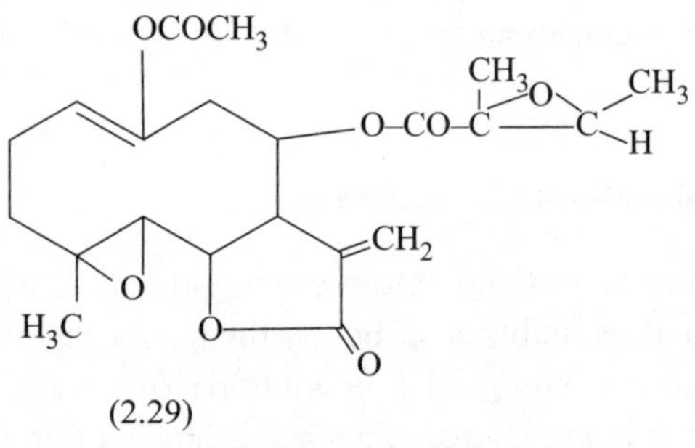

(2.29)

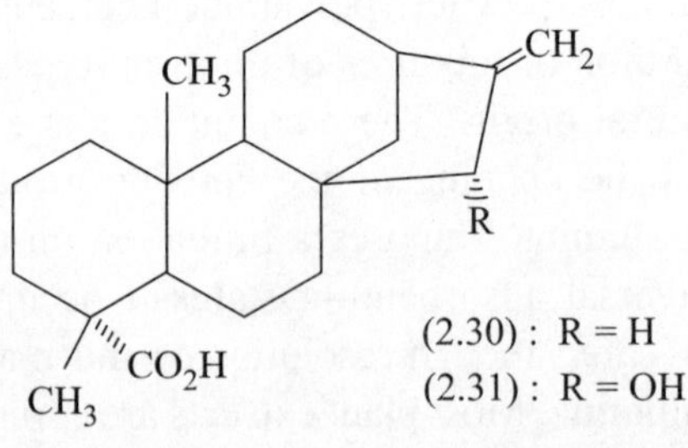

(2.30) : R = H

(2.31) : R = OH

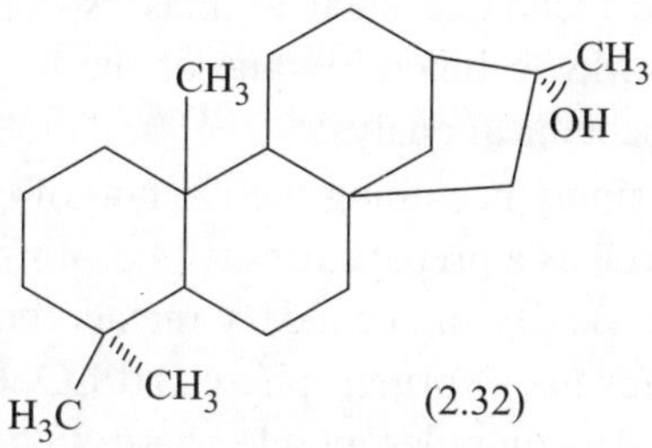

(2.32)

Pressure column chromatography

Flash chromatography is an expensive technique which is useful for the rapid resolution of samples weighing from 100 mg to 10 g in less than thirty minutes. Basically, it is an air pressure–driven hybrid of medium pressure and short column chromatography optimised for rapid separations. Since the use of gradients is possible, this technique can afford pure compounds in one single operation in the case of mixtures which are not too complex.

Low-pressure liquid chromatography (LOBAR) allows the use of numerous chemically bonded phases, besides silica. Repetitive injections of samples into small preparative columns allow the resolution of 200–300 mg quantities in less than one hour. Resolution is generally of a high order and in some cases comparable to that of HPLC.

HPLC and GC

High-pressure liquid chromatography (also known as high-performance or high-speed or high-efficiency liquid chromatography) and gas–liquid chromatography require comparatively more expensive equipment than any of the methods described above; they are also several times more efficient. Since its introduction by James and Martin in 1952, gas chromatography has continued to be used particularly for the separation of relatively volatile compounds, such as the terpenoid components of essential oils. Mixtures of fatty acids can also be analysed after conversion into their methyl esters. The technique can be used as an analytical tool, when it provides quantitative as well as qualitative data, and also as a preparative method. The separations brought about by GC can be monitored by a spectroscopic technique such as mass spectroscopy. Indeed, the combined GC–MS technique is one of the most powerful tools available for phytochemical analysis.

HPLC is increasingly becoming the method of choice, both as an analytical tool as well as a preparative method, for the separation and isolation of a wide variety of secondary metabolites from terrestrial and marine organisms. Normal phase HPLC employs a polar stationary phase and a non-polar mobile phase. In this mode, the least polar components of a mixture are eluted first. This is similar to what one observes in conventional column chromatography. As a matter of fact, experiences gained with TLC and column chromatography can be used to generate solvent combinations for bringing about optimum separations in HPLC in this mode. However, the technique more widely used is the reverse phase HPLC where the stationary phase is a non-polar one and the mobile phase is a polar solvent.

Chemically bonded octadecylsilane (C-18 ODS) is the most frequently used stationary phase. C-8 and shorter alkyl chains as also cyclohexyl and phenyl groups are alternative substitutes for the octadecyl functionality. Water is often used as the mobile phase. The retention time of a sample increases with increase in the water content of the mobile phase. In the order of increasing eluting power, methanol, acetonitrile, ethanol, isoropanol, dimethylformamide, *n*-propanol, dioxan and tetrahydrofuran are the other commonly employed mobile phases in reverse phase HPLC.

Particle size of the stationary phase is an important factor in HPLC as also in conventional column chromatography. The efficiency of the column increases with increasing surface area, that is with reduction in the particle size. The typical particle size used in HPLC columns is of the order of 3–10 μm. The small size of these particles leads to a resistance to the flow of the solvent, necessitating the use of a pump to push the solvent through the column under high pressure. Typically, a HPLC column made of stainless steel is 10–25 cms long and has an internal diameter of 4–6 mm and pressure of the order 10–400 bar is applied. Though expensive, these columns are reusable.

The mobile phase composition can be constant (isocratic) or can be varied in a predetermined manner to bring about gradient elution. With the availability of quaternary systems, four different solvents can be mixed in any combination, as long as the mixture is homogeneous. The solvents used should be of high purity and must be absolutely free of particulate matter. It is also necessary to de-gas the solvents as gas bubbles can disturb the flow rate. Dissolved oxygen also absorbs ultraviolet light below 200 nm and this leads to erroneous results when a diode array detector is used. De-gassing can be brought about by placing the mobile phase under vacuum, by ultrasonic stirring or by bubbling an inert gas like argon or helium through it.

Detector systems in HPLC An ideal detector should be sensitive to every single component of the mixture being separated. It must not be affected by changes in temperature or mobile phase composition which occur in gradient elution. It should also be able to identify small amounts of the sample and its response time must be very short. The most commonly used detector is the ultraviolet detector which is highly sensitive and has a wide linear range. UV detectors with a single wavelength detection (254 nm) were extensively used in the past.

The disadvantage of such a system is that components not absorbing at or near the specific wavelength would get eluted without detection. A diode array detector, on the other hand, makes it possible to detect every compound absorbing light anywhere in the UV–visible range. Refractive index (R1) detectors are non-selective and register all eluting components with refractive indices different from that of the pure mobile phase. RI detectors are much less sensitive than UV detectors. Fluorescent compounds are easily detected with the help of a light emission detector with sensitivity of a very high order. HPLC separations can also be monitored using a FT–IR instrument coupled to the HPLC system.

Recommended reading

1. Cannell RJP, (Ed.), *Natural Products Isolation*, Humana Press, New Jersey, 1998.
2. Cseke CS, *Natural Products from Plants*, 2nd Edition, CRC Press, Boca Raton, 2006.
3. Hostettmann K, Marston A and Hostettmann M, *Preparative Chromatographic Techniques*, 2nd Edition, Springer-Verlag, Berlin, 1998.
4. Houghton PJ and Raman A, *Laboratory Handbook for the Fractionation of Natural Extracts*, Chapman & Hall, London, 1998.
5. Markham KR, *Techniques of Flavonoid Identification*, Academic Press, London, 1982.
6. Sarkar SD, Latif Z and Gray AI, *Natural Products Isolation*, 2nd Edition, Humana Press, New Jersey, 2006.
7. Sherma J, *High Performance Liquid Chromatography in Phytochemical Analysis*, CRC Press, Boca Raton, 2010.
8. Waksmundzka-Hajnos M, Sherma J and Kowalska T, *Thin Layer Chromatography in Phytochemistry*, CRC Press, Boca Raton, 2008.

CHAPTER 3

Characterisation of Naturally Occurring Compounds

In this chapter, an outline of the various methods used for the characterisation of pure compounds isolated from natural sources is given. The earlier methods involved extensive use of chemical techniques such as derivatisation, functional group transformations, and degradations, mainly with the help of oxidising agents. Many of these methods continue to be used, though to a much reduced extent. By and large, the chemical methods have given place to spectroscopic techniques with a consequent dramatic reduction in time and the amount of a compound needed for a complete elucidation of its structure. In the following paragraphs brief descriptions of the different methods of characterisation, illustrated with the help of a few examples, are given.

3.1 CHEMICAL METHODS

3.1.1 Preliminary studies—colour reactions

Colour reactions give valuable clues to the chemical nature of several groups of secondary metabolites. Some of these are sensitive and adaptable enough to be carried out on TLC plates. Most others are test tube reactions which require larger amounts (several milligrams) of the compound. Colour reactions are particularly useful in the preliminary studies of flavonoids, sterols and alkaloids. Some functional groups can also be detected using specific colour reactions.

Flavonoids can be detected by the Shinoda test, where an alcoholic solution of the test material (even crude or partially fractionated extract), taken in a large test tube (preferably a boiling tube), is treated with magnesium metal powder followed by the cautious addition of concentrated hydrochloric acid. Since the reaction of the acid with the metal can be quite vigorous, it is desirable to add a few drops of *t*-butanol before running in the acid. The development of orange, red, pink or purple colours indicates the presence of a flavonoid in the test sample. It is instructive to carefully note the colour of the froth, particularly when the concentration of the compound is low.

The depth of colour depends on the degree of hydroxylation of the flavonoid; flavonols (3.1) give deeper colours than flavones (3.2). One of the contributing factors for the colour formation is the reductive transformation of the flavone to the corresponding anthocyanidin chloride (3.3). In a variant of the Shinoda test, an alcoholic solution of the flavone is treated with sodium amalgam, and after a few minutes, the mixture is acidified. Sodium borohydride has also been used as a reducing agent in this test. Dihydroflavonols (flavanonols, 3.4) as well as flavonol 3-glycosides (3.5) and 3-*O*-methyl ethers (3.6) give deep red or magenta colours in alcoholic solution when reduced with zinc metal dust and concentrated hydrochloric acid.

Flavonoid glycosides, and glycosides in general, answer the Molisch test described later. Flavones and flavonols dissolve in concentrated sulphuric acid giving dark brown–coloured solutions which exhibit green fluorescence. The exceptions are flavonols with a 2'-hydroxyl group in the side phenyl; such compounds yield coloured solutions without fluorescence. Flavones which contain one or more free phenolic hydroxyl groups dissolve in dilute aqueous alkali to give deep yellow–coloured solutions. The colour formed also depends on the hydroxylation pattern in the case of polyhydroxy flavones. 5,6,7-Trihydroxyflavones, such as

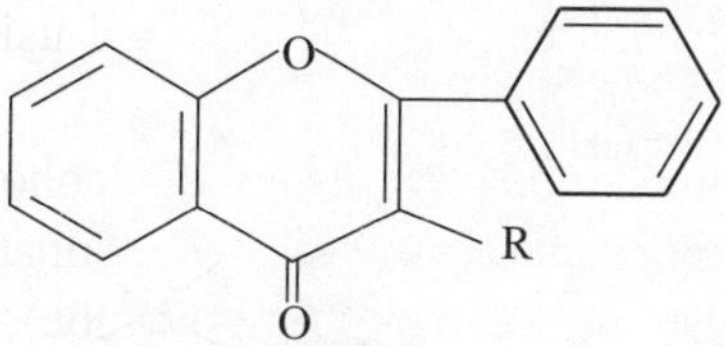

(3.1) : R = OH
(3.2) : R = H
(3.5) : R = O-gl
(3.6) : R = OCH_3

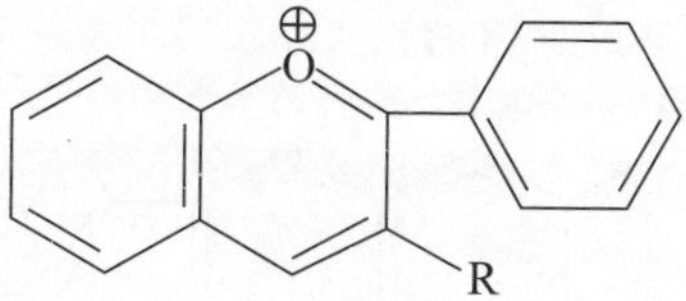

(3.3)

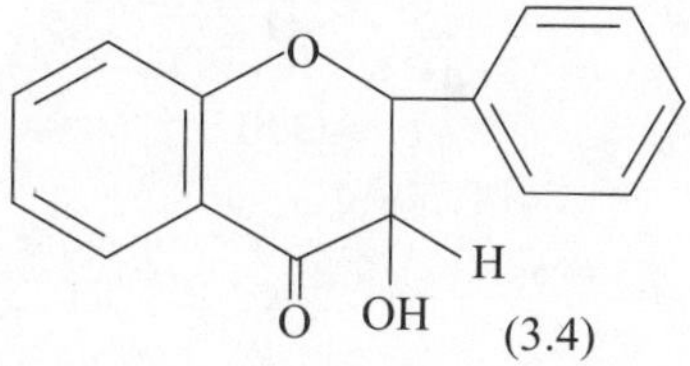

(3.4)

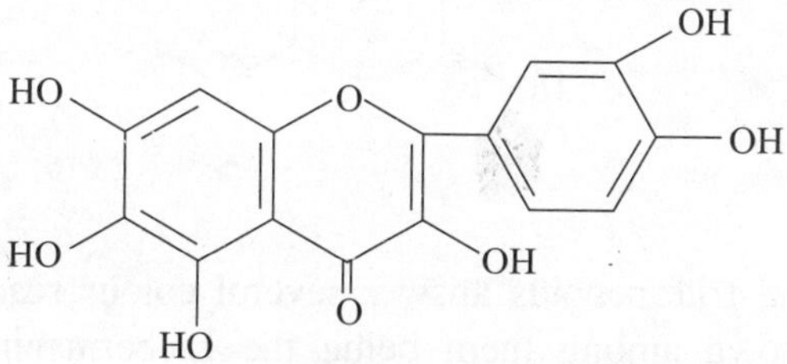

(3.7)

myricetin, which is 3,5,6,7,3',4'-hexahydroxyflavone (3.7), show a play of colours beginning with a transient green colour which turns blue, then violet and finally brown.

A related colour reaction is the Bargellini's test in which a solution of the compound in absolute alcohol is treated with sodium amalgam. The formation of a green flocculent precipitate indicates the presence of a 5,6,7-trihydroxyflavone. 5,7,8-Trihydroxyflavones, such as gossypetin (3,5,7,8,3',4'-hexahydroxyflavone, 3.8), on the other hand, give orange-red solutions in concentrated alkali which, on dilution with water, first turn green, then blue and finally brown. Alcoholic solutions of gossypetin and related compounds, with the 5,7,8- or 5,8-hydroxylation pattern, give a red-brown colour on treatment with alcoholic *p*-benzoquinone; this reaction is known as the Gossypetone test, which presumably involves oxidation of the quinol to a quinone moiety. Alcoholic ferric chloride is another useful reagent. The colour formed depends on the degree and pattern of hydroxylation and may range from brown to purple to green.

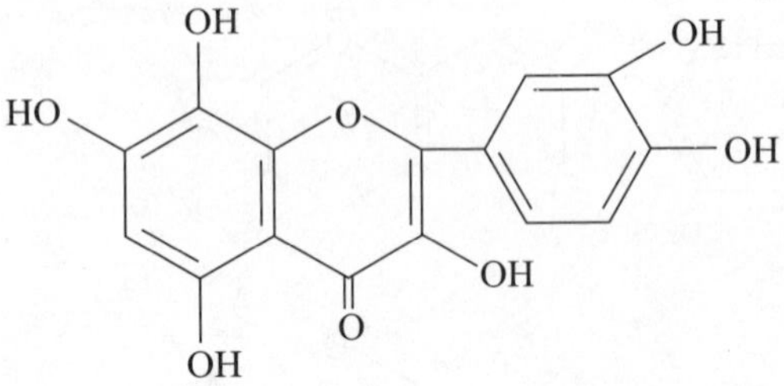

(3.8)

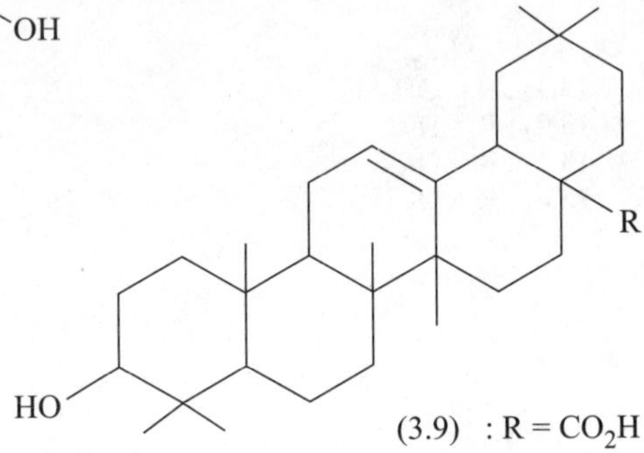

(3.9) : R = CO_2H
(3.10) : R = CH_3

Steroids and triterpenoids answer several colour reactions, the most well known among them being the Liebermann–Burchard reaction. In this test, the compound is first dissolved in a small quantity of concentrated sulphuric acid and then treated with acetic anhydride, added drop-wise. The majority of the compounds under these two categories exhibit a play of colours ranging from blue to red through green. For example, oleanolic acid (3.9) gives the following play of colours—red-violet-blue-green. Some compounds such as β-amyrin (3.10) give only a stable pink colour. α-Amyrin (3.11), on the other hand, gives a deep violet-red colour. The test can also be done in chloroform solution.

A carefully performed Liebermann–Burchard test can differentiate between cholest-5-en-3-ol (3.12) and cholest-7-en-3-ol (3.13). The latter reacts much faster than the former, with the colour attaining its maximum intensity within 2 minutes of mixing, whereas the 5-en isomer takes up to 30 minutes to develop the full colour. A related reaction is the Salkowski test in which a chloroform solution of the steroid compound is treated with concentrated sulphuric acid when a red or yellow colour forms. Another widely used reagent is a chloroform solution of antimony pentachloride with which, oleanolic acid,

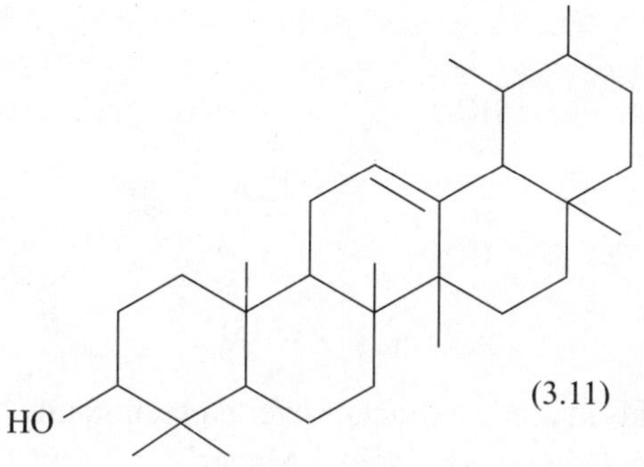

(3.11)

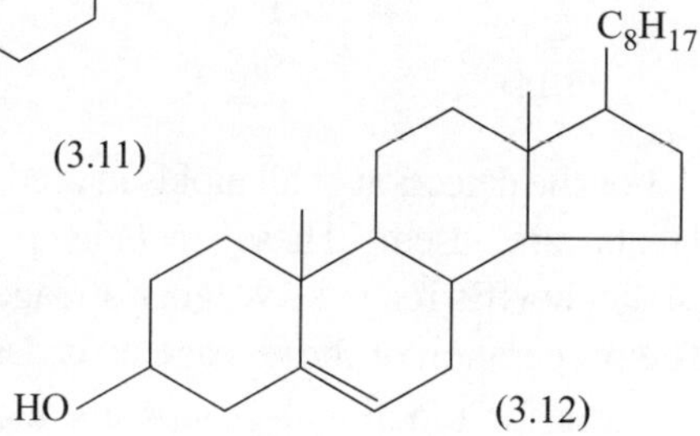

(3.12)

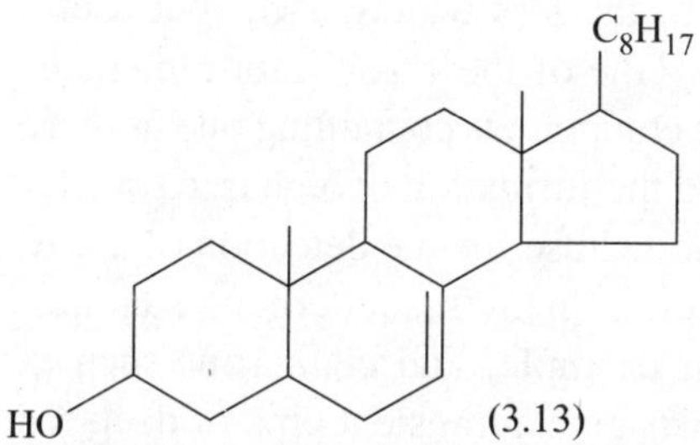

(3.13)

for example, gives a red-violet colour which turns an intense blue on addition of more chloroform.

For testing carbohydrates, besides the Molisch test, the following test is also useful. The reagent used for this colour test is a 0.1% solution of anthrone in concentrated sulphuric acid. To about 0.5 ml of this reagent, 0.5 ml of an aqueous solution or suspension of 1 mg of the test compound is added and mixed when a deep blue or green colour is obtained. Molisch test is the best known colour test for carbohydrates including phenolic and steroidal glycosides. In this test, to a solution of the sample dissolved in ethanol, a few drops of a 1% solution of alpha-naphthol in ethanol are added followed by the careful addition of concentrated sulphuric acid down the side of the test tube without disturbing the solution. At the interface of the acid and alcoholic layers, a brown to purple ring will appear if the sample is a carbohydrate.

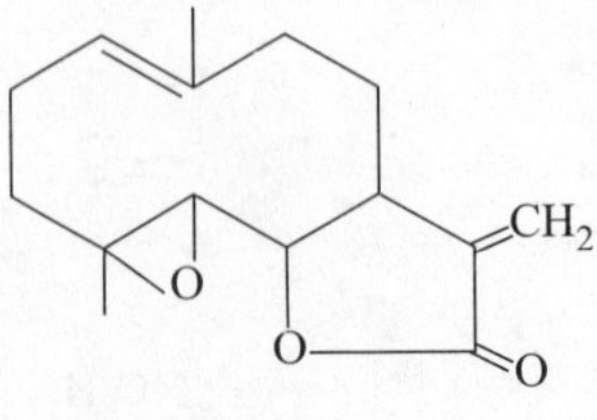

(3.14)

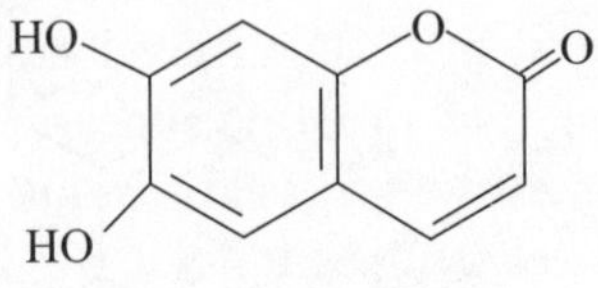

(3.15)

For the detection of alkaloids in crude extracts, several precipitating agents are used. These include picric acid, Mayer's reagent, Dragendorff's reagent, Wagner's reagent and ammonium reineckate. The preparation of these reagents is described in Appendix 2.

Tests for functional groups are too well-known to be described in detail here. However, some of the less widely used, but useful reactions, are mentioned below. One of these is tetranitromethane which gives a yellow colour with compounds containing one or more double bonds, presumably due to the formation of a charge transfer complex. The Legal test is of limited use for the detection of the α, β-unsaturated lactone moiety seen in many sesquiterpene lactones, such as parthenolide (3.14), for example, and coumarins such as esculetin (3.15). These compounds give a transient pink or deep red colour with freshly prepared alkaline sodium nitroprusside solution. The test is performed as follows: To a solution of the compound (2 mg) in pyridine (minimum quantity), one or two drops of freshly prepared 0.5% aqueous sodium nitroprusside is added, followed by four drops of a 0.2 N aqueous sodium hydroxide solution.

The Labat test which uses a sulphuric acid solution of gallic acid is useful for the detection of the methylene dioxy group often seen in flavonoids and lignans. Chromotropic acid is another colour developing reagent used for the detection of the methylene dioxy group.

3.1.2 Detection and derivatisation of functional groups

The presence of several functional groups can be detected on paper and TLC chromatograms using appropriate reagents. Derivatisation can also be brought about on TLC plates. The indicators, bromophenol blue and bromocresol green, are very useful for the detection of the carboxyl group. An acidic compound such as *p*-coumaric acid (3.16), appears as a yellow spot against a blue or green background. Esterification of an acid can be effected using ethereal diazomethane on a TLC plate before developing it. This is achieved by covering the spot of the compound being analysed by a few drops of ethereal diazomethane and allowing the solvent and the excess reagent to evaporate by gentle warming before developing the plate. Alternatively, the esterification of 1–2 mg of the compound can be brought about in a micro tube and the product spotted alongside the original on a TLC plate and identified by comparing the R_f values. Diazomethane can also be used for converting phenols into their methyl ethers.

Hydroxyl groups, both alcoholic and phenolic, can also be converted into their acetyl derivatives either on TLC plates or in micro tubes for comparison with the parent compounds. Generally, the product will have a higher R_f value than the parent. Phenolic hydroxyls can be detected on chromatograms using a variety of reagents, such as ammonia vapours, alcoholic ferric chloride, alcoholic aluminium chloride and the Boute reagent (ammonia followed by nitric oxide generated from concentrated nitric acid and copper) which gives a stable yellow colour. Aqueous or alcoholic 2,4-dinitrophenylhydrazine is the most convenient reagent for the detection of the carbonyl functionality of a ketone or an aldehyde. The colour and ease of formation of the 2,4-DNP derivative can indicate whether it is isolated or conjugated with a double bond or an aromatic ring. The colour of the derivative tends towards the red as the conjugation increases, while the rate of formation becomes slower.

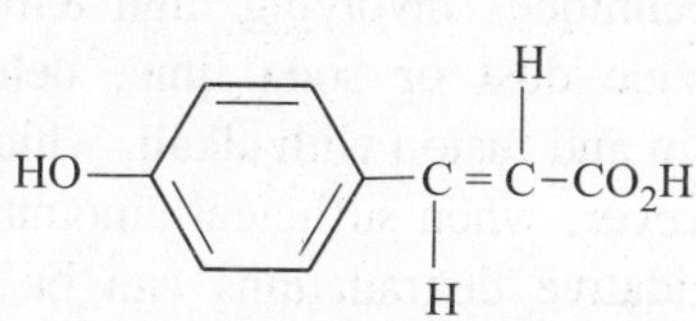

(3.16)

Derivatisation is also done to make the compound more amenable for subsequent spectral analysis. For example, the mass spectrum of an alcohol rarely shows the molecular ion signal. The corresponding acetate is more suitable. Further, the solubility of an acetate derivative in a non-polar solvent is usually more than that of the parent alcohol, which is also less volatile. Acetates are also easier to purify by crystallisation. The problems mentioned above are more acute in the case of polyhydroxy compounds, such as sugars whose acetyl and trimethylsilyl derivatives are much more amenable to spectral analysis. Polyhydric phenols can also be converted into their partial or complete *O*-methyl ethers. The one advantage of such derivatisation reactions is that in most cases the conversion is quantitative, unlike the degradation reactions described in the next section.

Hydrolysis of glycosides

If preliminary colour tests and solubility behaviour indicate that the compound under examination is a glycoside, the first step is to hydrolyse the compound using aqueous sulphuric acid to separate the aglycone from the sugar(s). The sugar portion can be easily identified by paper chromatographic analysis. The aglycone can be either identified, if it is a known compound, or characterised, if new, by further studies. Enzymatic hydrolysis is carried out to determine the type of glycosidic linkage.

3.1.3 Oxidative degradations

With the advent of spectroscopic methods, it is hardly necessary these days to resort to chemical degradations to obtain information regarding the structure of a compound. This is particularly true with regard to techniques involving high temperatures, such as distillation with zinc dust or soda lime, dehydrogenation with sulphur or selenium and fusion with alkali, which were in vogue in earlier days. However, when sufficient amounts of the compound are available, oxidative degradations can be carried out either to obtain further useful information or to confirm a part of the structure. Aqueous potassium permanganate is often used for this purpose but a number of other reagents, such as chromium trioxide, sodium or potassium dichromate and ozone can also be used. For instance, with 10 mg of terthienylmethanol (3.17), isolated from the plant *Eclipta alba*, it was possible to oxidatively break it—with the help of potassium permanganate—to thiophene 2,5-dicarboxylic acid (3.18) and bithienyl-2-carboxylic acid (3.19), which were identified by direct comparison with authentic samples.

Alkaline hydrogen peroxide has been used to break down isoflavones to characterise the side phenyl group in these compounds, which appears in the product mixture as a substituted benzoic acid. Coumarins, being lactones, can be methylated in an alkaline medium to obtain the corresponding 2-methoxycinnamic acid (3.20), which can either be identified as such or further degraded to identifiable products. This technique was successfully used for the elucidation of the structure of wedelolactone tri-*O*-methyl ether (3.21).

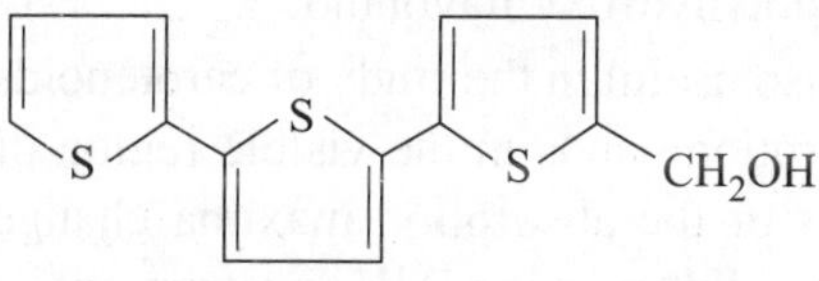

(3.17)

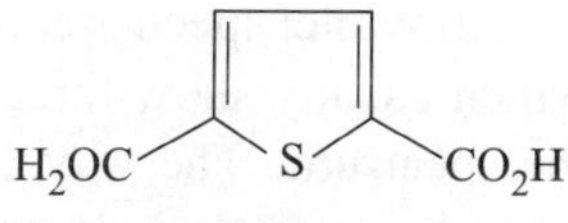

(3.18)

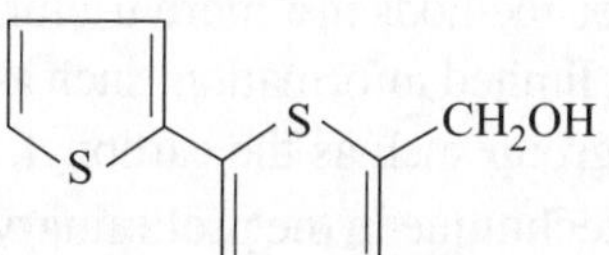

(3.19)

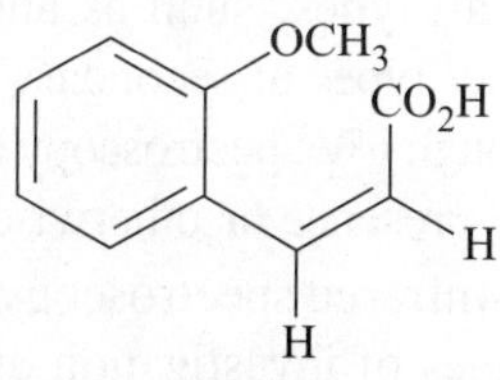

(3.20)

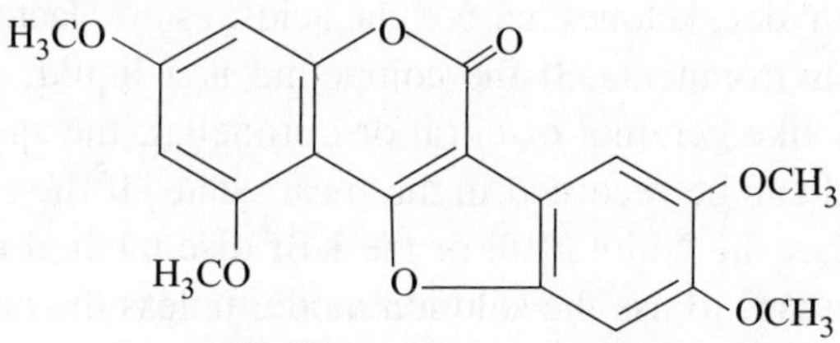

(3.21)

3.2 SPECTRAL METHODS

In the present day context, the use of spectral data for the determination of the structure of a new natural product hardly requires emphasis. In this book, where the emphasis is on practical details, it is not possible to go into the theory of the different types of spectroscopic methods available for structural studies. Spectral data have been given under individual compounds in later chapters. The most powerful and informative among the techniques available are nuclear magnetic resonance and mass spectroscopy in their full range. These are followed by infrared and ultraviolet spectroscopy in that order. The last mentioned technique, however, is very useful in the study of flavonoids. With the use of appropriate shift reagents, such as fused sodium acetate, sodium methoxide, sodium acetate–boric acid and aluminium chloride, with and without hydrochloric acid, it is possible to obtain information regarding the locations of different hydroxyl groups in a polyhydroxy flavonoid.

Ultraviolet spectroscopy is also useful in the study of carotenoids which usually show three absorption bands in the visible region of the spectrum. The wavelengths of the absorption maxima change with change in the solvent. Generally speaking, UV spectroscopy is more useful in the study of polyphenolic compounds and pigments of all types, such as anthocyanins, carotenoids and quinones. For other types of secondary metabolites, other methods are more useful, though UV spectroscopy can be used to get limited information, such as the presence or otherwise of a functional group such as the carbonyl.

Infrared spectroscopy is a very useful technique in the preliminary stages of investigation of a compound, as it provides data regarding the presence of functional groups, such as the hydroxyl, carbonyl of all kinds (aldehydes, ketones, carboxylic acids, esters, lactones, etc.) in different environments. If the compound is a liquid, such as a mono terpene like geraniol or citral or citronellal, the spectrum of the compound can be recorded in the 'neat' state. If the compound is a solid, either the Nujol Mull or the KBr disc method is used. It is rarely necessary to use the solution mode, unless the objective is to get accurate values of the absorption maxima.

Nuclear magnetic resonance spectroscopy is the most versatile among the physical methods available to a natural products chemist. Several excellent books and specialist monographs are available on the subject. It is too important a subject to be dealt with in a casual way in a paragraph or two. Suffice it to mention that with a combination of NMR techniques which include proton and carbon NMR spectra, double resonance methods and 2D-NMR techniques, it is possible to get almost all the information needed for elucidating the structure of a naturally occurring compound. For details, the books mentioned at the end of this chapter should be consulted. The majority of plant secondary metabolites dissolve in deutero chloroform or in deuterated dimethyl sulphoxide which are the most widely used solvents for recording NMR spectra. The internal reference compound is almost always tetramethylsilane.

The other physical method which in conjunction with NMR forms a powerful tool is mass spectroscopy. Here again, as in the case of NMR, there have been spectacular advances in instrumentation and modes of generation of spectra in recent years. As a consequence, it is possible to arrive at a structure, in favourable cases, on the basis of mass spectral data alone. By and large a combination of NMR and mass spectral data provides sufficient input for completely delineating the structure of a naturally occurring compound.

Recommended Reading

1. Derome AE, *Modern NMR Techniques for Chemistry Research*, Pergamon Press, Oxford, 1987.
2. Houghton PJ and Raman A, *Laboratory Handbook for the Fractionation of Natural Extracts*, Chapman & Hall, London, 1998.
3. Kemp W, *NMR in Chemistry: A Multinuclear Introduction*, Macmillan, London, 1986.
4. Krishnaswamy NR, *Chemistry of Natural Products: A Unified Approach*, 2nd Edition, Universities Press, Hyderabad; CRC Press, Boca Raton, 2010. [Chapter 2 (Section 2.1) of this book gives a comprehensive account of the methods, both classical and modern, used for the characterisation of different types of

natural products. Modern spectroscopic methods, including recent advances, have been adequately covered and explained with the help of a number of illustrative examples.]

5. Markham KR, *Techniques of Flavonoid Identification*, Academic Press, London, 1982.
6. McLafferty FW and Stauffer DB, *Registry of Mass Spectral Data*, Wiley, New York, 1989.
7. Nakanishi K and Solomon PH, *Infrared Absorption Spectroscopy —Practical*, 2nd Edition, Holden-Day, San Francisco, 1977.
8. Nakanishi K, (Ed.), *One-dimensional and Two-dimensional NMR Spectra by Modern Pulse Techniques*, Kodansha, Tokyo; University Science Books, Mill Valley, California, 1990.
9. Scott AI, *Interpretation of the Ultraviolet Spectra of Natural Products*, Pergamon Press, Oxford, 1964.
10. Van Middlesworth F and Cannell RJP, Cannell RJP, (Ed.), *Dereplication and Partial Identification of Natural Products in Natural Products Isolation*, Humana Press, New Jersey, 1998.
11. Wehrli FW, Wehrli S and Marchand AP, *Interpretation of Carbon-13 NMR Spectra*, 2nd Edition, Wiley, New York, 1988.

CHAPTER 4

Procedures for Isolation of Select Compounds

In this chapter, experimental procedures for the isolation and characterisation of a few compounds of different chemical types are described. The examples chosen cover a fairly wide spectrum of secondary metabolites of plant origin. The procedures are simple, do not require elaborate equipment and can be reproduced in any undergraduate laboratory. Success with these experiments should give students the confidence needed to tackle more difficult isolations which they may encounter in research investigations.

The most attractive part of a plant is the flower or any other brightly coloured part, such as a berry or a ripe fruit, or a leaf modification, as in the case of the Poinsettia. The colouring matter may belong to either of two broad types, differentiated from each other on the basis of their solubility characteristics. They are the sap-soluble and the fat-soluble pigments. The brightly coloured anthocyanins, the betacyanins and related polyphenolic compounds, such as the flavonoids and allied compounds, belong to the first type.

Fat-soluble compounds include the carotenoids and some quinonoid compounds. These compounds also possess useful biological properties. The heavily hydroxylated flavonoids are antioxidants and so also are the carotenoids. By virtue of this property they have been implicated in cancer chemotherapy. The carotenoids can also be used for colouring food materials as they are non-toxic.

The first experiment described below is for the isolation of a carotenoid pigment, namely, bixin from annatto seeds.

4.1 BIXIN FROM *BIXA ORELLANA* SEEDS (ANNATTO)

Bixin (4.1) is a carotenoid pigment. Carotenoids occur widely in plants, are biosynthetically derived from mevalonic acid (4.2) and can be classified as tetraterpenoids. β-Carotene (4.3), the characteristic pigment of carrots, and lycopene (4.4), the pigment of ripe tomatoes, are polyenes. Bixin, on the other hand, is an oxygenated compound with a shorter carbon chain. It is the monomethyl ester of a dicarboxylic acid and is closely related to crocin (4.5), the colouring matter of saffron (*Crocus sativus*). Its structure was determined by the German Nobel laureate, Richard Kuhn, and his co-workers. The structure is given below. In natural bixin, the double bond between positions 4 and 5 has the *cis* configuration. This stereochemical feature was established

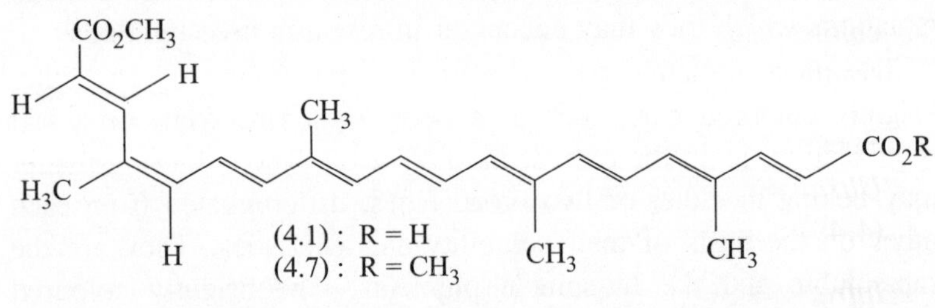

(4.1) : R = H
(4.7) : R = CH_3

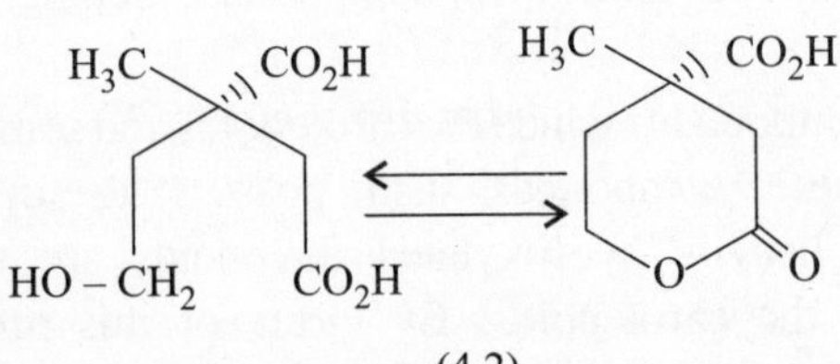

(4.2)

by Weedon on the basis of NMR spectral data. Natural bixin can be readily isomerised to the all-*trans* isomer (4.6) which was synthesised by another Nobel laureate, Paul Karrer, and his co-workers.

Experimental procedure

Whole seeds of *Bixa orellana* (they should not be powdered!) are boiled with ethyl acetate. The extract is decanted and concentrated to less than half its volume. The pure crystalline bixin which separates on cooling the concentrated extract is collected on a Buchner funnel under gentle suction and allowed to dry on the funnel itself. The average yield is 1.1 g from 10 g of the seeds. The filtrate is poured into light petroleum when a deep red-coloured solid separates out. This is impure bixin. Pure bixin can be obtained by redissolving it in the minimum quantity of ethyl acetate and precipitating it by the careful addition of light petroleum. By this procedure another 0.7–0.8 g of pure bixin can be obtained. Pure bixin crystallises from ethyl acetate–light petrol as deep red-coloured needles. It gives a blue colour with concentrated sulphuric acid. Its purity can be checked by thin layer chromatography on silica gel G, using chloroform–methanol (94:6) as the developing solvent; the pure compound gives a single spot.

Spectral properties of natural bixin

Ultraviolet spectrum λ_{max} (log ε); 446 (4.35), 471 (4.46) and 502 (4.49) nm.

Infrared spectrum γ_{max} 3300 (br, s), 1725 (s), 1660, 1615, 1575 (s), 1430, 1290, 1260, 1210, 1165 (s) and 965 (s) cm^{-1}.

Preparation of methylbixin (4.7; see p. 44)

To a solution of bixin (0.1 g) in dry acetone (30 ml), freshly ignited potassium carbonate (2 g) and pure dimethyl sulphate (Caution! highly toxic) (0.1 ml), are added and the mixture refluxed for 2 hours. Thereafter, it is filtered, the potassium salts washed with acetone and the combined filtrate concentrated on a water bath. To the residue, ice water is added with stirring. The methyl ester

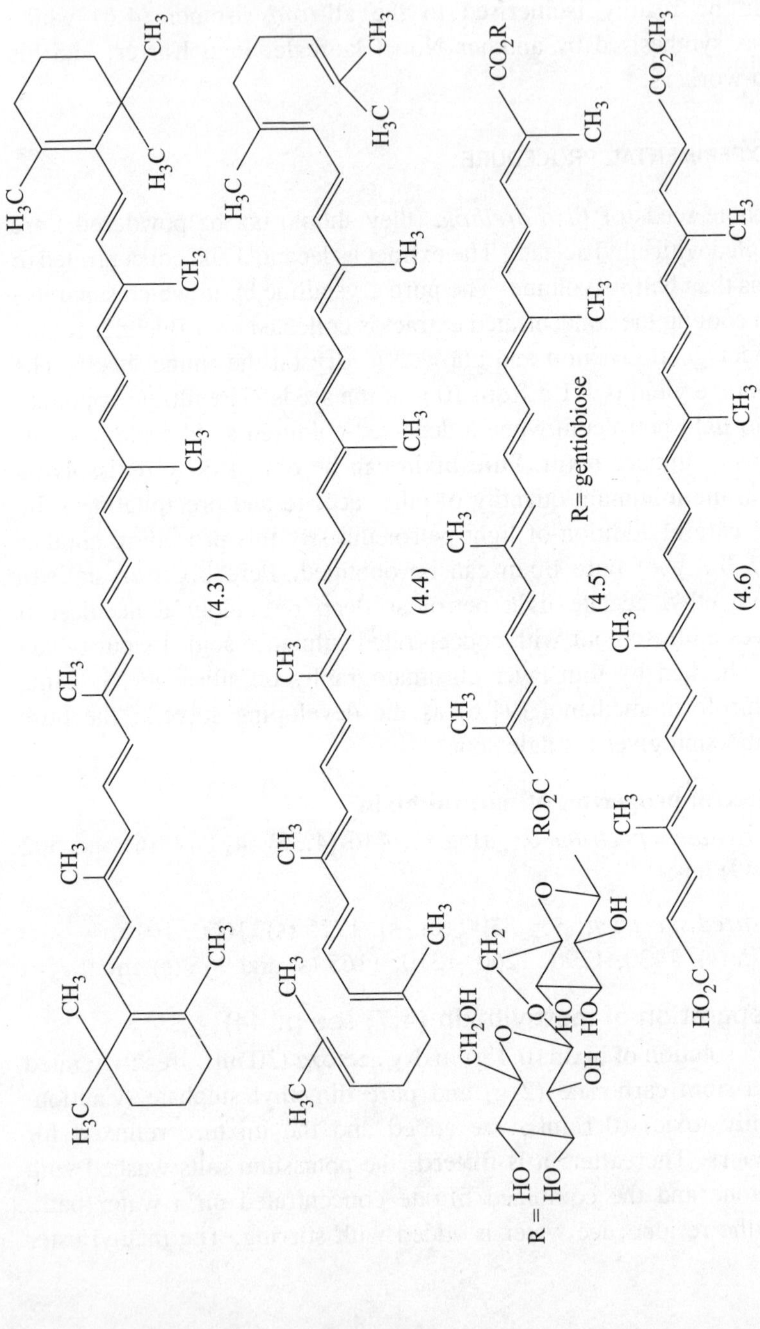

(4.3)

(4.4)

(4.5)

(4.6)

of bixin separates as a red-coloured crystalline solid, m.p. 161–62°C. It can also be prepared from bixin by reaction with ethereal diazomethane.

The proton NMR spectrum recorded in $CDCl_3$, with TMS as the internal reference, has the following signals: δ 1.98 (s, 12H), 3.77 (s, 6H), 5.89 (d, J = 15.5Hz, 2H), 6.57 (br, m, 10H), 7.41 (d, J = 15.5Hz, 1H) and 7.98 (d, J=15.5 Hz, 1H).

RELATED EXPERIMENTS

The pigments of red chilies, *Capsicum annuum*, capsanthin (4.8) and capsorubin (4.9), can be easily extracted and studied by TLC. A light petroleum extract of dry chilies (10 g), cut into small pieces, is made and concentrated to a small volume. A couple of drops of the extract is spotted on a TLC plate coated with silica gel G. The plate is developed with light petroleum as the irrigating solvent. Each of the two major spots is scraped out of the plate, extracted with light petroleum and the visible spectrum of each solution is recorded. The structures of these two compounds are shown below.

A similar extract of air-dried orange peels, free from the white pulpy matter, is made and examined by TLC. The main colouring matter of the material is citraurin (4.10).

Preparation of TLC plates

A slurry of silica gel G in distilled water is made by stirring in 30 g of the gel in 100 ml of distilled water. The consistence of the slurry can be adjusted by varying the amounts of the gel and water. It is then poured on clean, dry glass micro-slides with a deft movement of the hand; a uniform layer of the slurry is achieved on each plate. The plates are kept aside, without disturbance, on an even surface for about an hour. Thereafter, they are activated by heating in an oven at 120°C for 45 minutes to 1 hour.

Basic silica gel layers are prepared by mixing silica gel G with 0.1N aqueous sodium hydroxide, or 0.15M sodium acetate solution, or Sorensen buffer (pH 6.8), instead of water. Acidic silica gel layers can be prepared using 0.2 M oxalic acid or 2.5% (v/v) sulphuric acid solution in place of water.

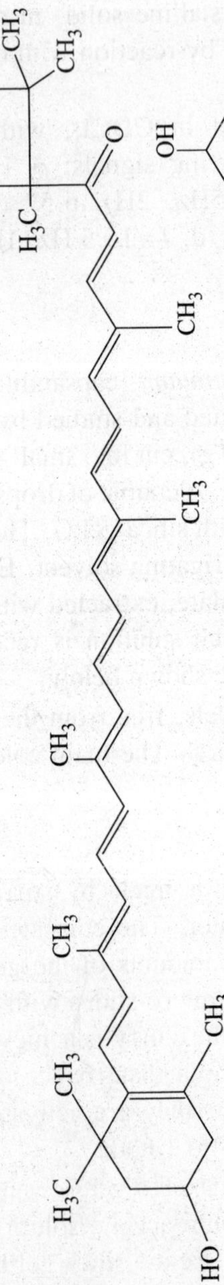

(4.8)

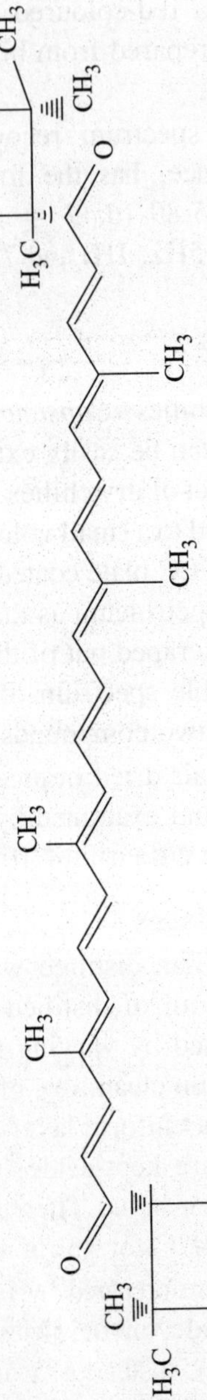

(4.9)

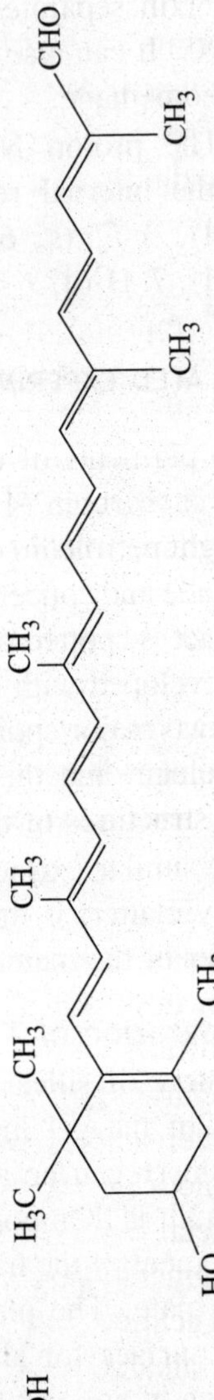

(4.10)

Reverse phase chromatographic plates are made by carefully immersing plates prepared as described above in a 5%–10% solution of the impregnating agent (liquid paraffin or silicone oil) in light petroleum (40–60) or diethyl ether. After removing the plates and allowing the solvent to evaporate, the plates are ready for use.

4.2 ANTHOCYANINS

Anthocyanins constitute a major group of sap-soluble plant pigments. These compounds are of widespread occurrence and are responsible for the orange, red, purple and blue colours (and different shades of these) of a large number of flowers, such as the rose, chrysanthemum, tulip, petunia, salvia, corn flower, and others, and also deeply coloured berries and fruits, such as black grapes, cherries, etc. A pioneer in the study of these compounds was the German Nobel laureate, Richard Willstatter, who isolated a number of these pigments and deduced their structures. They occur in nature as glycosides and in some cases, like the cornflower, as metal complexes.

Hydrolysis of the glycosides and removal of metals, if any, yields the corresponding anthocyanidins. The colour depends on the degree of hydroxylation and also on metal complexation. Partial methyl ethers and acyl derivatives are also known. Pelargonidin (4.11) derivatives exhibit orange and related shades, whereas cyanidin (4.12) derivatives are deep red in colour. Blue colour is characteristic of delphinidin (4.13) derivatives. Some metal complexes of cyanidin also show blue colour. Anthocyanin pigments are relatively unstable and their colours are pH dependent. In acidic solutions, cyanidin derivatives exhibit red colour, whereas in alkaline media, the colour changes to blue. Some anthocyanin structures and the effect of pH on structure are shown.

4.2.1 Isolation of cyanin (4.14) from red roses

The petals of deep red roses, free from stalks, are soaked in cold 2% methanolic hydrochloric acid. After 16 hours, the extract is

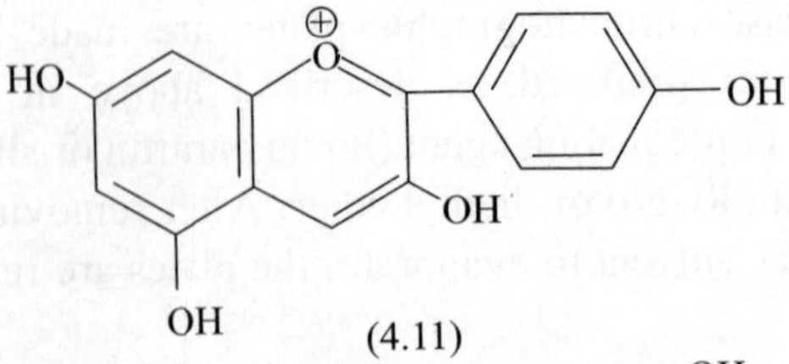

(4.11)

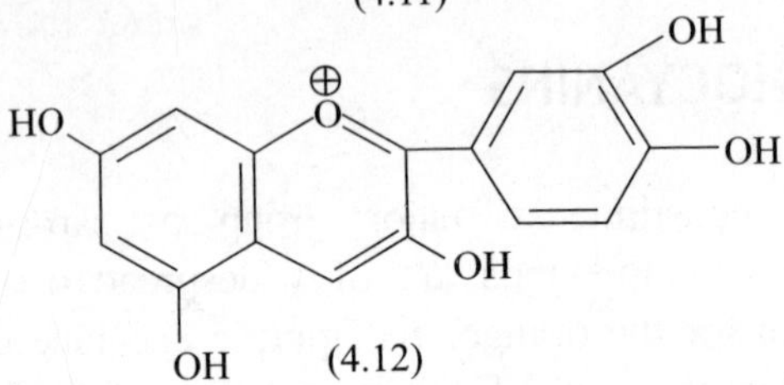

(4.12)

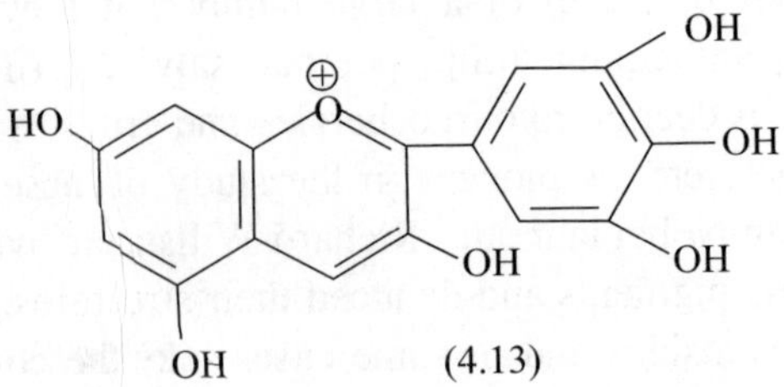

(4.13)

filtered and the residue washed with more solvent to complete the extraction. The combined solution is treated with two and half times its volume of diethyl ether, when crude cyanin separates as a red-coloured precipitate. The crude amorphous pigment is then covered with methanol containing 2% acetic acid for 24 hours, when most of the impurities dissolve, leaving behind the pigment as a deep brown microcrystalline solid. It is filtered, dissolved in boiling water and mixed with an equal volume of 3% ethanolic hydrochloric acid, when pure cyanin separates as fine, deep red glistening needles. The pure compound is collected on a Buchner funnel under suction and dried in a vacuum desiccator.

4.2.2 A blue pigment (4.15) from a blue flower

The above title was chosen by Prof. Hayashi for his lecture in which he first described the isolation of an anthocyanin pigment

(4.14)

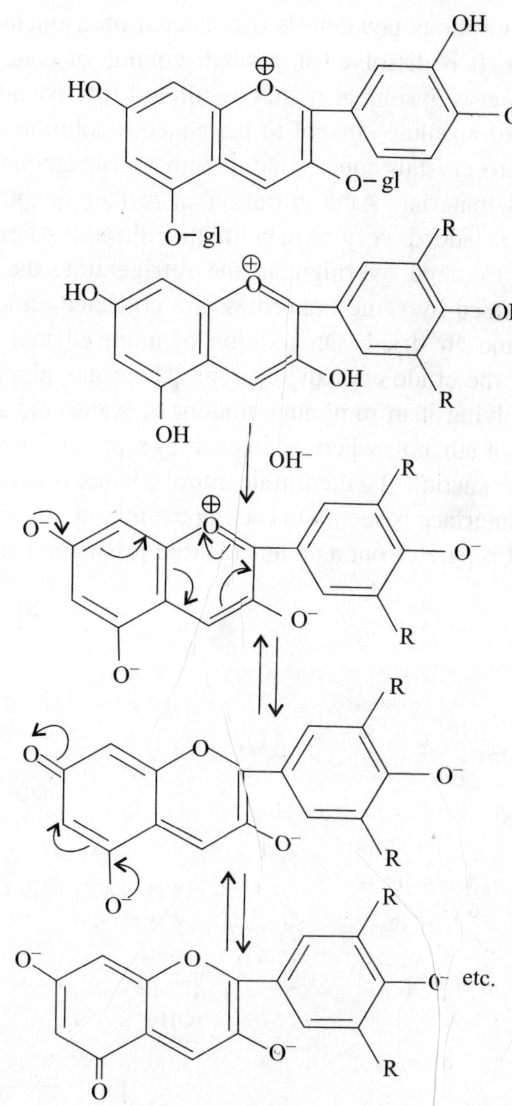

from cornflower, *Commelina communis*. Fresh crnflowers are pressed tightly in a gauze and the residue is triturаed with water and pressed again. The combined solution is filtered ad mixed with nine volumes of absolute ethanol, when the pigmet precipitates as an amorphous powder. It is collected on a Buchner funnel and air dried. It is dissolved in a small volume of cold water and the greenish gray insoluble matter is filtered off. By adding an equal volume of absolute ethanol to the aqueous solution and cooling it, blue micro-crystals appear, along with a large amount of colourless colloidal material. After filtration, a further quantity of absolute ethanol is added very slowly to the filtrate. After allowing the mixture to stand overnight in the refrigerator, the blue crystals, accompanied by some impurities, are collected on a sintered glass funnel and air dried. On addition of more ethanol to the filtrate, more of the crude crystals separate. The crude pigment is purified by dissolving it in minimum amount of water and adding a small amount of ethanol, when the impurities separate out and are filtered off under suction. To the filtrate, more ethanol is added, after which a clear interface is seen. On cooling the mixture overnight, the pure pigment separates out as blue-coloured prismatic needles.

(4.15)

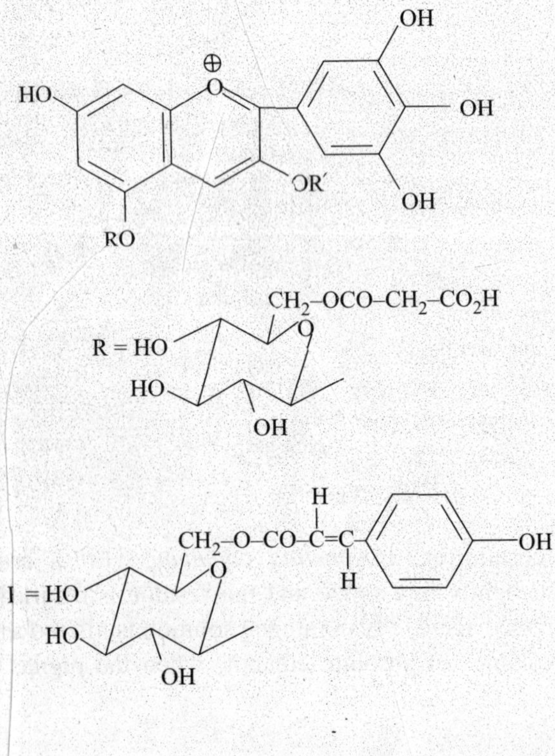

RELATED EXPERIMENTS

Crude anthocyanin pigments of the following plant materials are similarly extracted and examined by paper chromatography and visible spectroscopy: Flowers of jacaranda (blue), *Hibiscus rosa-sinensis* (red), salvia (scarlet red), purple Chrysanthemum, croton leaves (mottled), poinsettia leaves, and skins of fruits like cherries (reddish brown), grapes (dark purple), jasmine (purple) and ripe coffee berries (deep red). Alternatively, any of the above materials can be extracted by digesting them with up to ten times their weight of glacial acetic acid. When the plant tissues are completely decolourised, the extract is filtered and treated with diethyl ether, when the acetate of the anthocyanin pigment precipitates out. The solid is collected either by filtration or centrifugation (if it is fluffy and light) and dissolved in 0.5% methanolic hydrochloric acid and concentrated, if necessary, before subjecting it to paper chromatographic examination.

The anthocyanin pigments are hydrolysed by boiling in 20% aqueous hydrochloric acid for 10–15 minutes. The reaction mixture is cooled and extracted with *n*-amyl alcohol to remove the anthocyanidin chloride. The aqueous solution is carefully neutralised with aqueous sodium hydroxide and passed through short columns of anion and cation exchange resins to remove ionic impurities and concentrated. The concentrated residual solution is examined by paper chromatography using Whatman No.1 chromatographic paper. Either of the two solvent systems mentioned below can be used as the irrigating solvent. The paper, after spotting a few drops of the sugar solution at the centre of the paper, is developed using the horizontal mode of movement of the irrigating solvent (circular paper chromatography); the equipment comprises a small Petri dish to hold the solvent and a glass plate to cover the dish. The solvents which are useful for the examination of sugars are phenol saturated with water and the upper phase of butanol–acetic acid–water (4:1:5). After drying, the developed papers are sprayed with a solution of aniline phthalate and heated; the sugars appear as dark brown rings. Alternatively, the developed paper can be sprayed with silver nitrate–ammonium hydroxide solution. The sugars are identified by their R_f values, or by direct comparison with authentic samples.

For co-chromatography, the technique of ascending or descending chromatography is convenient. In the phenol–water system, for instance, glucose has an R_f of 0.5–0.55. The spray reagents are prepared as follows: Aniline phthalate reagent is prepared by dissolving 0.93 g of aniline and 1.66 g of phthalic acid in 100 ml moist butanol (butanol shaken with distilled water in a separatory funnel and separated from the aqueous layer). After spraying the developed chromatogram, it is heated for 10 minutes at 105°C. Ammonical silver nitrate is prepared by mixing 0.1N aqueous silver nitrate with an equal volume of 5N ammonium hydroxide. After spraying, the chromatogram is heated at 105°C for 5–10 minutes. Apart from butanol–acetic acid–water, the following solvents can also be used as irrigating solvents for the paper chromatographic separation and identification of reducing sugars.

1. Water (42), ethyl acetate (42), acetic acid (16)
2. Equal parts of water, 1-butanol and collidine
3. Ethyl acetate (60), pyridine (20) and water (20)

The components of each mixture are shaken together and allowed to stand for 24 hours, and if any separation occurs, the organic layer is separated and used as the solvent.

4.3 FLAVONOIDS

Naturally occurring flavones and flavonols are chemically related to the anthocyanins, but unlike the latter, they do not exhibit brilliant colours; at the most, they are coloured yellow, and hence, they are also known as *anthoxanthins*. The most well-known among these are quercetin, which is 3,5,7,3',4'-pentahydroxyflavone (4.16), and its glycosides. Other well-known and coloured flavonols include gossypetin (4.17) and its glycosides, which occur in cotton flowers and also in a number of species of Hibiscus and quercetagetin (4.18), for which the African marigold, *Tagetes patula*, is a good source.

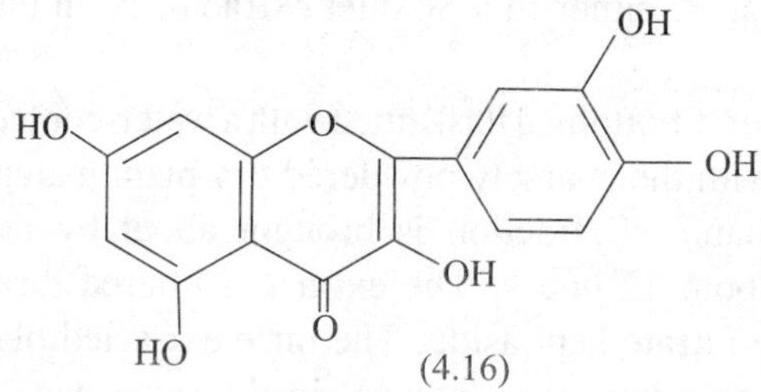

(4.16)

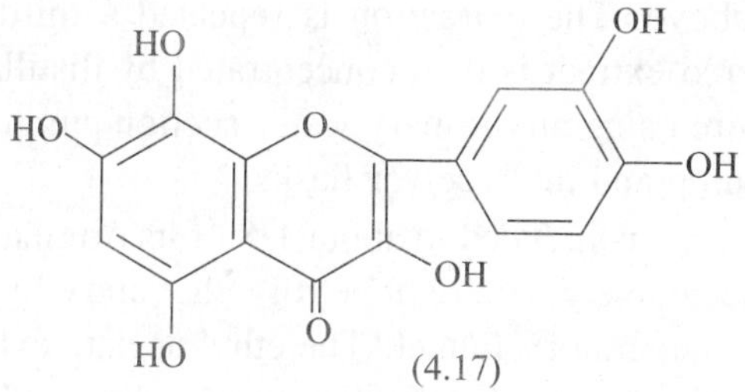

(4.17)

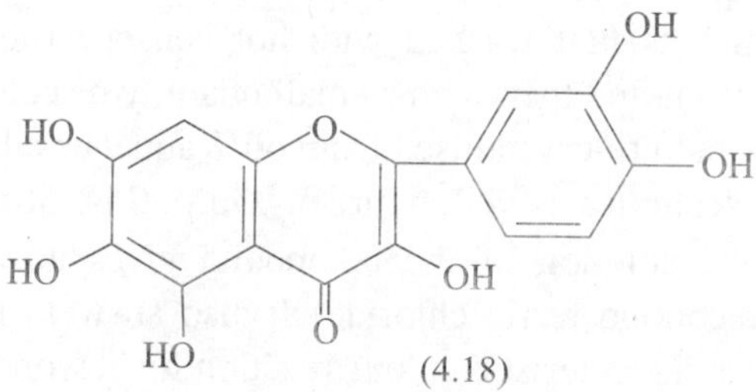

(4.18)

The following two procedures describe the isolation of two pale yellow-coloured flavone glucosides. These procedures have been chosen as they do not involve extensive fractionation and chromatographic procedures; the plant materials can also be easily procured.

4.3.1 Isolation of nepitrin (4.19) from *Nepeta hindustana*

Nepitrin is the 7-*O*-glucoside of 6-methoxy-5,7,3', 4'-tetrahydroxyflavone (4.20).

It is isolated as follows: Air-dried whole plant of the Indian medicinal plant, *Nepeta hindustana* (1 kg), is exhaustively extracted with 90% ethanol, either in a Soxhlet extractor or in the following manner.

A 5-litre round-bottomed flask fitted with a water-cooled condenser is half-filled with the coarsely powdered dry plant material covered with 90% ethanol. Extraction is brought about by refluxing the mixture for about 12 hours. The extract is filtered through cotton gauze and the filtrate kept aside. The once extracted plant material is extracted again with 90% ethanol in the same way and filtered as described above. The extraction is repeated a third time. The combined filtered extract is then concentrated by distillation under reduced pressure using an ordinary water-suction pump with a trap between the pump and the receiver flask.

After the extract is reduced to about 1/8 of its original volume, it is extracted successively with light petrol, ether and ethyl acetate, in that order, in a separatory funnel. The ethyl acetate extract yields, on removal of the solvent by distillation, a yellow-coloured solid (300 mg) which is first washed with hot benzene (do not inhale benzene vapours), and then with a small quantity of cold methanol. The residue is then re-crystallised from 60% aqueous ethanol, when pure nepitrin separates as yellow prisms, m.p. 254–56°C.

An alcoholic solution of the compound gives an olive green colour with alcoholic ferric chloride. It also answers the Shinoda test, which is a characteristic colour reaction for flavonoids. This is done as follows: To a solution of a few milligrams of the compound

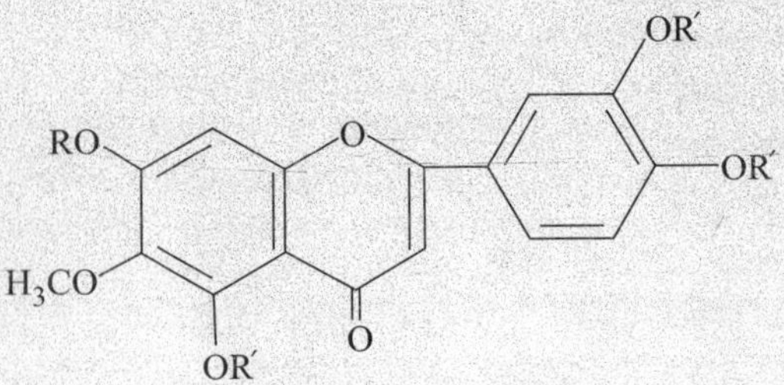

(4.19) : R = Glucosyl unit; R′ = H

(4.21) : R = H = R′

(4.20) : R = 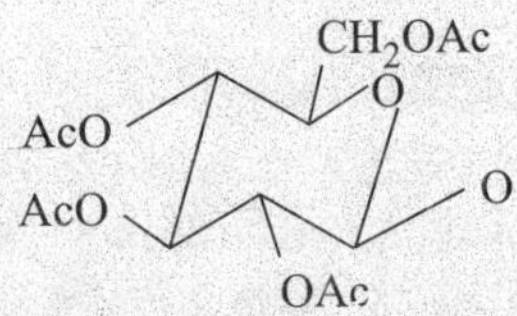

; R′ = Ac

in 2–3 ml of ethanol taken in a large test tube, a small amount of magnesium metal powder is added, followed by the addition of concentrated hydrochloric acid in drops. When all the magnesium has reacted, an orange-pink colour remains.

Nepitrin dissolves in 4% aqueous sodium carbonate solution giving a clear yellow-coloured solution from which it can be regenerated by acidification. It also answers the Molisch test for glycosides. For this test, the reagent required is a 10% solution of α-naphthol in pure methanol or chloroform. A couple of drops of the reagent is mixed with a couple of drops of an aqueous solution or dispersion containing 2–3 mg of the compound in a small test tube. This mixture is taken in a capillary pipette and allowed to slowly run down the side of a test tube containing 0.2–0.4 ml of concentrated sulphuric acid. The tube containing the acid is inclined at an angle of 45°, so that the test solution is stratified at the top of the acid. A violet-purple colour appears at the interface of the two layers. This is a useful diagnostic colour test for glycosides.

Characterisation of nepitrin

Paper chromatography: solvent: 25% acetic acid; R_f 0.3.

Thin layer chromatography: silica gel G; solvent: benzene–methanol (1:4); R_f 0.5; solvent: 15% acetic acid; R_f 0.8.

UV spectrum: λ_{max} MeOH(log ε) 272(4.33), 347(4.33); with sodium acetate: 272, 347; with sodium acetate–boric acid: 265(4.41), 375(4.34); with aluminum chloride: 280(4.3), 365(4.28) nm.

Nepitrin heptaacetate (4.20)

Nepitrin (100 mg), acetic anhydride (1ml) and pyridine (0.5 ml) are mixed together and warmed to get a clear solution, which is allowed to stand at room temperature for 24 hours. On pouring the mixture into water, a colourless solid separates. It is filtered, washed with ice-cold water and dried. Yield: 100 mg. On re-crystallisation from methanol, the acetate separates out in the form of long silky needles, m.p. 140°C.

Its proton NMR spectrum (in deuterated chloroform) shows the following signals: δ 2.05 (12H, s), 2.32 (6H, s), 2.45 (3H, s),

3.80 (3H, s), 4.25 (2H, br), 5.35 (5H, br), 6.60 (1H, s) and 7.15–7.80 (4H, complex).

HYDROLYSIS OF NEPITRIN—ISOLATION OF NEPETIN (AGLUCONE) (4.21) AND GLUCOSE

Nepitrin (0.1 g) is refluxed with 7% aqueous sulphuric acid (25 ml) for 2 hours. The mixture is cooled and filtered to collect the solid aglucone. The filtrate is extracted once with diethyl ether and the ether solution evaporated to recover more of the aglucone. Total yield of the yellow-coloured aglucone (nepetin) is 0.06 g. It can be purified by re-crystallisation from aqueous methanol, m.p. 264–65°C. It gives an olive-green colour with alcoholic ferric chloride and an orange-pink colour in the Shinoda test.

The UV spectrum in methanol has absorption maxima at 275(log ε 4.24) and 345(4.28) nm; with sodium acetate, 275(4.31), 375(4.20); with sodium acetate-boric acid, 267(4.29), 380(4.28) and with aluminium chloride, 262(4.14), 285(4.17), 360(4.26). The IR spectrum has a strong absorption maximum at 1660 cm^{-1}. Its acetate is prepared by warming 30 mg of the compound with acetic anhydride (0.5 ml) and a drop of pyridine, keeping it over-night with subsequent dilution with water. The product is collected using a micro-filtration apparatus; a micro -funnel fitted with a glass rod flattened at one end is convenient for collecting milligram quantities of a compound. Nepetrin tetraacetate melts at 170–72°C.

The filtrate remaining after removal of nepetrin is neutralised by the addition of barium carbonate till there is no further precipitation of barium sulphate, which is filtered off. The filtrate is concentrated in a porcelain dish over a water-bath to a small volume. The resulting solution is examined by circular paper chromatography in phenol saturated with water; the sugar has an R_f of 0.56 and is indistinguishable from chromatograms of glucose.

Estimation of glucose Alternatively, the filtrate after removal of nepetrin is made up to 25 ml in a measuring flask, and glucose is estimated colorimetrically by the Foilin–Wu method. Amount of glucose: 34.5%

Enzymatic hydrolysis of nepitrin

A solution of nepitrin (10 mg) in ethanol (5 ml) is treated with a citrate buffer (25 ml) and emulsin (from 15 almonds, as described below). The mixture is kept at 37°C for 4 days and then extracted with diethyl ether. Evaporation of the solvent from the ether extract gives nepetin. Paper chromatography of the aqueous layer shows the presence of glucose.

Preparation of emulsin Fifteen sweet almonds are immersed in boiling water for a minute. The water is poured off and the brown skins removed from the almonds. The almonds are then ground in a mortar, as thoroughly as possible, and made into a paste with 40 ml of water. Addition of 10 ml of 10% acetic acid to the paste causes coagulation of the proteins. After 10 minutes, the mixture is filtered through a Buchner funnel, the residue washed with a few millilitres of water and drained well. To the filtrate, a drop of 10% acetic acid is added and if the solution remains clear, no more acetic acid is added. To the solution, an equal volume of alcohol is added when the enzyme separates out as a solid. It is filtered on a Buchner funnel, washed with alcohol and ether and then dried in a vacuum desiccator. It is used for hydrolysis as described above.

4.3.2 Isolation of pedaliin (4.22)

This compound is closely related to nepitrin; the two are isomers with the positions of attachment of the glucose unit, and the *O*-methyl group, differing in them. Pedaliin is the 6-*O*-glucoside of 7-methoxy-5,6,3',4'-tetrahydroxyflavone (4.23).

It is isolated from the leaves of *Sesamum indicum* using the following procedure: Air-dried leaves of the plant (750 g) are extracted with boiling ethanol (3 × 4 litres; 12 hours each time) and the combined extract concentrated under reduced pressure as described under the isolation of nepitrin. The concentrated extract measuring one litre in volume is then cooled when a yellow-coloured solid (3 g) separates out. More of this compound

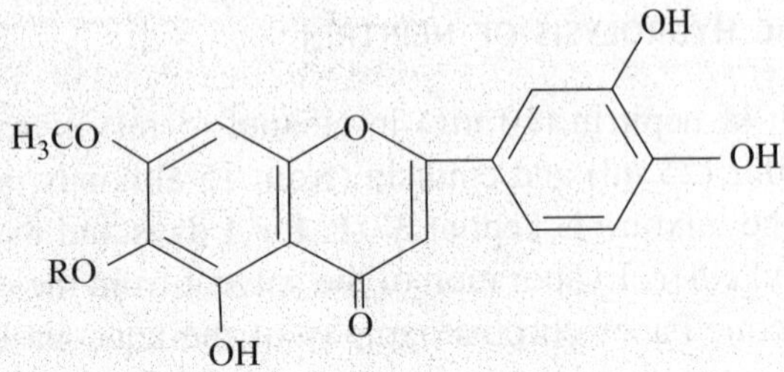

(4.22) : R = Glucosyl unit
(4.23) : R = H

(up to 2.5 g) is obtained from the filtrate by further concentration to 1/9 of the original volume, followed by cooling. The total solid is then refluxed with light petroleum in a small (100 ml) round-bottomed flask fitted with a water-cooled condenser till no more of the material dissolves in the solvent. The filtered solid is then repeatedly macerated with diethyl ether, filtered and washed with ether. The residue is crude pedaliin (5–5.5 g). It can be purified by dissolving in the minimum quantity of methanol, to which diethyl ether is added, when precipitation begins. The solution is then cooled when pedaliin slowly crystallises out. It can also be re-crystallised from 60% aqueous ethanol. It melts at 254–55°C, answers the Molisch test, gives an olive-green colour with alcoholic ferric chloride, and an orange-brown colour in the Shinoda test. Even though the melting points of nepitrin and pedaliin are the same, the fact that they are different compounds is shown by the determination of a mixed melting point which is depressed.

Characterisation of pedaliin The UV spectrum of pedaliin in methanol shows absorption maxima at 270–75 and 345–50 nm. On addition of sodium acetate, the spectrum shows maxima at 265 nm and 370 nm. Addition of aluminium chloride shifts the maximum at 350 nm to 425 nm.

Hydrolysis of Pedaliin—Isolation of Pedalitin (4.23)

A mixture of pedaliin (100 mg) and 7% aqueous sulphuric acid (50 ml) is refluxed for 2 hours, cooled and filtered. The filtrate is extracted once with diethyl ether and the solvent evaporated from the ether extract. The residue is mixed with the solid obtained by filtration and re-crystallised from methanol, when pedalitin, the aglucone, is obtained as yellow needles (ca 50 mg), m.p. 300–301 °C.

The UV spectrum shows absorption maxima at 285 nm and 345 nm. Paper chromatographic examination of the filtrate remaining after separation of the aglucone, neutralisation and concentration, shows the presence of glucose.

Pedalitin acetate is prepared using the same procedure as the one described under nepetin. The product melts at 242–43 °C.

4.3.3 Isolation of hesperidin (4.24)

Unlike flavones and flavonols (3-hydroxyflavones), flavanones (dihydroflavones) are colourless. One of these is hesperidin which is easily isolated from orange peels. It is a rhamnoglucoside of hesperetin, which is 4'-methoxy-5,7,3'-trihydroxyflavanone (4.25).

Peels from fresh orange fruits (*Citrus aurantium*) are carefully dried in the shade by spreading them out on a table. The peels are cut into small pieces, packed into a Soxhlet extractor and extracted with light petroleum (b.p. 40–60 °C) till the siphonings are colourless. The petroleum extract is kept aside for the isolation of limonene described later. The de-fatted peels present in the Soxhlet extractor are then extracted with methanol till the extraction is complete, as shown by the absence of any colour in the siphonings. The methanolic extract is concentrated by distillation under reduced pressure, using a water-suction pump. The syrupy residue is

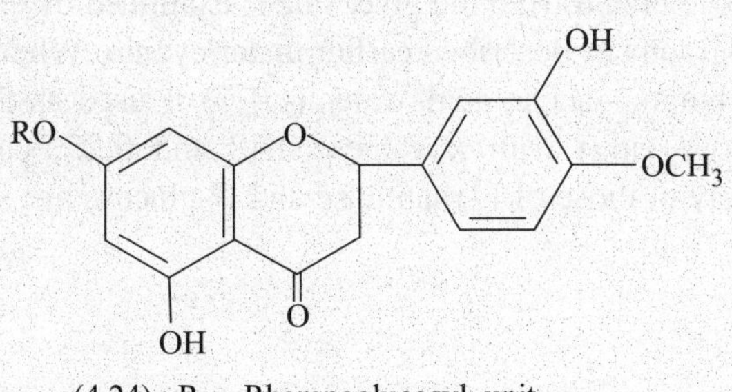

(4.24) : R = Rhamnoglucosyl unit
(4.25) : R = H

dissolved in hot aqueous acetic acid and the solution filtered hot. On cooling the solution, hesperidin crystallises out as colourless needles, m.p. 252–54°C. It answers the Molisch test, gives a wine-red colour with alcoholic ferric chloride and a purple colour in the Shinoda test. Its UV spectrum shows absorption maximum at 283 nm with a shoulder at 326 nm.

Hydrolysis of Hesperidin—Isolation of Hesperetin

In a 50-ml round-bottomed flask, a solution of 1 g of hesperidin in 20 ml of ethylene glycol is taken. To this solution, 1 ml of concentrated sulphuric acid is added and the mixture is refluxed on a boiling water bath for 45 minutes. The clear yellow solution is poured into 50 ml of cold water in a 100 ml beaker and cooled. Hesperetin, the pure aglycone, separates out as a colourless precipitate which is filtered under suction using a small Buchner funnel. It is washed free of acid, using small quantities of ice-cold water, on the funnel itself. The compound is re-crystallised from ethanol, when it is obtained as colourless crystals (0.35 g), m.p. 224–26°C.

The proton NMR spectrum of the compound has signals at δ 2.6–2.8 (2H, m), 3.8 (3H, s), 5.2 (1H, dd), 5.8 (1H, d, J = 3 Hz), 6.0 (1H, d, J = 3 Hz) and 6.8 (3H, m).

The aqueous filtrate obtained after filtering the precipitated hesperetin is neutralised by the addition of barium carbonate. After filtering the precipitated barium sulphate, the filtrate is concentrated in a porcelain dish on a water bath. The syrupy solution containing the sugars liberated from the glycoside is examined by circular paper chromatography as described earlier under cyanin. When the organic phase of butanol–acetic acid–water (4:1:5) is used as the irrigating solvent, two rings with R_f values, 0.48 and 0.29, corresponding respectively to those of L-rhamnose and D-glucose are seen.

4.3.4 Isolation of a biflavone—Cupressuflavone (4.26)

Biflavones are dimeric flavonoids with a C–C or a C–O linkage connecting two monomeric flavone moieties. These compounds have a rather restricted distribution in plants and are mainly confined to the Gymnosperms. One such compound is cupressuflavone. As can be seen from the structure, cupressuflavone is a C–C (8, 8") linked biflavone. Another example of a C–C linked biflavone is amentoflavone (3', 8" linked) (4.27). A biflavone having an ether linkage is hinokiflavone (4.28).

Clean leaves of *Cupressus torulus*, free from dirt, are air-dried and cut into small pieces. The material (200 g) is then extracted with acetone in a Soxhlet extractor. The extract is distilled to remove the solvent. The gummy residue is boiled with light petroleum (100 ml) to remove chlorophyll and waxy matter. The remaining solid is then refluxed with ethanol (100 ml) and the alcoholic extract decanted off. The procedure is repeated a second time. Cupressuflavone remains as a greenish-yellow solid (1.5 g). The compound is sparingly soluble in most organic solvents and can be purified by refluxing with acetone to remove the impurities. Cupressuflavone does not melt up to 360°C. With alcoholic ferric chloride it gives a green colour and dissolves in aqueous sodium carbonate and sodium hydroxide to yield yellow-coloured solutions.

The UV spectrum in ethanol has maxima at 226 (log ε 4.68), 274(4.58) and 330(4.55) nm. With sodium acetate, these maxima shift to 231(4.56), 285(4.60) and 335(4.33) nm. With aluminium chloride, the maxima are seen at 231(4.62), 281(4.55) 304(4.42) and 341(4.51) nm.

Cupressuflavone hexaacetate (4.29)

A mixture of cupressuflavone (100 mg), acetic anhydride (2.5 ml) and dry pyridine (1.5 ml) is gently refluxed for 3 hours and then poured into ice water. The colourless precipitate that separates is filtered, washed with water and dried. It is re-crystallised from

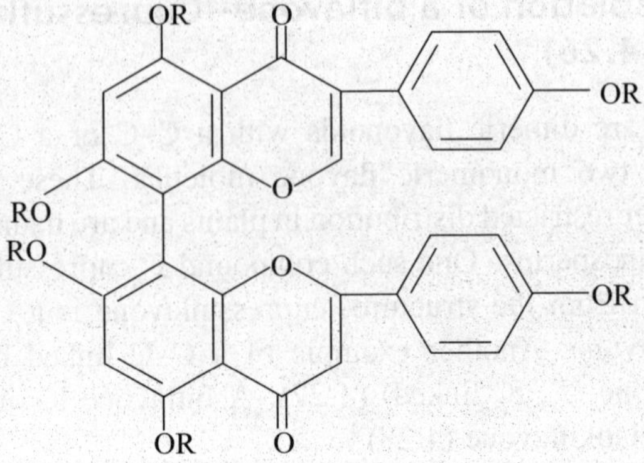

(4.26) : R = H
(4.29) : R = $COCH_3$
(4.30) : R = CH_3

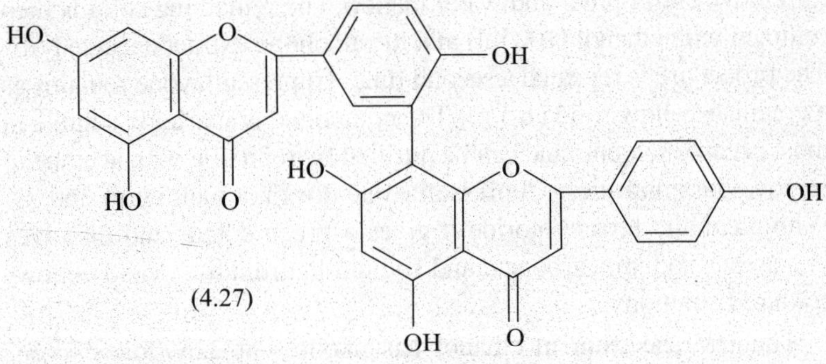

(4.27)

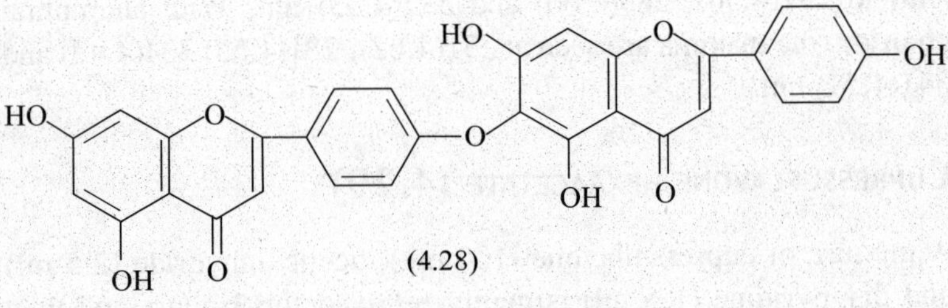

(4.28)

ethyl acetate when it is obtained as colourless needles (75 mg), m.p. 252–54°C.

CUPRESSUFLAVONE HEXAMETHYL ETHER

To a suspension of cupressuflavone (200 mg) in dry acetone (30 ml), dimethyl sulphate (0.6 ml) is added, followed by anhydrous (freshly ignited) potassium carbonate (1.6 g), and the mixture refluxed for 72 hours. The mixture is then filtered hot and the residue washed with warm acetone. The combined filtrate is distilled and the residue treated with water. The greenish-yellow solid separating out is filtered, dried and dissolved in chloroform. It is passed through a short column of silica gel and the adsorbed material eluted out using chloroform. Removal of the solvent from the chloroform eluate yields cupressuflavone hexamethyl ether (4.30; see p.64) as a yellow solid (120 mg). It is re-crystallised from methanol. The pure product melts at 295–97°C.

The UV spectrum in ethanol has maxima at 225 (log ε 4.75), 269(4.68) and 320(4.60) nm. Its proton NMR spectrum has signals at δ 3.7 (6H, s), 3.8 (6H, s), 4.1 (6H, s), 6.6 (4H, s), 6.8 (4H, d) and 7.3 (4H, d).

4.3.5 Isolation of catechins from green tea

Catechins are optically active flavonoids which lack the pyrone carbonyl function of flavones. They are accordingly classified as flavans or 2-phenylchromans. In recent years, these compounds have assumed much importance by virtue of their antioxidant activities and consequent use as dietary supplements. Green tea is a good source for these compounds which can be isolated as a mixture of closely related compounds. The main components of this mixture are epi-catechin (4.31), epi-gallocatechin (4.32) and the gallate esters (4.33 and 4.34) of these two compounds.

Fresh, green tea leaves are air-dried at room temperature and the dry material (10 g) is extracted with distilled methanol (free from water; 100 ml). After an hour the solution is filtered, water (10 ml) is added and the mixture distilled on a boiling water bath to remove

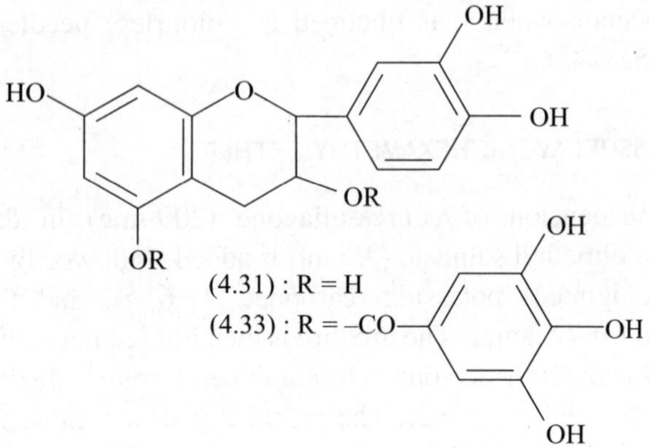

(4.31) : R = H
(4.33) : R = –CO–

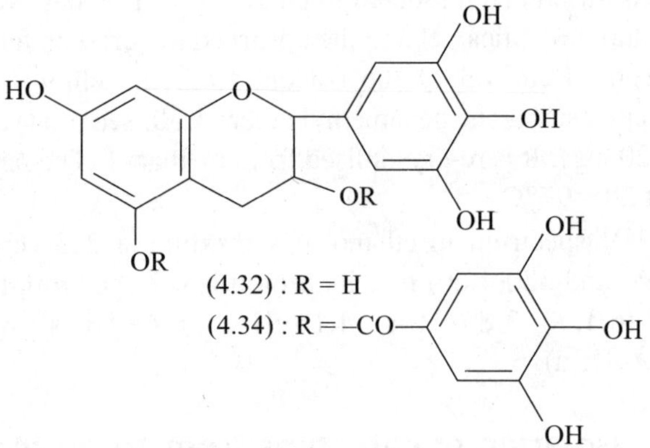

(4.32) : R = H
(4.34) : R = –CO–

the methanol. To the residual aqueous solution of the catechins, hexane (10 ml) is added and the mixture shaken well in a separatory funnel. After removing the organic layer, the aqueous layer is once again shaken with a fresh quantity of hexane to ensure the complete removal of caffeine. To the aqueous solution, which can be diluted if necessary, sodium chloride (1 g) is added, followed by the addition of phosphoric acid in drops, till the pH of the solution reaches 3.5. The mixture is then extracted in a separatory funnel with ethyl acetate twice, each time using 10 ml of the solvent. The combined ethyl acetate extract is washed a couple of times with ice-cold water till the washings are free from acid. Removal of the solvent from the ethyl acetate extract by distillation yields a solid catechin mixture. Yield: 1.5–2 g.

About 0.5 mg of the product is dissolved in 10 ml spectroscopic grade methanol and the UV spectrum recorded. For estimating the amount of epi-catechin, the absorbance at 278 nm is measured. The mixture is also examined by circular paper chromatography using Whatman No. 1 paper and the upper layer of benzene–acetic acid–water (2:2:1) as the developing solvent. The developed paper is sprayed with alcoholic ferric chloride. Epi-catechin gives a green colour, whereas epi-gallocatechin gives a bluish-green colour.

4.4 ISOFLAVANONES

Isoflavanones, as the name indicates, are isomers of flavanones and occur in several plants of the family Leguminosae (Fabaceae). They are dihydro derivatives of isoflavones, typical examples of which are daidzein (4.35) and genistein (4.36). In this section the isolation of two isoflavanones, homoferreirin (4.37) and ougenin (4.38) from the heartwood of *Ougenia dalbergioides* Linn. is described.

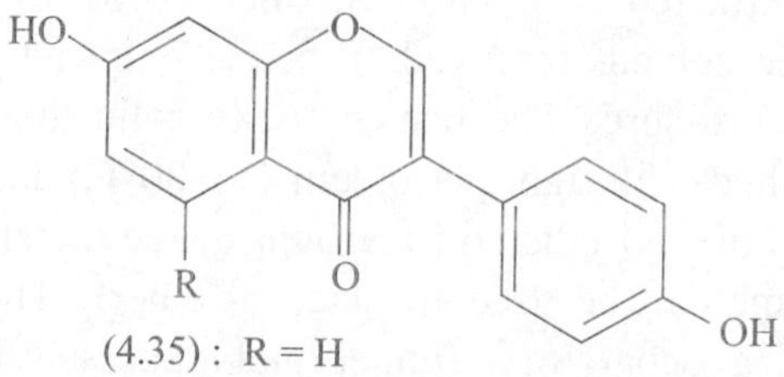

(4.35) : R = H
(4.36) : R = OH

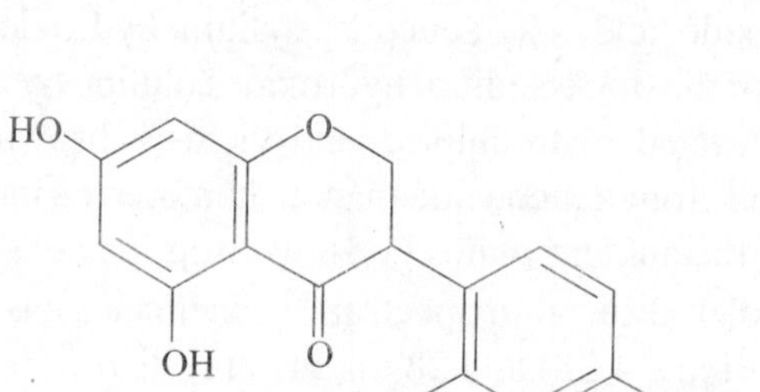

(4.37)

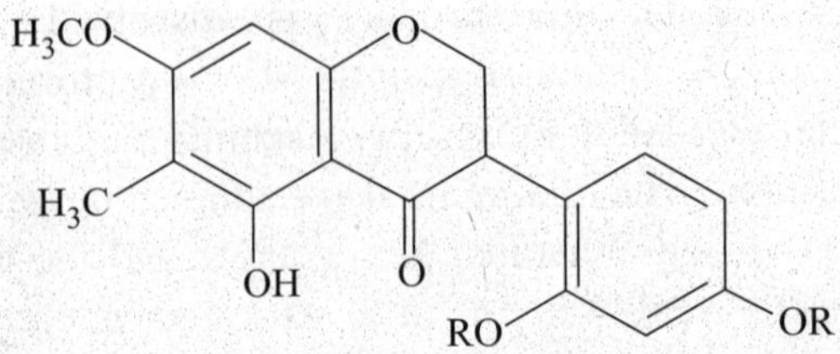

(4.38) : R = H
(4.40) : R = CH_3

This durable heartwood, known as Tinsha in Hindi, is used for making furniture.

4.4.1 Isolation of homoferreirin from *Ougenia dalbergioides*

(The quantities of plant materials given under this and the following experiments can be reduced. Alternatively, a group of students can be assigned one isolation experiment.)

Dry heartwood chips (550 g) of *Ougenia dalbergioides* are exhaustively extracted in a large Soxhlet extractor with boiling acetone and the solvent removed from the extract by distillation under reduced pressure. The brown sticky solid thus obtained is repeatedly washed with light petroleum (60–80°C) and the residue macerated with diethyl ether till the bulk of the material dissolves (dichloromethane can be used in place of ether). The solution is transferred to a separatory funnel and successively extracted with 20% aqueous sodium carbonate solution, 0.4% aqueous sodium hydroxide and 4% aqueous sodium hydroxide. Careful neutralisation of the 0.4% sodium hydroxide solution by the addition of cold concentrated hydrochloric acid yields a brown solid. On recrystallisation from aqueous methanol, homoferreirin is obtained in the form of rectangular plates (1.18 g), m.p. 147–48°C.

The ultraviolet absorption spectrum in methanol has absorption maxima at 229(log ε 4.38) and 287(4.31) nm. Its infrared spectrum (in KBr) shows a strong absorption band at 1643 cm^{-1}. It is optically active; $[\alpha]_D$ at 28° (in chloroform) is – 27°.

Dehydrogenation of homoferreirin

Formation of 5,7-dihydroxy-2',4'-dimethoxyisoflavone (4.39)

To a solution of homoferreirin (550 mg) in acetic acid (50 ml) taken in a 100-ml round-bottomed flask, freshly fused potassium acetate (1 g) is added, followed by the gradual addition of a solution of iodine (300 mg) in acetic acid (6.5 ml) over a period of 30 minutes. The mixture is refluxed for 6 hours, the solvent removed under reduced pressure, and the residue treated with water when the product separates out. It is recrystallised from methanol when 5,7-dihydroxy-2',4'-dimethoxyisoflavone is obtained as a colourless crystalline solid, m.p. 220–21°C. With alcoholic ferric chloride it gives a reddish violet colour.

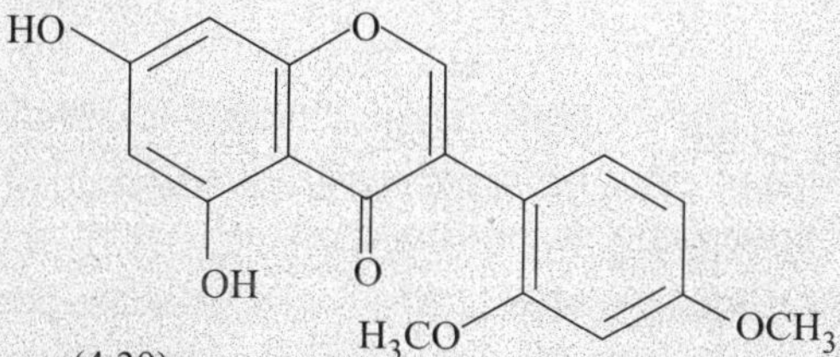

(4.39)

4.4.2 Isolation of ougenin

Acidification of the 4% aqueous sodium hydroxide extract gives a pale brown solid (3 g). On recrystallisation from methanol–benzene, ougenin separates out as pale yellow prismatic crystals, m.p. 238–40°C. Its UV spectrum in methanol has an absorption maximum at 291 nm (log ε 4.15). Its IR spectrum has a strong absorption band at 1627 cm^{-1}.

Preparation of ougenin dimethyl ether

A solution of ougenin (1.5 g) in the minimum amount of methanol–diethyl ether is treated with freshly prepared ethereal diazomethane solution till the yellow colour of diazomethane remains undischarged. The reaction mixture is allowed to stand at room temperature for

24 hours and thereafter the solvent is removed by distillation on a water-bath (Caution: ether is highly inflammable). The residue is washed with 10% aqueous sodium hydroxide solution and filtered, and the solid is washed free of alkali with cold water. After drying in a vacuum desiccator, it is recrystallised from methanol. The yield of ougenin dimethyl ether (4.40; see p. 68), m.p. 143–44°C, is 1 g.

4.5 XANTHONES

Xanthones are closely related to the flavonoids and form an important group of naturally occurring oxygen-containing heterocyclic compounds. They exhibit yellow or deeper colours depending on the degree of hydroxylation. They occur widely in several plants of the Guttiferae family. Well-known examples are gentisin (4.41), which occurs in the roots of *Gentiana lutea*, mangostin (4.42), isolated from *Garcinia mangostana,* and mangiferin (4.43), which is a chemical constituent of the leaves, heartwood and stem bark of

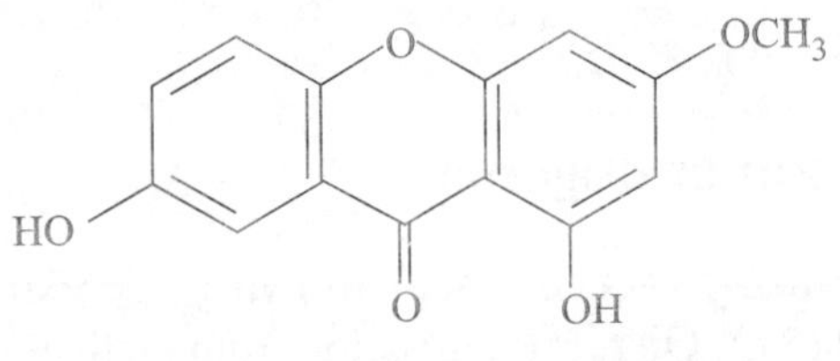

(4.41)

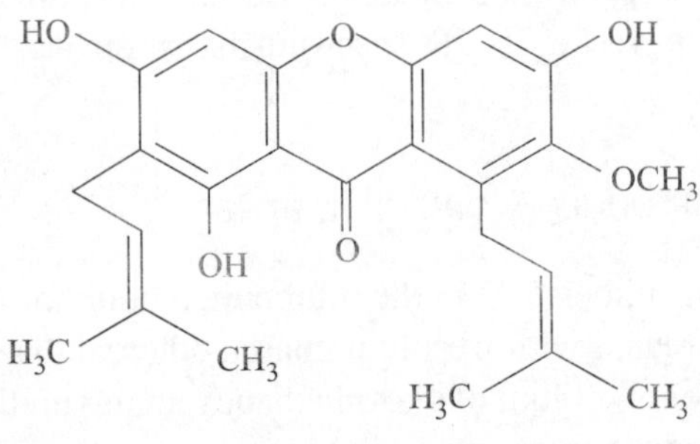

(4.42)

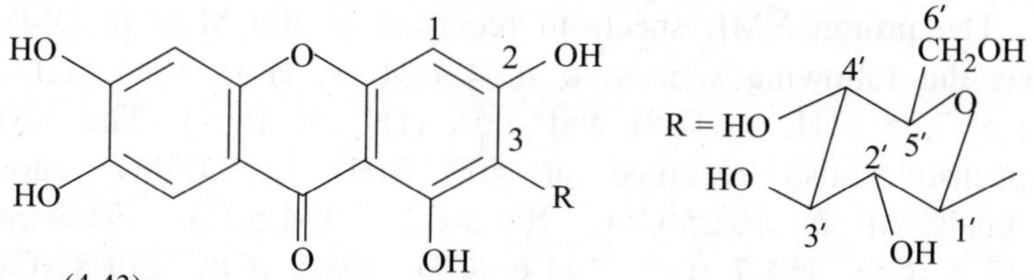

(4.43)

the mango tree, *Mangifera indica*. Its isolation from the bark of the mango tree is described.

4.5.1 Isolation of mangiferin

Air-dried fresh bark (120 g) of *Mangifera indica* is pulverised to a coarse powder and extracted in a Soxhlet extractor with light petroleum (60–80°C) to remove fatty matter. The defatted bark is then transferred to a percolator and repeatedly extracted with cold acetone to get rid of tannins; the extraction with this solvent is stopped when no residue is left behind on removal of the solvent. The material is then transferred back to the Soxhlet extractor and exhaustively extracted with 70% aqueous ethanol. The ethanolic extract is concentrated—preferably in a rotary evaporator—under reduced pressure. The distillation is stopped when mangiferin separates as a yellow amorphous powder (3.2 g). On recrystallisation from 70% aqueous ethanol, the compound is obtained as pale yellow needles, m.p. 270–272°C.

The IR spectrum of this compound (in KBr) has major absorption bands at 3413 (s), 2924 (m), 1645 (s), 1613 (s), 1486 (s), 1295 (m) and 1250 (s) cm^{-1}. The UV spectrum (recorded in 60% aqueous ethanol) shows absorption maxima at 239(log ε 4.35), 257(4.52), 314(4.15) and 360(4.10) nm. It is optically active, $[\alpha]_D$ at 32°C is +32° (in aqueous ethanol). In circular paper chromatography, with 60% acetic acid as the irrigating solvent, it appears as a pale yellow ring with R_f 0.60; the colour changes to a deeper yellow on exposure to ammonia vapours. With alcoholic ferric chloride it gives a deep green colour, and in the Shinoda test (magnesium and hydrochloric acid) it develops an orange-red colour. It answers the Molisch test for glycosides.

The proton NMR spectrum recorded at 400 MHz in DMSO has the following signals: δ 6.34 (1H, s, H-4), 6.84 (1H, s, H-5),7.35 (1H, s, H-8) and 4.56 (1H, d, H-1'). The NMR spectrum, also recorded at 400 MHz in DMSO, shows signals at δ 162.5(C1), 108.3(C2), 164.5(C3), 93.8(C4), 103.3 (C5), 154.7 (C6), 144.6 (C7), 108.8 (C8), 179.8 (C9), 156.9 (C4a), 151.5 (C4b), 112.4 (C8a), 102.0 (C8b), 82.3 (C1'), 73.8 (C2'), 71.3 (C3'), 70.9 (C4'), 79.7 (C5') and 62.2 (C6').

4.6 BETANINS

Betacyanins like betanidin (4.44), and betaxanthins such as indicaxanthin (4.45), collectively known as the betanins, are tinctorially related to the anthocyanins and the anthoxanthins, and like the latter are classified as sap-soluble pigments of plant origin. However, chemically and biosynthetically, the two groups of pigments are unrelated. The betacyanins and the betaxanthins are nitrogenous compounds derived from the amino acid proline (4.46). They are useful as chemotaxonomic markers as they are confined to plant families of the order Centrospermae. The chemistry of

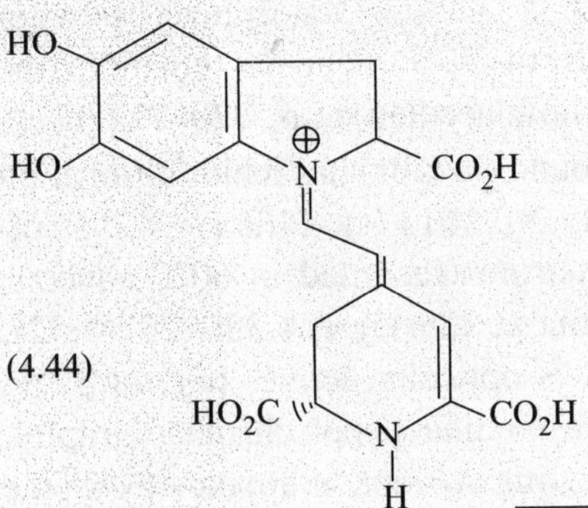

(4.44)

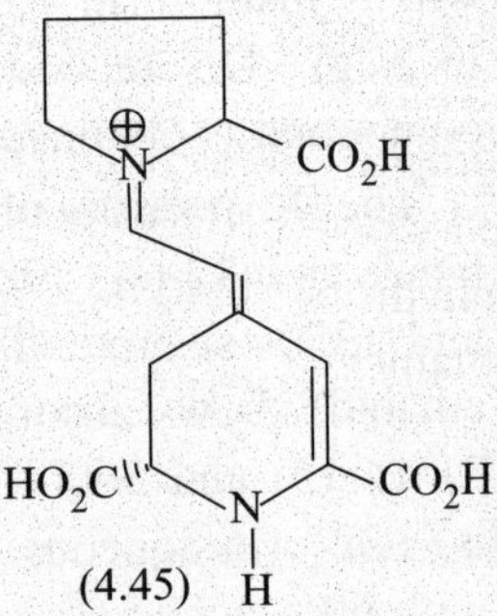

(4.45)

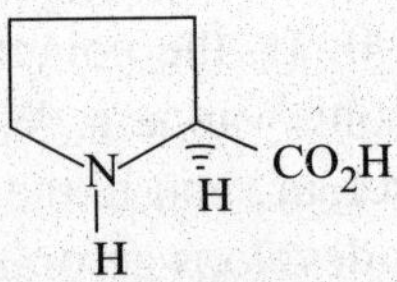

(4.46)

these compounds remained obscure for a long time and they were considered to be nitrogen-containing anthocyanins. Pioneering studies by the Swiss chemist, AS Dreiding and his co-workers, resulted in the elucidation of the structures of these compounds. Common sources for these pigments are the bougainvillea flowers, the beet root and species of the genus Amaranthus.

4.6.1 Isolation of crude betanins from Bougainvillea flowers

Air-dried bracts of coloured *Bougainvillea glabra* are immersed in 1% methanolic hydrochloric acid in a beaker. After allowing the mixture to stand for a day, the coloured solution is decanted and filtered to remove any plant debris. To the beaker containing the once-extracted flowers, a second lot of the solvent is added. After a day, the second extract is decanted and added to the first extract. The combined extract is then concentrated by distillation under reduced pressure (water-suction pump), and then treated with a mixture of diethyl ether and light petroleum (2:1 ratio). After a couple of hours, the supernatant liquid is decanted and the residue is re-dissolved in minimum quantity of 1% methanolic hydrochloric acid. The pigment is re-precipitated by the addition of an ether–petroleum mixture. This procedure is repeated 5 to 8 times to completely remove any ether and petrol-soluble compounds accompanying the betanins. Finally, the deep bluish red-coloured viscous residue is dried in a vacuum desiccator over anhydrous calcium chloride. The dark purple–coloured solid thus obtained is a mixture of betacyanins and betaxanthins.

4.7 QUINONES

Benzoquinones, naphthoquinones, anthraquinones and related compounds also form an important group of plant pigments and occur fairly widespread in almost all parts of plants, including underground parts. They impart deep yellow, orange or red colour to the plant tissues in which they occur. Well-known benzoquinones

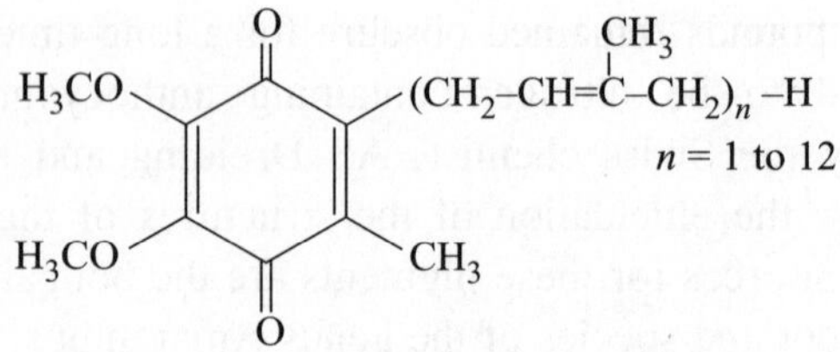

(4.47)

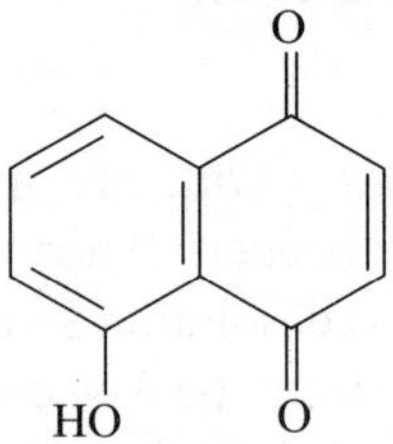

(4.48)

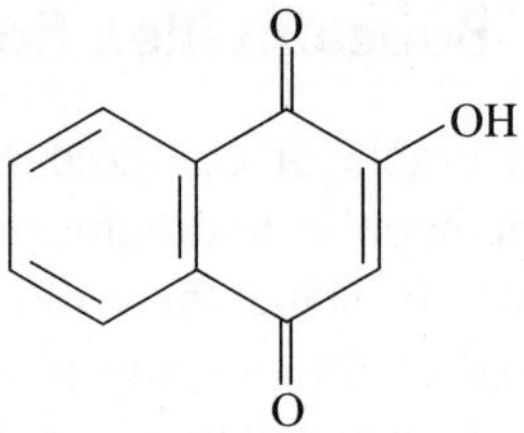

(4.49)

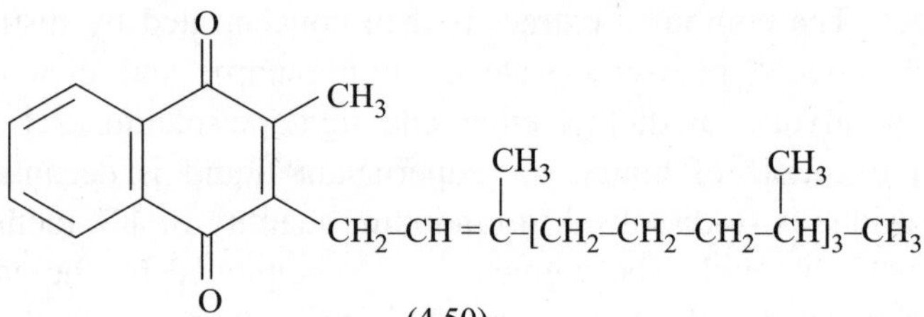

(4.50)

include the ubiquinones (4.47), lawsone (4.48), juglone (4.49) and vitamin K (4.50), which are examples of naphthoquinones.

Among plant pigments, anthraquinones occupy a prime place as they have the potential of being used as dyes. A classic example is alizarin (4.51)—the pigment isolated from madder roots. Plants belonging to the Rubiaceae and Rhamnaceae families are particularly rich in these compounds, several of which have also been isolated from some lichens. In this section, the procedure for the isolation of morindonin (4.52), a diglucoside of morindone (4.53), which is 2-methyl-1,5,6-trihydroxyanthraquinone, from the root bark of *Morinda tinctoria* Roxb. is described.

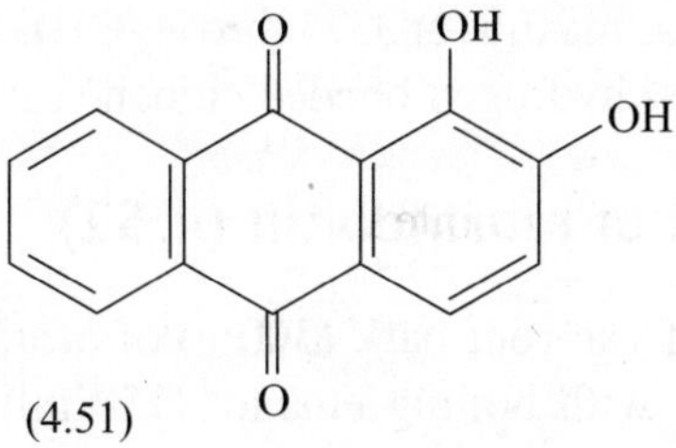

(4.51)

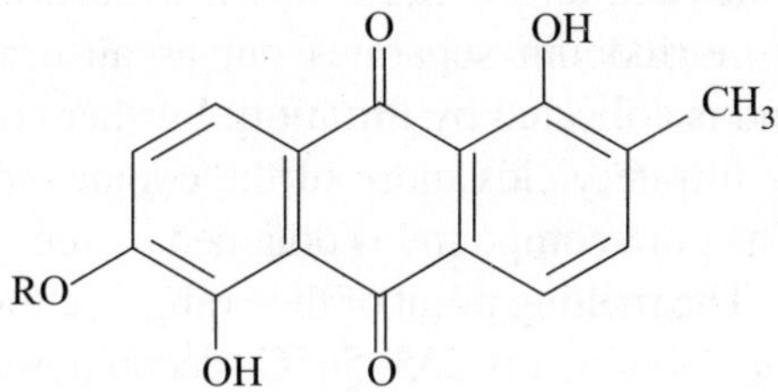

(4.52) : $R = C_{12}H_{12}O_{10}$
(4.53) : $R = H$

4.7.1 Isolation of lawsone (4.48) from *Lawsonia alba*

5 kg of fresh leaves of *Lawsonia alba* are cut into small pieces and kept immersed in aqueous saturated sodium bicarbonate solution for 24 hours in a large beaker or basin. After filtering off the extract, a fresh quantity of the sodium bicarbonate solution is added to the plant material and the extract collected after 24 hours. The combined extract is cooled and carefully acidified by slow addition of 50% aqueous sulphuric acid, with stirring. After allowing the precipitate to settle, it is collected on a Buchner funnel by filtration under suction. It is washed with ice-cold distilled water till the washings are not acidic. It is purified by dissolving it in minimum amount of aqueous ammonia, and re-precipitated by the addition of concentrated hydrochloric acid. The precipitate is filtered, washed with ice-cold water and dried. It is then boiled with benzene (care is to be taken when benzene is used as a solvent as it is carcinogenic) and the benzene solution concentrated by distillation to a small volume and cooled. Lawsone separates out as orange-yellow crystals (2.5 g), m.p. 185–86°C.

The IR spectrum has maxima at 3375 (broad, OH), 1650 (s, quinone carbonyl) and 1621 (s, hydrogen-bonded quinone carbonyl) cm^{-1}.

4.7.2 Isolation of morindonin (4.52)

Coarsely powdered fresh root bark (300 g) of *Morinda tinctoria* is extracted four times with boiling ethanol (750 ml), each time for 6 hours. The combined extract is concentrated to a fourth of its volume and cooled when morindonin separates out as an orange-yellow crystalline solid and is collected by filtration. Further concentration and cooling of the filtrate yields more of the compound. The total yield is 750 mg. The pure compound is obtained by recrystallisation from 65% ethanol. The melting point of the orange-yellow prismatic crystalline solid thus obtained is 255–56°C (decomposes).

Morindonin gives a rose colour with methanolic magnesium acetate and a deep purple colour with concentrated sulphuric acid. It dissolves in aqueous sodium hydroxide to form a deep red solution.

Hydrolysis of morindonin

Morindonin (100 mg) is refluxed with 20 ml of 7% ethanolic sulphuric acid in a 50-ml round-bottomed flask for 10 hours. Removal of ethanol from the solution, followed by dilution with a small amount of ice-cold water, results in the separation of the aglycone, morindone (4.53), as a red crystalline solid (40 mg). It can be recrystallised from glacial acetic acid. The melting point of pure morindone is 280–81°C.

The aqueous filtrate obtained after filtering off morindone is treated with barium carbonate, filtered and concentrated in a porcelain basin on a water-bath. Paper chromatographic examination (circular) using the lower layer of phenol–water as the irrigating solvent reveals the presence of only one sugar, detected by spraying with aniline hydrogen phthalate. The R_f value (at 30°C), 0.57, shows that it is glucose. The identity can be confirmed by the preparation of the osazone derivative, m.p. 204°C.

Enzymatic hydrolysis of morindonin

To a solution of morindonin (50 mg) in 10% aqueous ethanol, emulsin (obtained from 10 almonds) is added and the solution kept at 37°C for four days. On removal of ethanol from the reaction mixture, morindone separates as a brownish-red solid. Paper chromatographic examination of the filtrate shows the presence of glucose.

4.8 ESSENTIAL OILS

If colour is a pleasure to the eyes, good smell is a feast to the olfactory sensory organs. Plant products, such as camphor, have been used from ancient times, along with flowers, in the worship of God and in religious practices. Indeed, for worship, flowers which combine colour with aroma, like the rose, are considered superior to those devoid of smell. Compounds which exhibit aroma belong to different chemical types, such as the terpenoids, phenolics and several types of benzene derivatives. Several of these compounds occur as constituents of the so-called essential oils, which have to be distinguished from fixed oils, where the characteristic constituents are the glycerides.

Essential oils are derived from a wide variety of plant materials such as flowers, seeds, barks, roots and rhizomes. These in turn serve as source materials for the isolation of individual chemical compounds, often involving sophisticated fractionation procedures. Gas chromatography is a versatile method of analysing the composition of complex essential oils. In the following paragraphs, the general methods of obtaining essential oils from a plant source, followed by procedures for the isolation of individual compounds are described.

The most widely used method for the extraction of an essential oil is steam distillation. This method, however, is not suitable when heat-labile compounds are present in the oil. In such cases, solvent extraction at a low temperature is the method of choice. The equipment needed for steam distillation can be easily assembled in the laboratory. Any textbook of practical organic chemistry, such as the one by Vogel, gives a description of the apparatus.

The physical characteristics and the main chemical components of some of the well-known and widely used essential oils are described below.

1. **Oil from the lemon-scented eucalyptus (*Eucalyptus citriodora*)** It is a colourless or pale yellow mobile liquid with a strong, fresh, citronella-like odour and sweet balsamic undertone. The major chemical component is citronellal (4.54) which occurs to the extent of 80%–95%. The minor components are citronellol (4.55), geraniol (4.56) and α-pinene (4.57). The gum or 'kino' contains the antibacterial substance, citriodorol, which has been identified as methyl *p*-coumarate (4.58).
2. **Oil from blue gum Eucalyptus (*Eucalyptus globulus*)** It is a colourless mobile oil which turns yellow on aging. It has a sharp camphoraceous odour with a woody undertone. The chief chemical constituent is cineole (70%–85%) (4.59) accompanied by small quantities of pinene, limonene (4.60), *p*-cymene (4.61), phellandrene (4.62), and terpinene (4.63).
3. **Lemon grass oil** It is obtained by steam distillation of fresh or partially dried leaves of lemon grass, *Cymbopogon citratus*, and is a yellow or reddish-brown liquid with a fresh grassy lemony scent and an earthy undertone. 65%–85% of the oil is made of citral (4.64). The other chief constituents are myrcene (12%–25%) (4.65; see p.80), dipentene (racemic limonene), linalol (4.66; see p.80), geraniol, nerol (4.67; p.80), citronellol and farnesol (4.68; see p.80).
4. **Citronella oil** The leaves of *Cymbopogon nardus* yield citronella oil which is a yellow, mobile liquid with a strong and fresh lemony scent. The principal chemical constituents are geraniol (up to 45%), and citronellol (50%); minor components are limonene, geranyl acetate (4.69; see p.79) and camphene (4.70; see p.81).
5. **Oil of turpentine** This is the essential oil obtained by the steam distillation of the oleo resin which appears as a gummy exudate on the trunks of various species of the genus Pinus. It is a colourless liquid with a pleasant, balsamic scent. Apart from α-pinene, which occurs to the extent of 50%, the oil also contains β-pinene (25%–35%) (4.71; see p.81) and

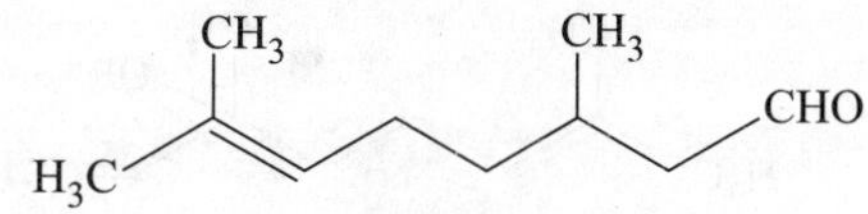

(4.54)

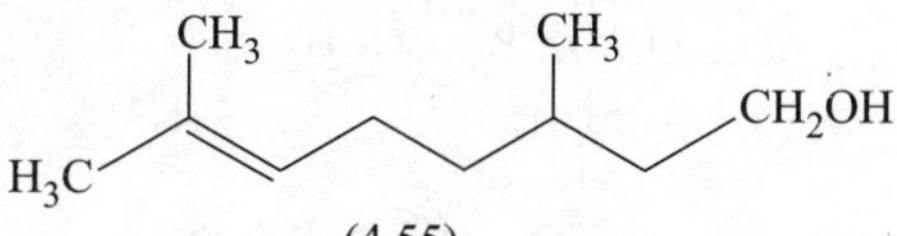

(4.55)

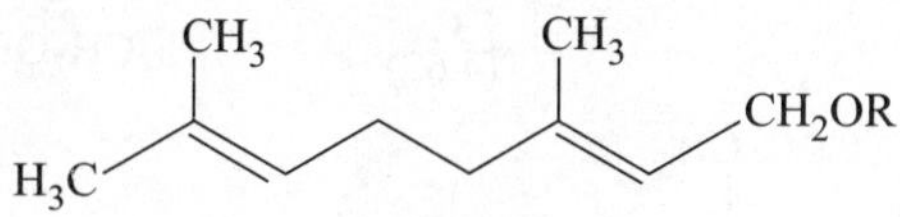

(4.56) : R = H
(4.69) : R = $COCH_3$

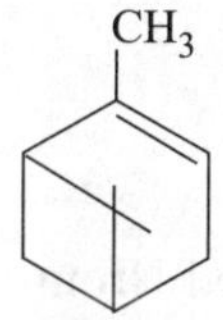

(4.57)

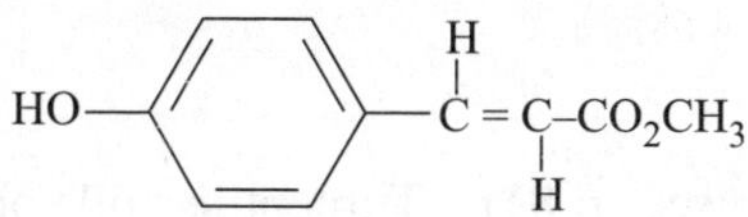

(4.58)

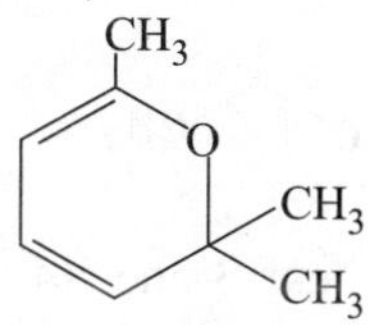

(4.59)

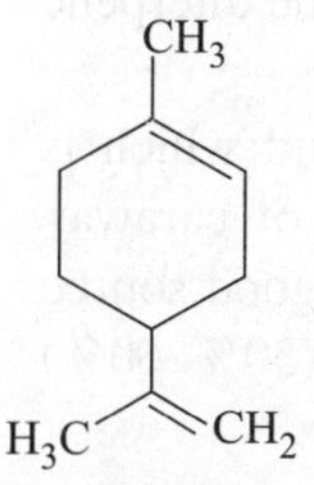

(4.60)

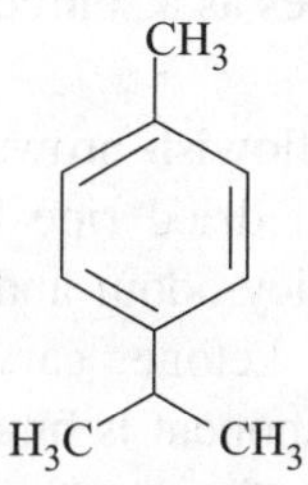

(4.61)

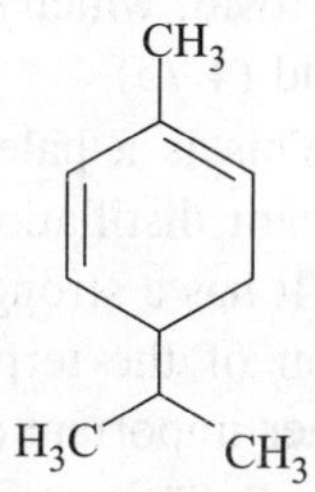

(4.62)

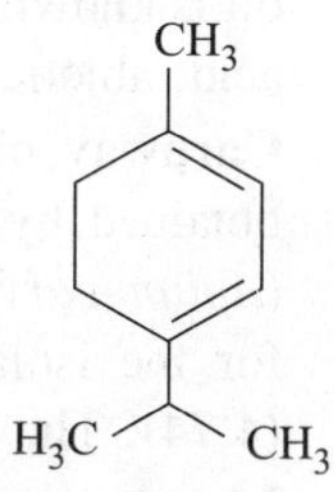

(4.63)

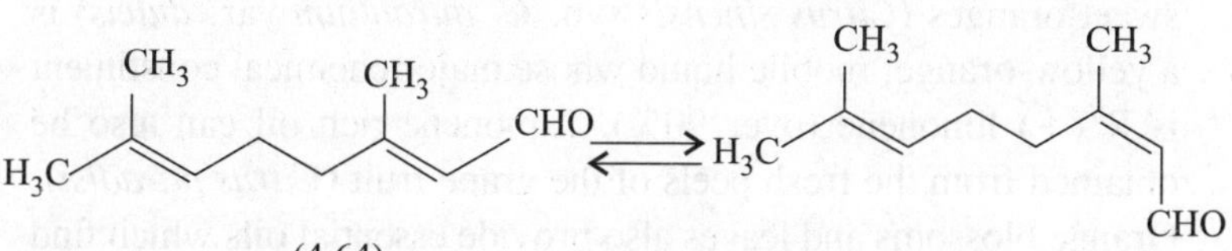

(4.64)

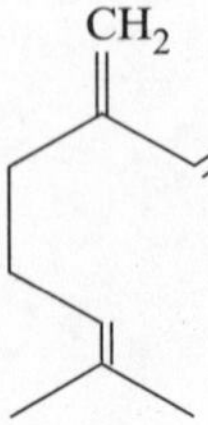

(4.65)

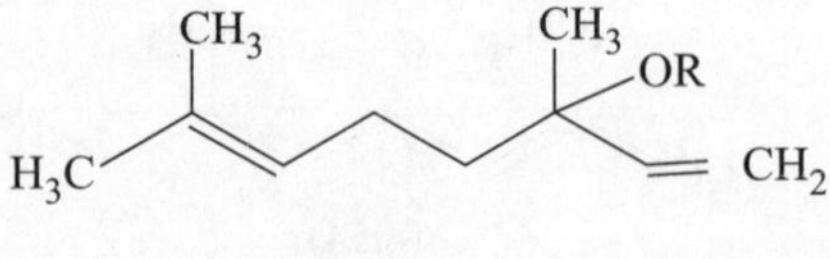

(4.66) : R = H
(4.75) : R = $COCH_3$

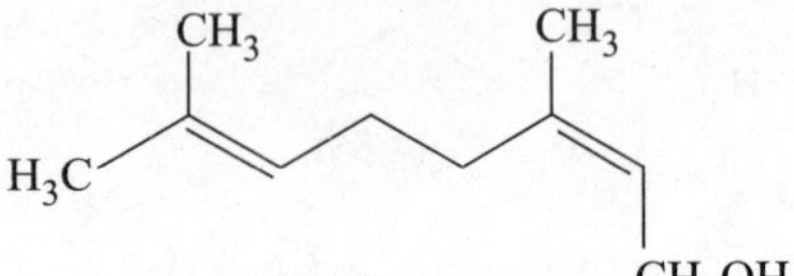

(4.67)

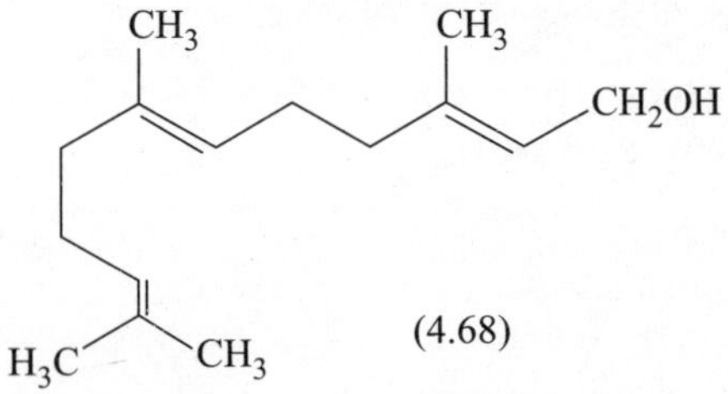

(4.68)

car-3-ene (4.72; see p.81). Turpentine oil obtained from European pines may contain up to 95% of α-pinene. The gummy residue remaining after removal of the steam volatile oil is known as rosin, which serves as a source for the diterpene acid, abietic acid (4.73)

6. **Caraway oil** This is a pale yellowish-brown liquid which is obtained by steam distillation of dried ripe fruits of caraway (*Apium carvi*). It has a strong spicy odour and is a good source for the isolation of the terpene ketone, carvone (50%–60%) (4.74). The other important component is limonene.
7. **Limonene-rich oil** The essential oil obtained either by expression (hand or machine) or steam distillation of the outer peels of ripe, sweet oranges (*Citrus sinensis* syn. *C. aurantium* var. *dulcis*) is a yellow-orange, mobile liquid whose major chemical constituent is R (+) limonene (over 90%). Limonene-rich oil can also be obtained from the fresh peels of the grape fruit (*Citrus paradisi*). Orange blossoms and leaves also provide essential oils which find applications in the perfumery industry. The flower oil has linalol

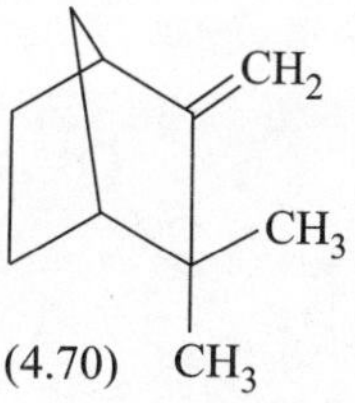

(4.70)

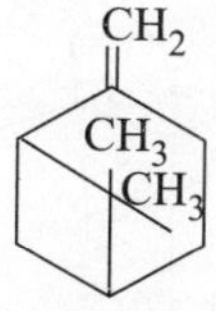

(4.71)

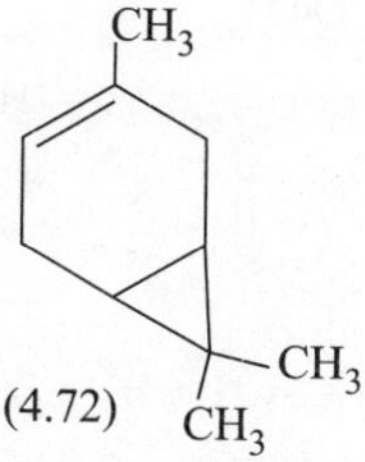

(4.72)

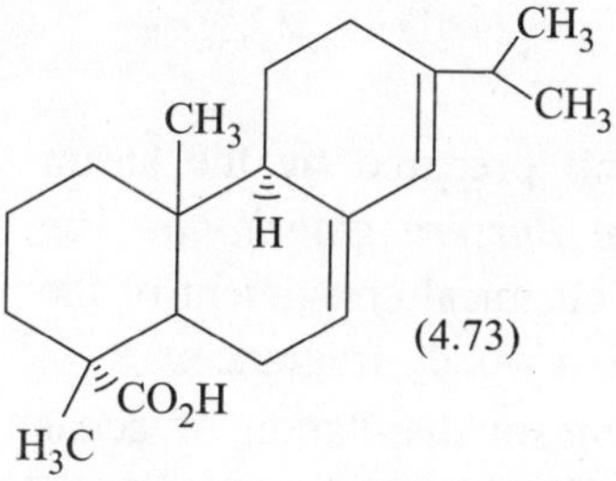

(4.73)

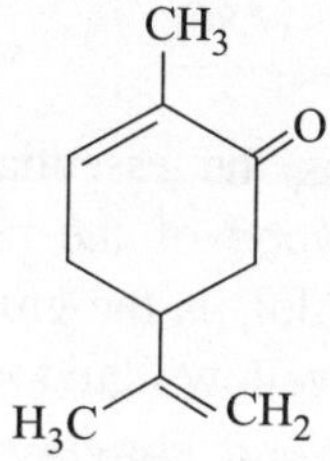

(4.74)

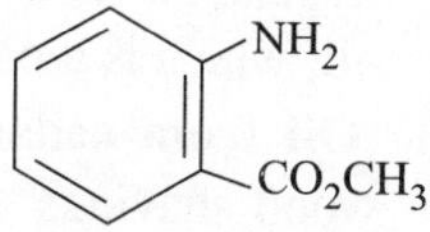

(4.77)

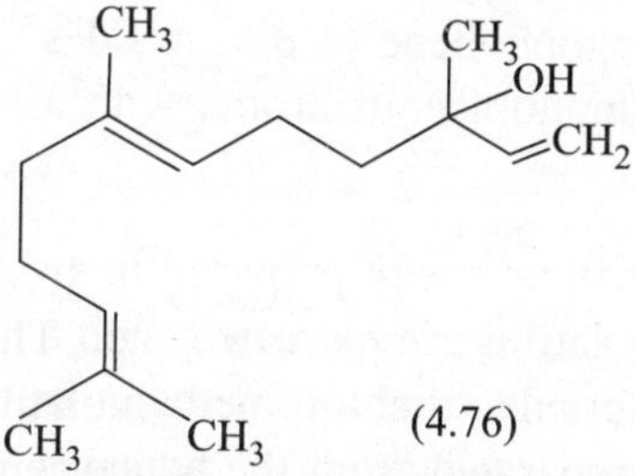

(4.76)

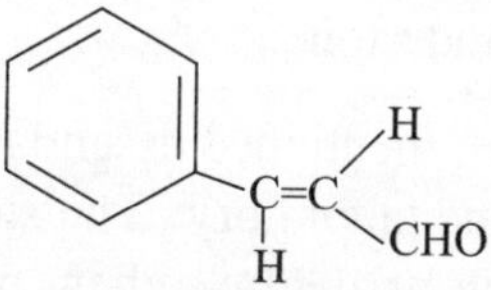

(4.78)

as the main component (34%), accompanied by linalyl acetate (ca.12%) (4.75), limonene (15%), pinene, nerolidol (4.76), geraniol, nerol, citral and methyl anthranilate (4.77). The oil of petitgrain is produced by steam distillation of leaves and twigs of the orange tree. It is a good source for monoterpene esters, linalyl acetate and geranyl acetate.

8. **Cinnamon oil** This is obtained by steam distillation of the dried inner bark of the cinnamon tree, *Cinnamomum zeylanicum*. The yellow liquid with a spicy odour, has cinnamaldehyde (4.78) as the major component (40%–50%).
9. **Tarragon oil** This is the essential oil obtained by steam distillation of the leaves of *Artemisia dracunculus*. It is a colourless or pale yellow mobile liquid containing up to 70% of estragole (4.79).

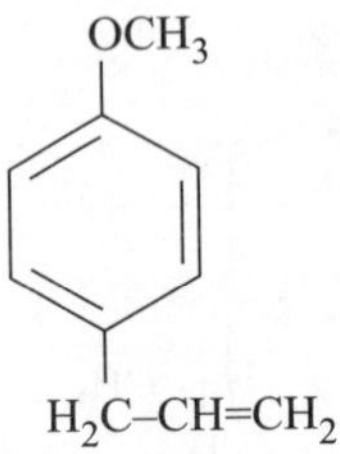
(4.79)

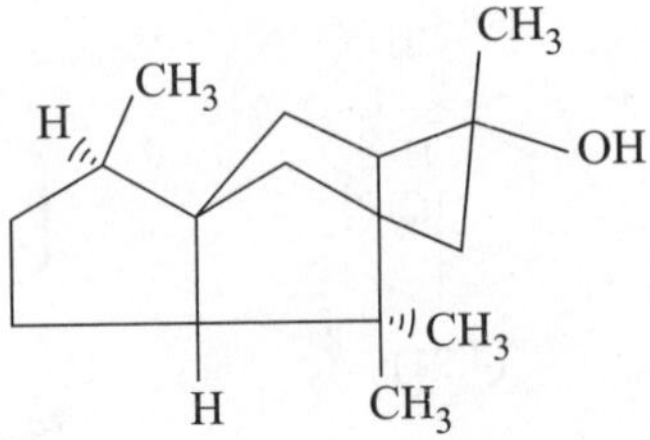
(4.80)

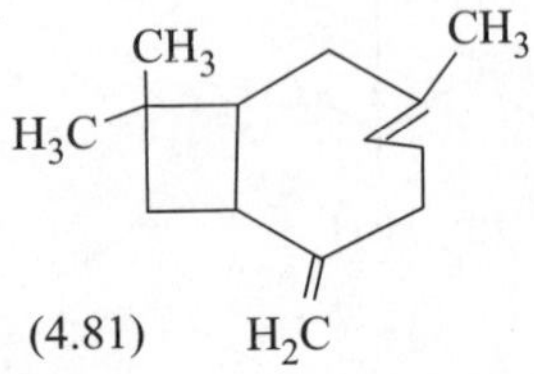
(4.81)

10. **Linaloe oil** This is the essential oil prepared by the steam distillation of the wood of the plant *Bursera glabrifolia*. The terpene alcohol, linalol, is the chief chemical constituent of the oil, which is a pale yellow liquid with a woody fragrance.
11. **Oil from cedar wood shavings** Steam distillation of cedar wood shavings yields a dark yellow liquid which contains the sesquiterpenes cedrol (4.80) and caryophyllene (4.81), besides other terpenoids. It has a warm camphoraceous aroma with a woody undertone.

All the above mentioned essential oils can be easily prepared in an undergraduate laboratory. The steam volatiles are extracted with a solvent, such as diethyl ether, or preferably, dichloromethane in a separatory funnel, the organic layer separated from the aqueous layer, the solvent removed by evaporation, and the residue examined for its chemical components by thin layer chromatography. Some of the compounds like citral, citronellal, carvone and cinnamaldehyde can be easily detected on the TLC plates by spraying with a solution of 2,4-dinitrophenylhydrazine. Unsaturated terpene hydrocarbons like limonene and α- and β-pinenes can be detected by spraying the developed TLC plates with bromine water or aqueous potassium permanganate. A list of spraying agents for TLC examination is given at the end of this chapter.

4.8.1 Isolation of limonene

The essential oil obtained from orange peels (100 g) is taken in a 250-ml round-bottomed flask fitted with a short fractionating column attached through a water-cooled condenser to a receiver flask with a side arm, which in turn is connected through a trap to a vacuum pump. The flask is heated on a boiling water bath (or an electrically heated mantle with a thermostat attachment) at a pressure of 27 mm. Pure *d*-limonene distills over at 75°C and collects in the receiver flask which is cooled in a cold water bath to prevent loss of the compound. Its specific rotation, $[\alpha]_D$, is +126.8°. The average yield from a good grade orange oil is 75 g.

In the proton NMR spectrum, the two methyl groups appear as 3H singlets at δ 1.65 and 1.72, whereas the olefinic hydrogens give rise to signals at δ 4.66 (2H, s) and 5.35 (1H, t).

Bromination of Limonene

10 ml of limonene is diluted with 40 ml of diethyl ether and cooled in an ice bath. To this solution, 0.7 ml of bromine is added drop-wise. After all the bromine is added, the ether is evaporated and the reaction mixture is allowed to stand for 1–2 hours. Limonene tetrabromide (4.82) which separates out is filtered and washed with cold alcohol. It is recrystallised from ethyl acetate and melts at 104–5°C.

4.8.2 Isolation of geraniol

Geraniol is an acyclic monoterpenoid alcohol. Biosynthetically, geranyl pyrophosphate (4.83) is the first member of the monoterpene family, and all the other monoterpenoids are derived from it. Geraniol is an allylic primary alcohol and can be readily oxidised to the aldehyde, geranial, which together with its geometrical isomer,

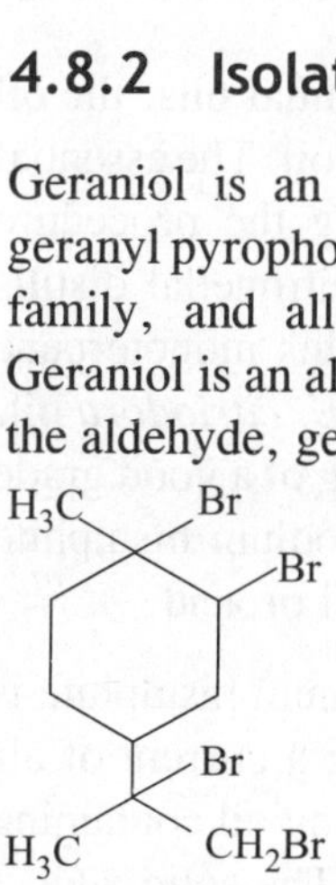

(4.82)

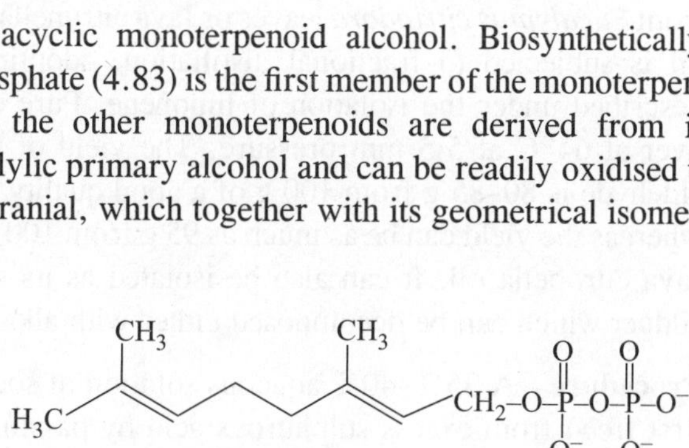

(4.83)

neral, constitutes citral (4.64; see p.79). Geraniol can be easily isolated from essential oils, such as palmarosa oil, by virtue of the fact that it yields a crystalline derivative with anhydrous calcium chloride. This derivative is insoluble in petroleum, benzene, chloroform and ether, and can be decomposed by treatment with water to obtain pure geraniol.

Procedure Equal parts of carefully dried palmarosa oil and finely powdered anhydrous calcium chloride are mixed thoroughly and ground in a mortar. Once the reaction starts, the temperature of the mixture rises to 30–40°C. The mixture is then placed in a desiccator and set aside for a few hours in a cool place. The resulting mass is triturated and ground with light petroleum and filtered under suction on a Buchner funnel. The solid is repeatedly washed with light petroleum and then with diethyl ether. It is then added to warm water and extracted with diethyl ether in a separatory funnel. The ether extract is washed with water and evaporated, after drying over anhydrous sodium sulphate, to obtain geraniol. If necessary, it can be further purified by distillation under reduced pressure. Its boiling point is 229–30°C at 757 mm, and 114–15°C at 12 mm pressure.

4.8.3 Isolation of citronellal

Citronellal can be isolated from either of two essential oils: the oil from *Eucalyptus citriodora* leaves or Java citronella oil. The essential oil is subjected to fractional distillation, adopting the procedure described under the isolation of limonene. Pure citronellal distills over at 64°C at 5.5 mm pressure. The yield of this monoterpene aldehyde is 80–85 g from 100 g of a good quality *E. citriodora* oil, whereas the yield can be as much as 95 g from 100 g of a good grade Java citronella oil. It can also be isolated as its sodium bisulphite adduct which can be decomposed either with alkali or acid.

Procedure A 35%–40% aqueous solution of sodium bisulphite is first freed from excess sulphurous acid by passing a current of air through it. It is then added to crude citronellal or any oil containing the compound till there is no more precipitation. The solid adduct

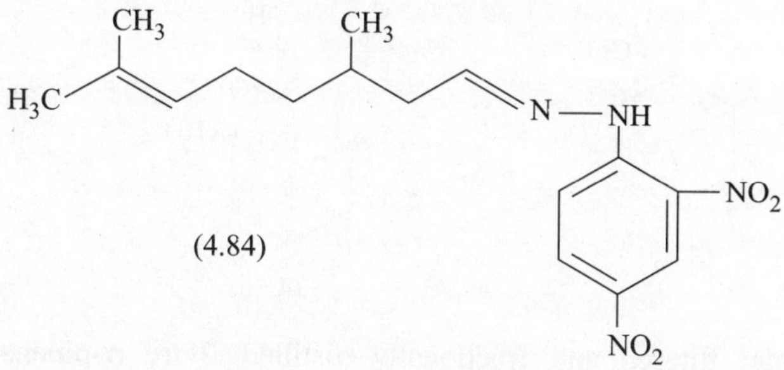

(4.84)

separating out is collected by filtration on a Buchner funnel under suction and washed with diethyl ether. The dry adduct is dissolved in a small amount of boiling water, cooled and shaken in a separatory funnel with ether and 10% sodium hydroxide solution. The ether solution is quickly separated from the aqueous layer, washed repeatedly with cold water till the washings are neutral to litmus; removal of the solvent gives citronellal.

Characterisation of citronellal

For the preparation of 2,4-dinitrophenylhydrazone derivative (4.84), the reagent is prepared by dissolving 0.25 g of 2,4-dinitrophenylhydrazine in 5 ml methanol containing a few drops (0.4–0.5 ml) of concentrated sulphuric acid and warming the mixture. It is filtered and used. For the preparation of the derivative, the reagent is added to a solution of 0.2–0.3 g of citronellal dissolved in minimum amount of methanol. Mixing the two solutions and keeping the mixture aside, the derivative slowly crystallises out. In the case of citral, it may be necessary to warm the mixture. The 2,4-DNP derivative of citronellal melts at 78°C.

The UV spectrum shows an absorption maximum with a low value at 285 nm. Its proton NMR spectrum has the following signals: δ 0.9 (3H, d), 1.65 (3H, s), 1.75 (3H, s), 5.1 (1H, t) and 9.75 (1H, t), besides multiplets between 1.2 and 2.4.

4.8.4 Isolation of α-pinene

Commercially available turpentine oil, obtained by the steam distillation of pine oleo resin, is first dried over anhydrous sodium

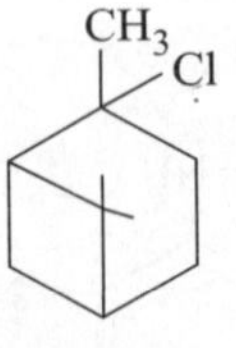

(4.85)

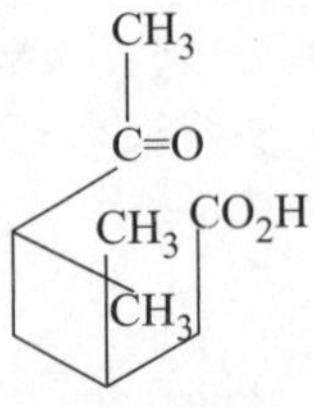

(4.86)

sulphate, filtered and fractionally distilled. Pure α-pinene distills over at 154–55°C at atmospheric pressure. The yield depends upon the source of the turpentine oil and varies from 50 g to as much as 90 g per 100 g of the oil. β–Pinene has a boiling point of 163–64°C.

Preparation of α-Pinene Hydrochloride (4.85)

Dry hydrogen chloride gas is bubbled through a solution of pinene (10 g) in chloroform (10 ml), keeping the temperature below 0°C, till the solution gets saturated with the gas. After addition of water (10 ml), the excess acid is neutralised by the addition of solid sodium bicarbonate. The mixture is immediately subjected to steam distillation. The product solidifies on cooling and is re-crystallised from alcohol, m.p. 130–31°C. Instead of chloroform, diethyl ether can also be used as the solvent for the pinene.

Oxidation of α-Pinene

An emulsion of α-pinene (5 g) in 30 ml of water is gradually added to 12 g of potassium permanganate in 100 ml of water. The mixture is cooled in an ice bath and stirred continuously during the addition. After completion of the oxidation, the manganese dioxide sludge is removed by filtration. The filtrate is saturated with carbon dioxide gas and distilled with steam to remove any unoxidised compounds. The liquid is evaporated in a current of carbon dioxide to a volume of 40 ml and extracted twice with diethyl ether (5 ml each time). The aqueous layer is acidified by the addition of dilute sulphuric acid and extracted with ether. The ether solution is washed with cold water, dried and evaporated. The residue is recrystallised from petroleum. α-Pinonic acid (4.86) melts at 68°C.

4.8.5 Isolation of citral

A convenient source for this monoterpene aldehyde is the essential oil obtained by the steam distillation of lemon grass. Wild varieties of lemon grass which are common in several parts of India are easy to collect but the yield of oil from these varieties is low. Cultivated varieties based on botanical selection yield an essential oil which can provide as much as 85 g of citral per 100 g of the oil. Such varieties can be obtained from the Central Institute of Aromatic and Medicinal Plants (Bengaluru station). Pure citral has a boiling point of 118–120°C at 20 mm. Citral can also be isolated from lemon grass oil as its solid bisulphite adduct, obtained by adding a 35% aqueous solution of sodium bisulphite to the oil, stirring all the while till there is no more precipitation. The solid is filtered, washed with light petroleum and dried. Since the conversion is quantitative, by weighing the solid, the percentage of citral content in a sample of oil can be calculated. Thus, 1.52 g of pure citral should yield 2.4 g of the bisulphite adduct. The ultraviolet spectrum of citral has an absorption maximum at 238 nm in good accordance with the Woodward–Fieser rules.

The infrared spectrum of citral has a strong band at 1680 cm^{-1}, attributed to the stretching vibration of the conjugated carbonyl group. The medium intensity band at 1620 cm^{-1} is due to the olefinic double bond. In the proton NMR spectrum, there are two one proton doublets at δ 9.9 and 10.0, attributable to the aldehyde hydrogens in the *cis*- and *trans*-isomers, neral and geranial; natural citral is an inseparable mixture of the two isomers, with geranial being the major component. The olefinic proton at position 2 gives rise to the signal at 5.9 (d), whereas the one on carbon 6 appears at δ 5.1 as a triplet.

4.8.6 Isolation of carvone

Coarsely powdered, fresh caraway seeds (25 g) are taken with 250 ml of distilled water in a 500-ml round-bottomed flask fitted with a distillation head and a water-cooled condenser. The distillate (about 100 ml) is collected in a receiver flask and shaken with 20 ml

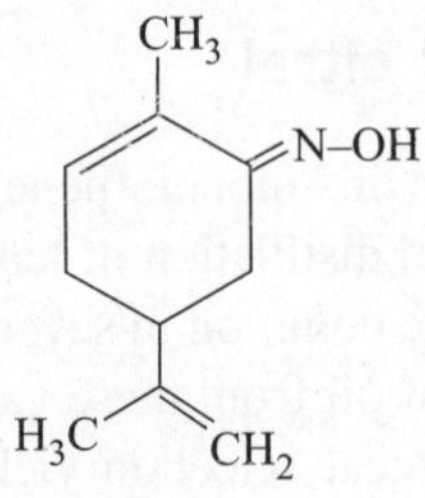

(4.87)

of dichloromethane in a 250-ml separatory funnel. After separating the organic layer, the aqueous layer is once again extracted with a fresh quantity (20 ml) of dichloromethane. The combined extract is dried over anhydrous magnesium sulphate for about 10 minutes, and filtered and distilled on a water bath to remove the solvent. The recovered dichloromethane can be used for extracting another batch of steam distillate. The crude essential oil thus obtained is subjected to fractional distillation, when pure carvone boils over at 230°C at 760 mm (88–90°C at 4 mm). The yield varies from 70 g to 80 g per 100 g of the essential oil.

The uv spectrum of carvone has two absorption maxima, one at 235 nm with a large ε value, similar to the 238 nm band in the spectrum of citral, and the other at 318 nm with a low ε value; the latter is due to n–π^* excitation of the conjugated carbonyl group. The carbonyl stretching vibration band in the ir spectrum is seen at 1675 cm^{-1}. In the ^{13}C NMR spectrum the carbonyl carbon atom gives rise to a signal at δ 198.0.

PREPARATION OF CARVONE OXIME (4.87)

To a solution of 1 g of carvone in 5 ml of ethanol is added, with shaking, a hot solution of 1 g of hydroxylamine hydrochloride in 1 ml of water. To the clear liquid, a warm solution of 1 g of KOH in 8 ml of water is added at once. The liquid turns yellow and potassium chloride precipitates out. After cooling, the liquid is poured into cold water and carvone oxime separates out as solid flakes. It is collected by filtration on a Hirsch funnel, washed with ice water and sucked dry. It melts at 92–93°C.

4.9 HIGHER TERPENOIDS

Among the higher terpenoids, the triterpenoids and the related phytosterols occur widely in the plant kingdom, though, most often in small quantities. They are also easier to isolate and purify, as the majority of them, with the exception of triterpenoid and steroid esters of long-chain fatty acids, are solids with considerable affinity for non-polar solvents. They can also be readily detected by means of colour tests, such as the Liebermann–Burchard reaction. On the other hand, since they usually occur in the form of mixtures of closely related compounds, chromatographic methods are often necessary to isolate pure compounds. However, in an undergraduate laboratory, it is sufficient if the students learn how to isolate crude fractions containing these compounds, and how to analyse them using thin layer chromatography with the help of appropriate spraying reagents. The most common among the phytosterols is sitosterol (4.88) which occurs free, and as glycosides. Stigmasterol (4.89) is another widely occurring sterol. Among the triterpenoids,

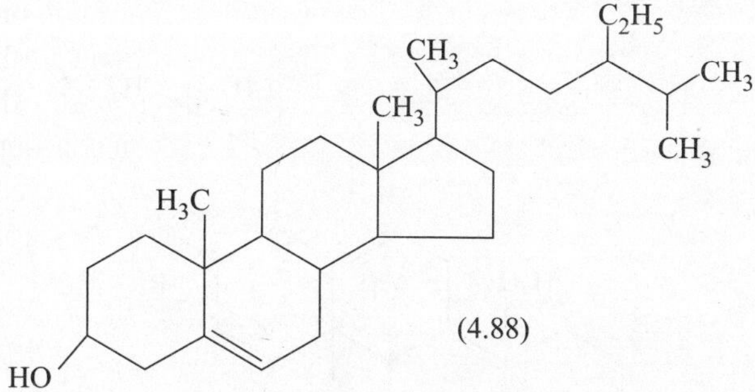

(4.88)

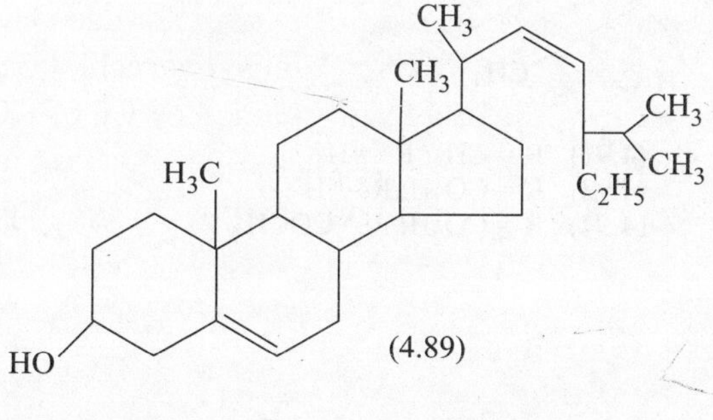

(4.89)

the most widespread are the α- and β-amyrins (4.90 and 4.91), oleanolic acid (4.92) and lupeol (4.93).

The following examples have been chosen with the objective of giving the students some degree of familiarity with this important group of compounds. One exercise also involves a simple chromatographic fractionation.

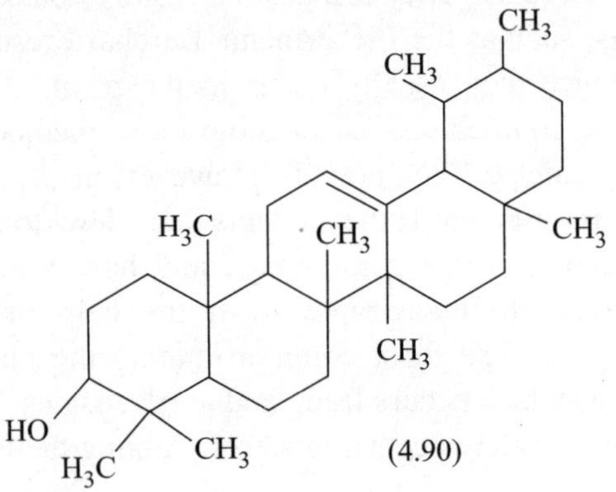

(4.90)

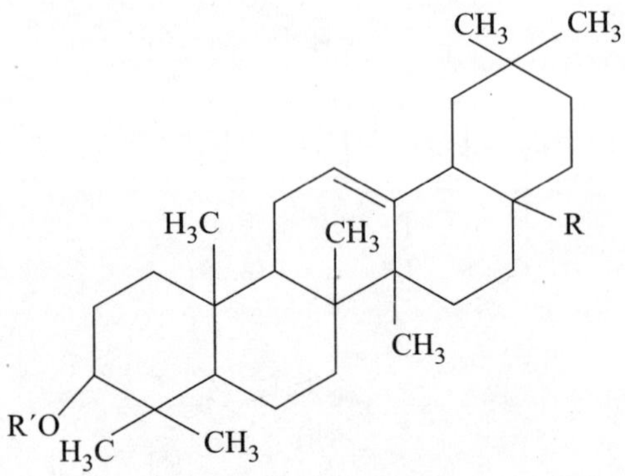

(4.91) : R = CH_3; R′ = H
(4.92) : R = CO_2H; R′ = H
(4.97) : R = CO_2H; R′ = $COCH_3$

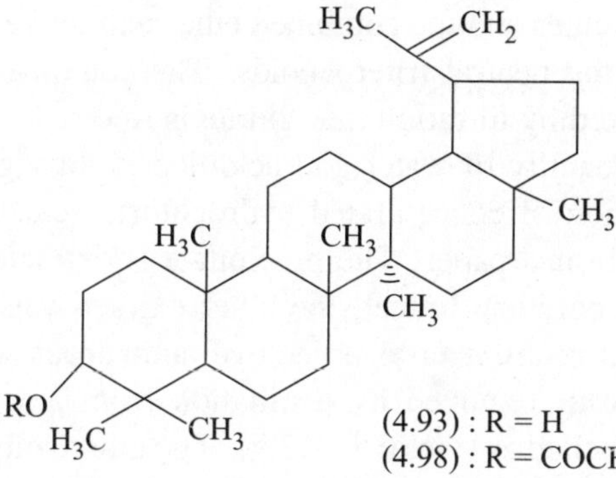

(4.93) : R = H
(4.98) : R = $COCH_3$

4.9.1 Isolation of all the triterpenoids in birchwood bark

Species of Betula, commonly known as birch, are indigenous to America and the Himalayan region of North India. This forest tree is well-known for its soft white bark and very durable wood. The bark, on extraction, yields a mixture of triterpenes, of which the major component is the pentacyclic triterpene diol, betulin. The following procedure describes the isolation of all the terpenoids present in the outer barks of *Betula papyrifera* and further fractionation into acidic and neutral triterpenes. The plant material can be procured from suppliers in the USA.

Procedure The coarsely powdered outer bark of *B. papyrifera* (10 g) is extracted in a Soxhlet extractor with light petroleum (40–60°C). Three to five siphonings should ensure complete extraction. The extract is distilled from a water bath and the recovered solvent kept aside for future use with another fresh batch of the bark. The residue (5–6 g) is dissolved in diethyl ether (Caution: ether is highly inflammable) and the solution shaken with 10% aqueous sodium hydroxide in a separatory funnel. At the interface of the organic and aqueous layers, a fluffy solid of the sodium salts of the acidic compounds can be seen. The aqueous layer, along with the solid, is separated from the organic layer and filtered. The organic layer is also filtered, the residue washed with diethyl ether and the combined ether extract kept aside for the isolation of the neutral triterpenoids. The combined solid sodium salt is collected by filtration (the filtrate is rejected). It is suspended in a small quantity of water and acidified, with vigorous stirring, by the addition of concentrated hydrochloric acid till the mixture is acidic to litmus paper. The precipitate is extracted with diethyl ether in a separatory funnel, the ether extract washed with water till the washings are neutral, dried over anhydrous sodium sulphate and the solvent removed by distillation from a water bath. The residue is labelled A (yield: 1–1.2 g). The ether solution remaining after the removal of the sodium salt is thoroughly washed with cold water till the washings are free from alkali, dried over anhydrous sodium sulphate and distilled to remove the solvent. The residue is labelled N (yield 4.5 g).

TLC EXAMINATION OF N—ISOLATION OF BETULIN (4.94)

Thin layer chromatographic analysis of N using silica gel G and chloroform–benzene (1:1) as the developing solvent shows three spots that become visible on exposure to iodine vapours, or after spraying with 10% sulphuric acid. The major component has the lowest R_f value. Comparison with authentic samples, if available, shows that this corresponds with betulin; the other two are lupeol (highest R_f value) and sitosterol. The crude solid is directly re-crystallised from hot methanol, when pure betulin separates out as colourless needles (3.5–4 g), m.p. 259–61°C. It gives a yellow colour with tetranitromethane, showing the presence of a double bond, and answers the Liebermann–Burchard reaction (yellow-brown-deep red-brown).

Betulin diacetate (4.95) is prepared as follows. A solution of betulin (0.1 g) in dry pyridine (2 ml) is mixed with acetic anhydride (2 ml) and the reaction mixture maintained at 35°C for 12 hours. Thereafter, it is poured into ice-cold water, the precipitated solid filtered, washed with water and dried. It melts at 219–21°C. Its proton NMR spectrum has signals at δ 0.87 (9H, s = 3 tertiary methyls), 1.01 (3H, s), 1.08 (3H, s),1.71 (3H, s), 2.04 (3H, s) and 2.09 (3H, s).

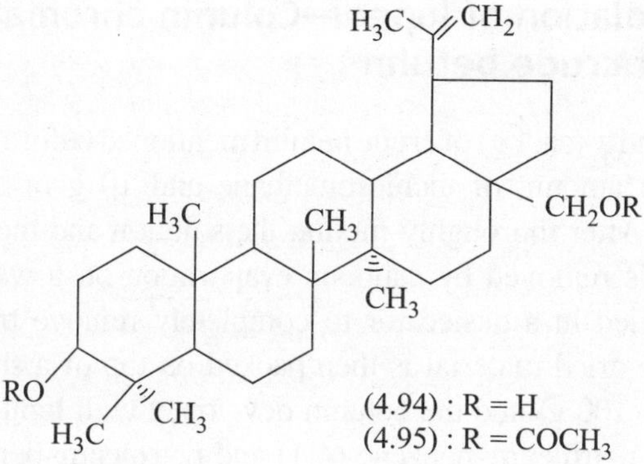

(4.94) : R = H
(4.95) : R = $COCH_3$

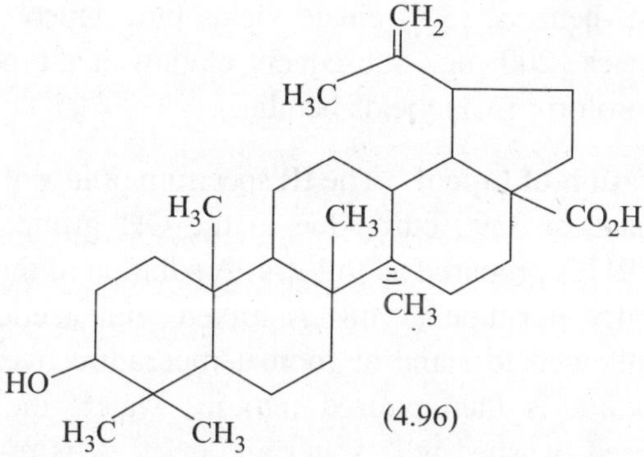

(4.96)

TLC EXAMINATION OF A

Thin layer chromatography of A on silica gel G with chloroform-methanol (99:1) as the developing solvent shows the presence of three acidic compounds which can be detected by spraying the plate with bromophenol blue. The spot with the lowest R_f value corresponds with that of oleanolic acid. The middle spot is due to betulinic acid (4.96), and the spot with the highest R_f value coincides with that of acetyloleanolic acid (4.97; see p. 90). The compounds can be isolated by preparative TLC.

4.9.2 Isolation of lupeol—Column chromatography of crude betulin

A small quantity (ca. 1 g) of crude betulin mentioned before is dissolved in minimum amount of dichloromethane and 10 g of silica gel is added to it. After thoroughly mixing the solution and the adsorbent, the solvent is removed by cautious evaporation on a water bath. It is further dried in a desiccator to completely remove traces of the solvent. The dried material is then packed on top of a short column of silica gel (100 g) and the column developed with light petroleum, followed by petroleum–benzene (4:1) and petroleum–benzene (3:1). Fractionation is monitored by TLC. Evaporation of the solvent from the petroleum–benzene (3:1) eluate yields pure lupeol, m.p. 208–10°C. Yield: ca. 200 mg. Subsequent elution of the column with benzene–chloroform (3:1) yields betulin.

Characterisation of lupeol The IR spectrum of lupeol has a broad absorption band at 3390 cm^{-1}, due to the OH group. Its acetate (4.98; see p.91) is prepared as follows. A solution of the compound (50 mg) in dry pyridine (1 ml) is mixed with acetic anhydride (1 ml) and allowed to stand at room temperature overnight. The reaction mixture is then poured into ice water, the precipitate (45 mg) filtered, washed with water and dried. It is re-crystallised from methanol, m.p. 215–17°C.

Oxidation of lupeol to lupenone (4.99)

A solution of lupeol (100 mg) in pure acetone (30 ml) is mixed with Jones reagent (0.8 ml) (prepared by dissolving 2.67 g of chromium trioxide in 2.3 ml of concentrated sulphuric acid). The mixture is stirred well and maintained at room temperature for 30 minutes. It is then diluted with water and shaken with diethyl ether in a separatory funnel. The ether extract is washed with water till the washings are neutral to litmus, dried and evaporated. The residue is re-crystallised from light petroleum to obtain pure lupenone, m.p. 170–71°C. Its IR spectrum has an absorption band at 1715 cm^{-1}.

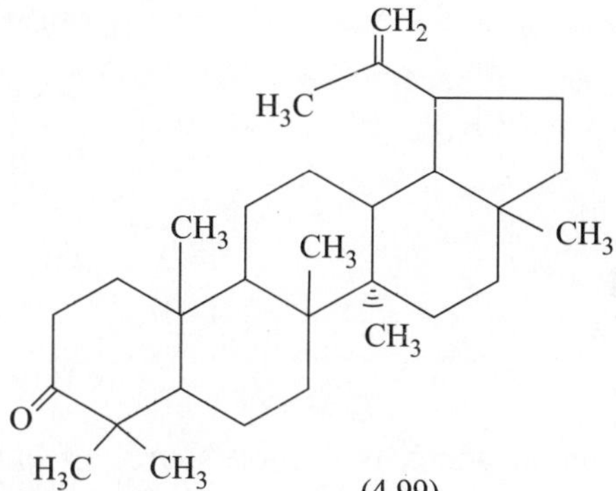

(4.99)

4.9.3 Isolation of sitosterol

Sitosterol can be isolated from a petroleum extract of the powdered seeds of *Trifolium alexandrinum* by column chromatography over neutral alumina. The seeds can be obtained from any Agricultural Research station (for example, in India, ICAR). Details of the chromatography have been deliberately left out as this exercise could be used to test the students' skill and capacity to experiment and innovate. Sitosterol melts at 135–37°C.

The IR spectrum has a broad band around 3350 cm^{-1} and the mass spectrum shows the molecular ion signal at m/z 414. Its benzoate prepared by treatment with benzoyl chloride and pyridine melts at 144–46°C.

4.10 NON-TERPENOID COMPONENTS OF ESSENTIAL OILS

Several essential oils—particularly those derived from spices—contain, apart from terpenoids, benzenoid compounds which impart the characteristic aroma and flavour to the oils. Typical examples are the oil of clove, which contains eugenol (2-methoxy-4-allylphenol; 4.100), oil of cumin seeds, the main constituent of which is 4-isopropylbenzaldehyde (cuminaldehye; 4.101), and

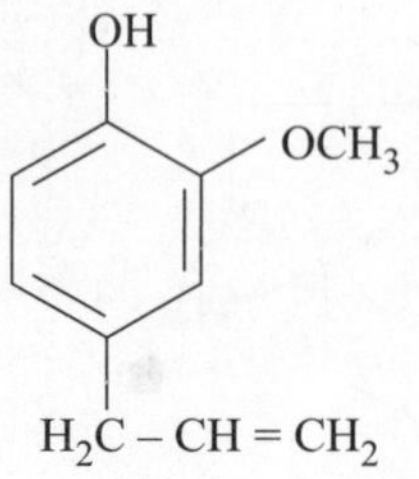

(4.100)

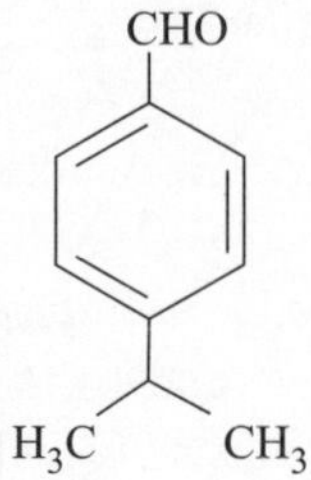

((4.101)

the oil of cinnamon which is a good source of cinnamaldehyde. The structures of these three compounds have been shown and the procedure for the isolation of eugenol is given below. The same procedure can also be used for the other two oils.

4.10.1 Isolation of eugenol

In a 500-ml 3-neck round-bottomed flask, coarsely powdered cloves (10 g) are taken, along with 150 ml of water. Through one neck, a dropping funnel is inserted to let in extra water, as and when needed. Through the middle neck, the flask is connected to a still head, and a water-cooled condenser to the other end of which a receiver flask is attached. The third neck is stoppered. The mixture is heated and the distillate is collected in the receiver flask. When the distillate is clear of oily drops, the operation is stopped and the distillate transferred to a separatory funnel, where it is extracted with dichloromethane. The extraction is done twice or thrice to extract all the oily matter. The organic layer is then dried over anhydrous sodium sulphate, filtered and heated on a steam bath to remove the solvent. The major component of the oil is eugenol, whose proton NMR spectrum shows a sharp 3H singlet at δ 3.80, due to the methoxyl group. It can be directly converted into its benzoyl derivative as follows.

The crude eugenol (0.2 g) is taken in a test tube to which 1 ml of water and a few drops of 1M aqueous sodium hydroxide are added till the mixture becomes a clear solution. Thereafter, 0.1 ml of benzoyl chloride is added and the mixture gently heated on a steam bath for about ten minutes. After cooling, the inside of the test tube is scratched with a glass rod to induce crystallisation of the benzoyl derivative, which separates as a colourless solid. Since the derivative has a low melting point, the cooling will have to be done in an ice bath. The solid is collected on a Hirsch funnel and washed free of alkali with ice-cold water. The conversion is quantitative and from the yield, the percentage of eugenol present in the oil can be calculated. The benzoate melts at 70°C.

4.11 ALKALOIDS

Alkaloids form a very large and diverse group of secondary metabolites, predominantly of plant origin. The only common factor is that their biosynthetic origin can be traced to an amino acid. The exceptions are the so-called pseudo-alkaloids, such as the Solanum and the Kurchi alkaloids, which are better classified as nitrogenous steroids; the source of the amino functionalities in these compounds is not an amino acid but inorganic in nature. The earlier definition that alkaloids are basic is not comprehensive enough to include alkaloids like colchicine (4.102), which is biosynthetically derived from two units of phenylalanine. Alkaloids were probably the first among

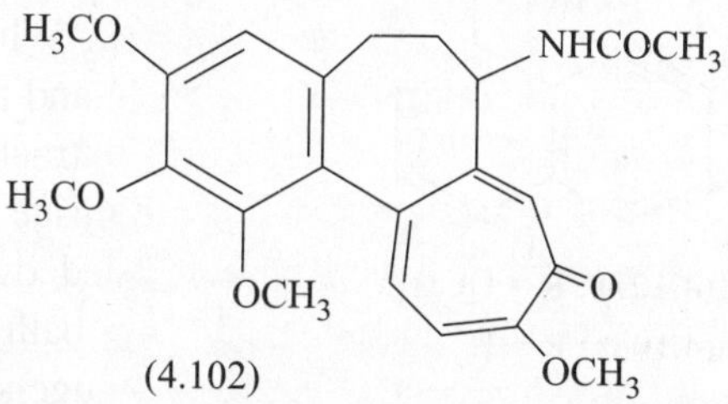

(4.102)

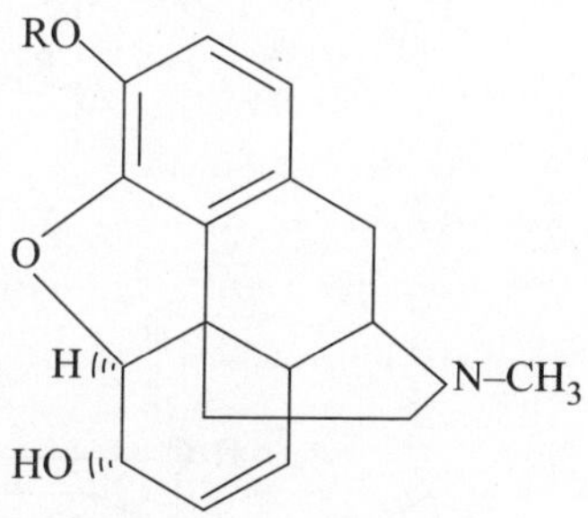

(4.103) : R = H
(4.104) : R = CH₃

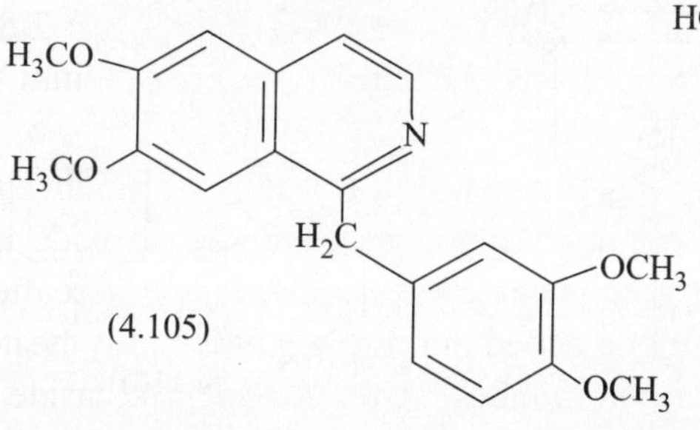

(4.105)

secondary metabolites to attract the attention of organic chemists by virtue of their pronounced biological activities. Morphine (4.103) was the first alkaloid to be isolated in the pure state. It is the kingpin among narcotic analgesics and serves as the model for a large number of synthetic analogues and substitutes. Opium, which is the source of morphine, also contains the anti-tussive codeine (4.104), papaverine (4.105) and narcotine (4.106). Other important alkaloids include the cinchona alkaloids [the anti-malarial quinine (4.107) and cinchonine (4.108)], the highly toxic strychnine (4.109), the tobacco alkaloid nicotine (4.110), atropine (4.111), the local anaesthetic cocaine (4.112),

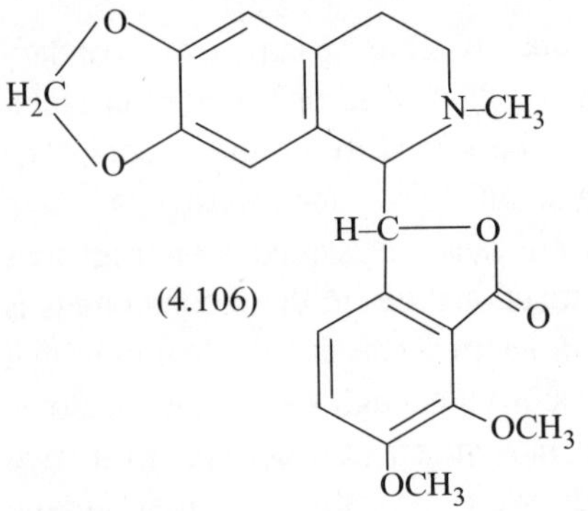

(4.106)

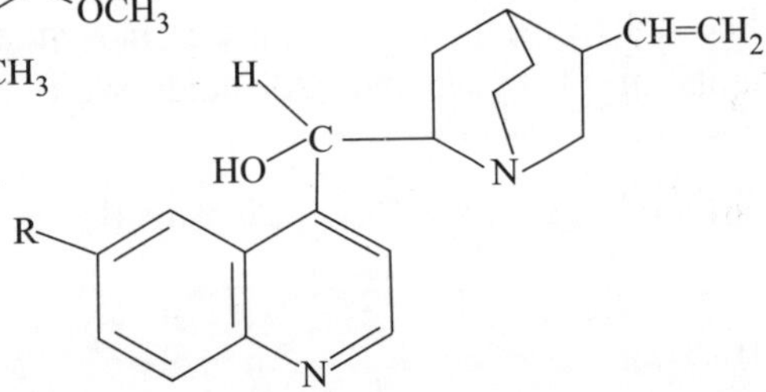

(4.107) : R = OCH_3

(4.108) : R = H

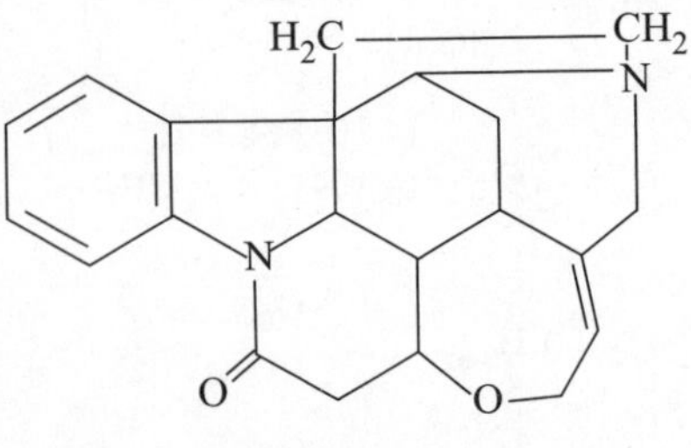

(4.109)

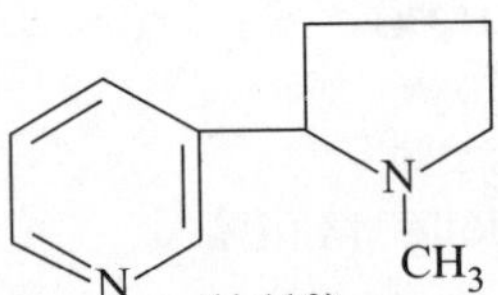

(4.110)

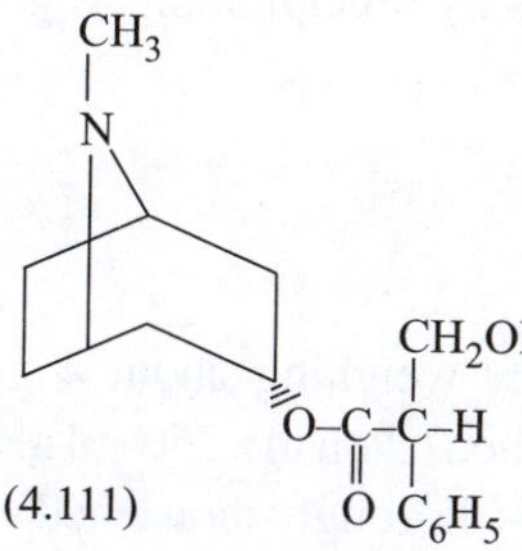

(4.111)

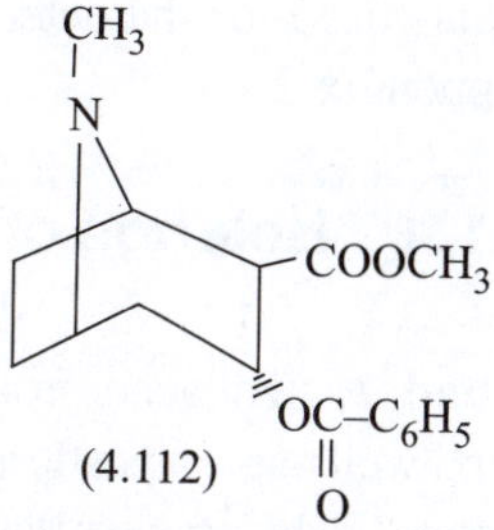

(4.112)

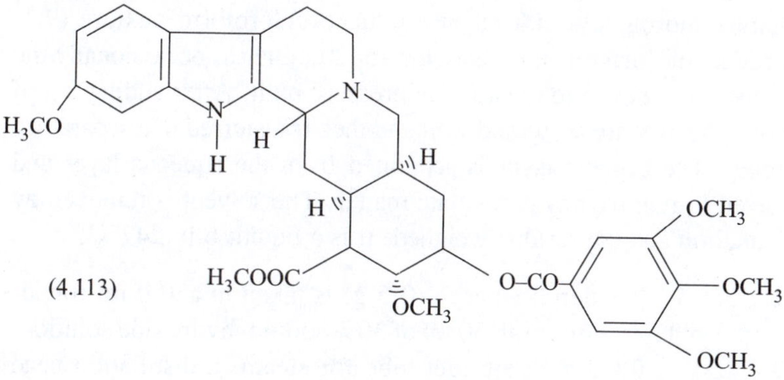

(4.113)

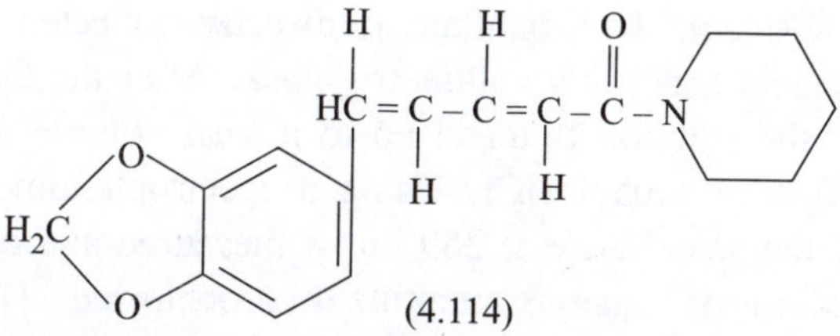

(4.114)

and the Rauwolfia alkaloids [reserpine (4.113) and related compounds], to name a few. Among these, strychnine is fairly easy to isolate, but considering its toxicity, it is not included in this book. However, an experiment describing the isolation of nicotine—which is also toxic, but less so than strychnine—from cigarettes, is included, along with that of piperine (4.114) from pepper. The preparation of reagents used for the detection of alkaloids by precipitation, is given in Appendix 2.

4.11.1 Isolation of nicotine

Method 1 Tobacco from 3–4 cigarettes, weighing about 4 g, is ground well using a pestle and mortar, and then taken in a 250-ml glass-stoppered Erlenemeyer flask. The tobacco is thorougly moistened with 15–20 ml of a saturated solution of barium hydroxide followed by the addition of 1 g of solid barium hydroxide. After shaking the mixture thoroughly, 100 ml of a toluene–chloroform mixture (9:1) is added and shaken vigorously for 15–20 minutes; occassionally the stopper is removed to release any pressure built. After adding 2 g of celite, the mixture is swirled well and then transferred to a separatory funnel. The organic layer is separated from the aqueous layer and filtered to remove any particulate matter. The solvent is removed by distillation and the residue weighed. It is a liquid; b.p. 247°C.

Method 2 Powdered tobacco (0.5 g) is taken in a 100-ml round-bottomed flask, along with 30 ml of 30% sodium hydroxide solution. The flask is fitted with an inlet tube for steam, a distillation head and a water-cooled condenser. The solution is first boiled and then distilled with steam. The distillate is directly collected in 0.1N hydrochloric acid taken in a volumetric flask. After the distillation is complete, the solution is made up to a final volume of 1 litre by the addition of 0.05N HCl. Using a spectrophotometer or a colorimeter, the absorbance at 259 nm is measured and compared with a standard of aqueous nicotine hydrochloride. Using the following equation, the amount of nicotine in the sample prepared can be estimated.

$$c = \frac{(A_{259})\,(c')}{(A'_{259})}$$

4.11.2 Isolation of piperine

Finely powdered black pepper (10 g) is taken in a Soxhlet extractor and extracted once with distilled ethanol. The extract is filtered to remove any fine particulate matter and distilled under reduced pressure. To the concentrated solution, 10 ml of 10% alcoholic potassium hydroxide solution is added, and after some time filtered by decantation. On allowing the clear solution to stand overnight, yellow-coloured needles of piperine separate and are collected by filtration. Yield: 0.3 g. Pure piperine melts at 125–26°C.

Hydrolysis of piperine—Isolation of piperic acid (4.115)

A mixture of piperine (100 mg) and 10% alcoholic potassium hydroxide (1 ml) is gently refluxed for 90 minutes. After evaporating the solvent, the solid residue is stirred with hot water and acidified with hydrochloric acid. Piperic acid which precipitates out as a yellow solid is collected by filtration on a Buchner funnel. It is washed with ice-cold water till the washings are neutral and the residue re-crystallises from ethanol. Pure piperic acid crystallises as yellow needles, m.p. 216–17°C.

4.11.3 Isolation of a purine derivative

Purines are fairly widespread in nature, both as free bases as well as their ribosides or deoxyribosides, which are known as nucleosides. Apart from caffeine (4.116) and the related theobromine (4.117) and theophilline (4.119), other common purine bases are adenine (4.119) and xanthine (4.120). The ribosides of adenine and xanthine are known as adenosine (4.121) and xanthosine (4.122), respectively.

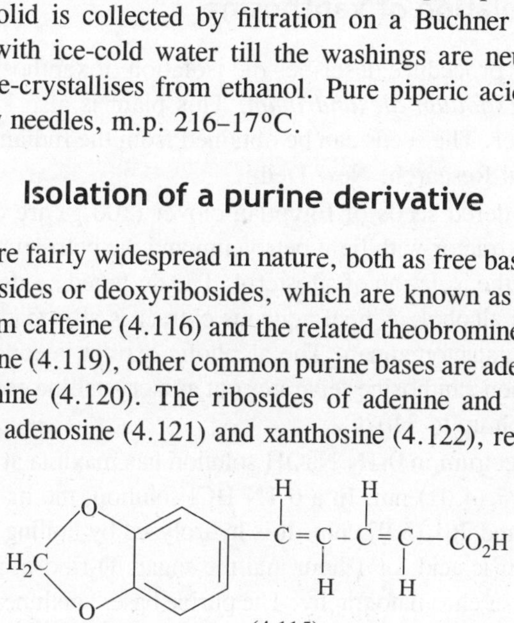

(4.115)

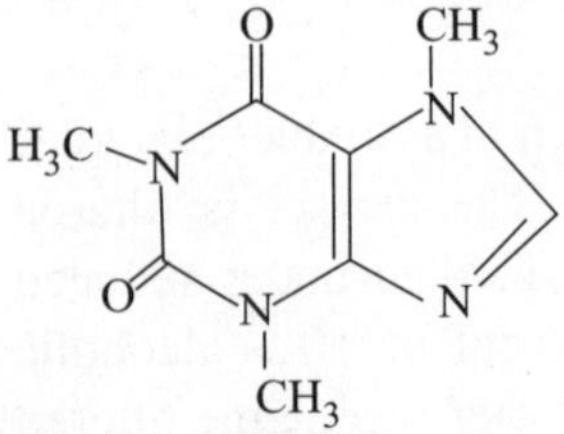

(4.116)

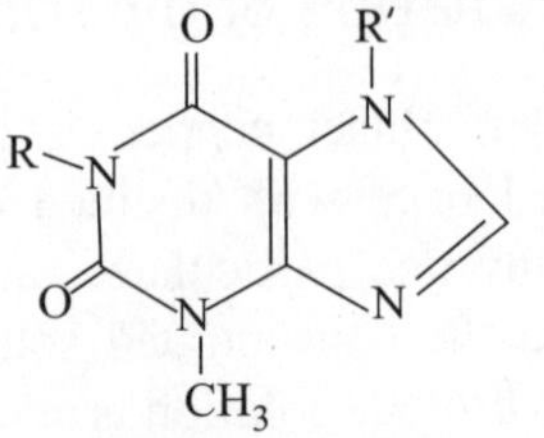

(4.117) : R = H; R′ = CH_3
(4.118) : R = CH_3; R′ = H

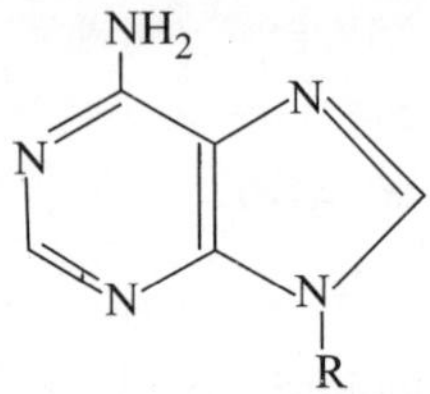

(4.119) : R = H
(4.121) : R = D-ribose

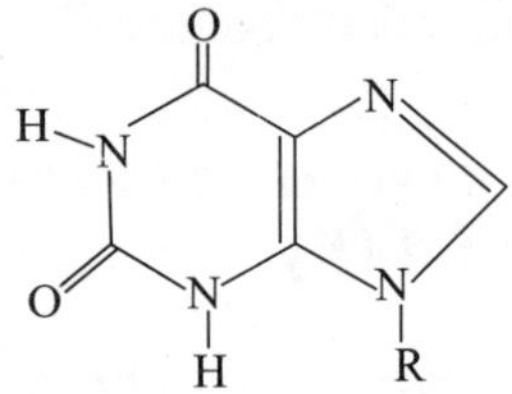

(4.120) : R = H
(4.122) : R = D-ribose

4.11.4 Isolation of xanthosine

The following procedure describes the isolation of xanthosine from the seeds of *Trifolium alexandrinum*. This plant is also known as Egyptian clover. The seeds can be obtained from the Indian Council of Agricultural Research, New Delhi.

Finely powdered seeds of Egyptian clover (100 g) are extracted in a Soxhlet extractor with light petroleum and the petroleum extract kept aside for the isolation of sitosterol. The de-fatted seeds are then extracted with alcohol. A final aqueous extract is also made for the isolation of a galactomannan. The alcoholic extract is concentrated and cooled when xanthosine separates out as a crystalline compound. It does not melt up to 340°C.

The UV spectrum in 0.1N NaOH solution has maxima at 248 (log ε 4.06) and 277 (4.01) nm. In a 0.1N HCl solution, the maxima are at 235 (3.93) and 261 (3.97) nm. It is hydrolysed by boiling with 7% aqueous sulphuric acid for 1 hour and the sugar, D-ribose, identified by circular paper chromatography. The purine base, xanthine, can also be detected by paper chromatography using butanol–water (86:14) as the developing solvent; the R_f value is 0.18. It forms a crystalline perchlorate, m.p. 262–63°C. Its UV spectrum in a 0.1N NaOH solution shows an absorption maximum at 282 nm, whereas in 0.1N HCl, the maximum is seen at 263 nm.

4.12 OXYGEN HETEROCYCLICS OTHER THAN FLAVONOIDS

The coumarins, including the coumestans, which are biosynthetically related to the isoflavonoids, fall in this category. Coumarins exhibit a wide range of pharmacological activities which include anti-coagulant activity [for example, dicoumarol (4.123) and related compounds], antibiotic activity (novobiocin, 4.124), photodynamic action [psoralen (4.125)] and related furanocoumarins and chromones] and estrogenic activity (as shown by coumestrol, 4.126). The isolation of psoralen and wedelolactone-desmethylwedelolactone (4.127 and 4.128) is described.

4.12.1 Isolation of psoralen

Seeds of *Psoralea corylifolia* (100 g) are crushed and extracted with light petroleum (60–80°) in a Soxhlet extractor. Removal of the solvent by distillation on a water bath yields an oil weighing about 10 g. After standing for a few days, the oil deposits a pale yellow crystalline solid which is collected by decanting the supernatant oil. The solid is washed with a small quantity of cold petroleum. The crude psoralen thus obtained (250 mg) melts at 135°C. On re-crystallisation from alcohol, the pure compound is obtained (m.p. 162°C).

Psoralen exhibits a bright blue fluorescence in the solid state and when dissolved in neutral solvents. It can be easily detected on TLC plates by viewing under UV light. It is sparingly soluble in petroleum and diethyl either but soluble in alcohol and chloroform.

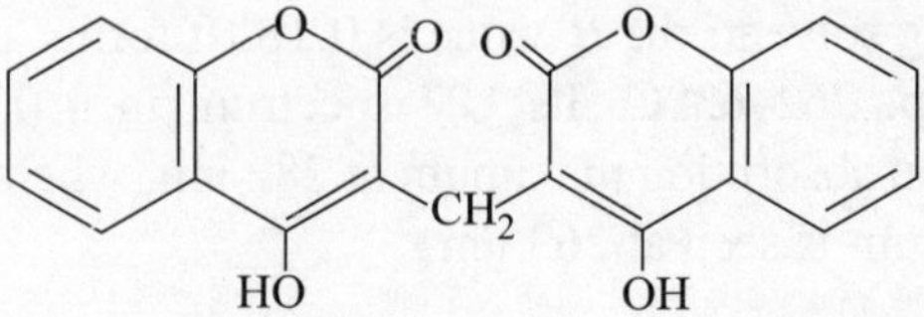

(4.123)

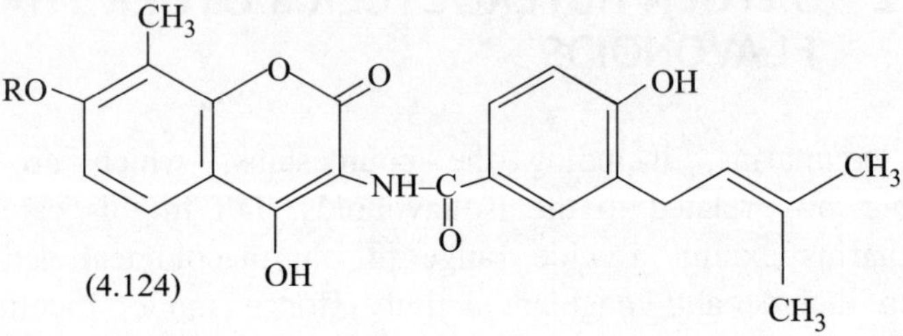

(4.124)

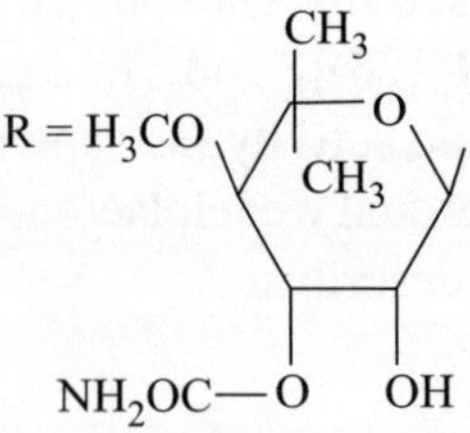

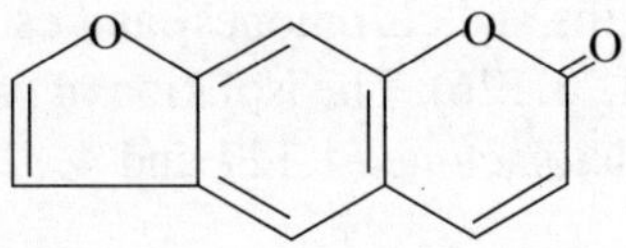

(4.125)

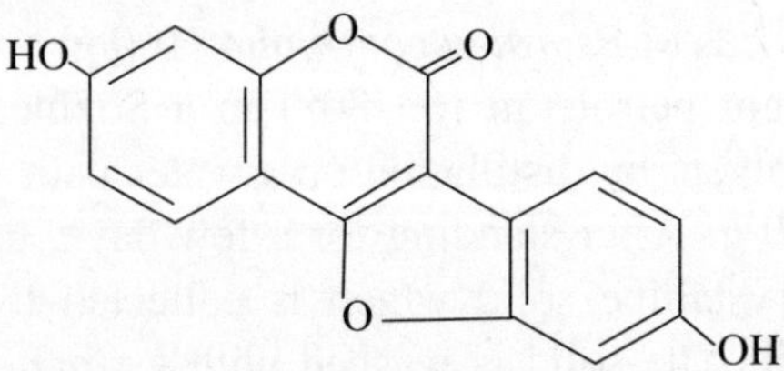

(4.126)

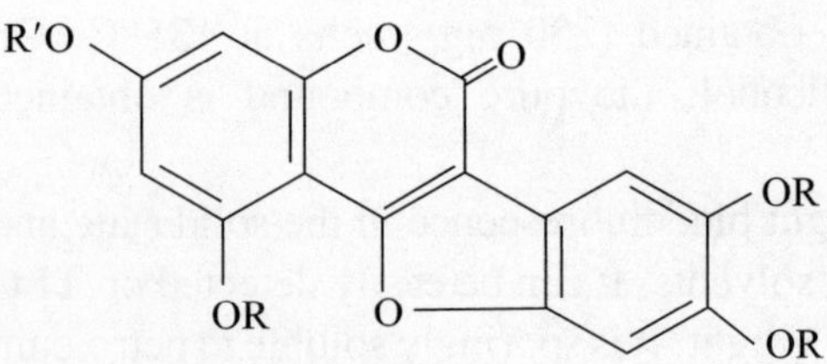

(4.127) : R′ = CH_3; R = H

(4.128) : R = R′ = H

(4.129) : R = R′ = CH_3

(4.130) : R′ = CH_3; R = $COCH_3$

(4.131) : R′ = R = $COCH_3$

4.12.2 Isolation of Wedelolactone–Desmethylwedelolactone

Fresh leaves of *Wedelia calendulaceae* (500 g) are cut into small pieces and extracted with 90% ethanol containing 2% acetic acid, until the extract is no longer coloured green. The extract is filtered hot and concentrated until the separation of solid matter begins. The solid, which is a mixture of chlorophyll and a waxy material, is filtered off and the filtrate further concentrated under reduced pressure. It is then extracted with diethyl ether in a separatory funnel, till the ether extract is no longer fluorescent. Removal of the solvent from the ether extract yields wedelolactone as a pale green solid (250 mg). It is re-crystallised from methanol (m.p. 327–330°C).

When the leaves of the related plant, *Eclipta alba*, are used in place of *W. calendulaceae*, the solid obtained by the same procedure described above, is a mixture of wedelolactone and desmethylwedelolactone. The two compounds separate out on paper chromatography using the lower phase of benzene–acetic acid–water (2:2:1) as the developing solvent. On Whatman No.1 paper, wedelolactone has a R_f value of 0.55, whereas desmethylwedelolactone has a R_f of 0.45. Both the compounds exhibit bright blue fluorescence under UV light and turn green on exposure to ammonia.

The composition of the mixture varies from batch to batch, depending on factors such as season and place of collection. For example, the South Indian variety of the plant has desmethylwedelolactone as the major component, whereas wedelolactone constitutes bulk of the mixture obtained from North Indian varieties. The material obtained from plants growing in and around Bengaluru yields a mixture of the two compounds which on re-crystallisation from ethanol yields pure desmethylwedelolactone, the yield of which is about 300 mg from 1 kg of the leaves. It does not melt up to 360°C. The mixture itself can be used as such for conversion into tri-*O*-methylwedelolactone (4.129; see p.104) and also for studying the colour reactions mentioned below. An alcoholic solution of the mixture gives a dark green colour with alcoholic ferric chloride. Other colour reactions are performed with the solid material (a few milligrams for each test).

1. **Saturated sodium bicarbonate solution** The solid slowly dissolves giving a green-coloured solution which turns yellow and finally red on standing. The same colour changes are also seen in aqueous sodium carbonate.
2. **Concentrated nitric acid** A blue-green solution is obtained, which turns brown, then yellow, and finally almost colourless on standing.
3. **Alcoholic *p*-benzoquinone** A bluish green solution, which fades on keeping, is obtained.

HPLC analysis of Wedelolactone–Desmethylwedelolactone mixture

1 mg of the crude mixture of wedelolactone and desmethylwedelolactone (along with traces of other compounds) is dissolved in 1 ml of methanol. 5 μl of this solution is used for HPLC analysis on an instrument equipped with a high-speed diode array detector. The column used is ODS RP-18 (Altex ultrasphere 5 μm particle size; 25 cm × 4.6 mm ID). The solvent system consists of acetonitrile and distilled water containing 10 ml of 0.1N phosphoric acid per litre. A linear gradient of 60%–80% acetonitrile is used for the run. The flow rate is controlled at 0.8 ml per minute. Under these conditions, the retention time of wedelolactone is 2.5 minutes and that of desmethylwedelolactone is 2.9 minutes. The UV maxima for both the compounds are 245, 305 and 350 nm.

Characterisation of Wedelolactone triacetate (4.130; see p.104) and Desmethylwedelolactone tetraacetate (4.131; see p.104)

Wedelolactone (0.1g) is dissolved in warm acetic anhydride (2 ml) containing a few drops of pyridine. The mixture is allowed to stand overnight and then diluted with ice-cold water till the precipitation of the acetate is complete. It is filtered using a micro-funnel, washed with a small quantity of ice water, dried and re-crystallised from ethyl acetate, m.p. 248–50°C.

Desmethylwedelolactone prepared in the same way as described above melts at 271–72°C.

Preparation of tri-*O*-methylwedelolactone

The crude mixture of wedelolactone and desmethylwedelolactone (0.1 g) is dissolved in 50 ml of dry acetone (prepared by allowing purified acetone to stand over ignited potassium carbonate for a few hours, before use). After the addition of anhydrous potassium carbonate (ca. 2 g) and dimethyl sulphate (2.5 ml), the mixture is refluxed for 6 hours. It is then filtered hot, the potassium salts washed with hot acetone, and the filtrate concentrated by distillation on a water bath. Addition of water to the residual solution causes the methyl ether to separate out as a colourless solid. It is collected by filtration, dried and re-crystallised from methanol. The yield is 0.1 g. It melts at 250–51 °C.

Its proton NMR spectrum has signals at δ 3.9(12H, s), 6.9 (1H, d, J=3 Hz), 7.2 (1H, d, J=3 Hz), 7.5 (1H, s) and 7.8 (1H, s).

Recommended reading

1. Balakrishna S, Ramanathan JD, Seshadri TR and Venkataramani B, *Proc. Royal Soc.*, A, 268: 1–20, 1962 (for isolation of homoferreirin and ougenin).
2. Balakrishna S, Seshadri TR and Venkataramani B, *J. Sci. Ind. Res.*, 19B: 433–36, 1960 (for isolation of morindonin).
3. Bhatia VK, Ramanathan JD and Seshadri TR, *Tetrahedron, 23*: 1263–68, 1967. (for isolation of mangiferin).
4. Cannell RJP, (Ed.), *Natural Products Isolation*, Humana Press, New Jersey, 1998.
5. Geissman TA, (Ed.), *The Chemistry of Flavonoid Compounds*, Pergamon Press, New York, 1962 (for the isolation of some anthocyanins and flavonoids).
6. Guenther E, *The Essential Oils*, Van Nostrand, New York, 1948.
7. Houghton PJ and Raman A, *Laboratory Handbook for the Fractionation of Natural Extracts*, Chapman & Hall, London, 1998.
8. Ikan R, *Natural Products—A Laboratory Guide,* 2nd Edition, *Academic Press,* London, 1991.

9. Krishnaswamy NR, *Chemistry of Natural Products—A Unified Approach,* 2nd Edition, Universities Press, India, 1999 (for original references to pedaliin, nepitrin, wedelolactone and desmethylwedelolactone).
10. Lawless J, *The Illustrated Encyclopedia of Essential Oils, The Complete Guide to the use of Oils in Aromatherapy and Herbalism*, Harper Collins, 1995. (This book makes delightful reading and has a wealth of information on all aspects of essential oils.)
11. The *Merck Index*, 11th Edition, Merck & Co., Inc., New Jersey, 1989 (for physical constants and important references to the compounds discussed in this chapter).

CHAPTER 5

Chemical Transformations of some Natural Products

5.1 HYDROXYCITRONELLAL FROM CITRONELLAL

Citronellal (5.1) which is the chief terpene constituent of the oil of *Eucalyptus citriodora* leaves has little value as a perfumery chemical. It is, however, used in mosquito repellent formulations. Hydroxycitronellal (5.2), on the other hand, has a very pleasant, pervading and lingering odour, which resembles the exotic smell of the lily of the valley. However, this compound does not occur in nature and has to be prepared from citronellal by hydration across the double bond. Such a hydration, however, cannot be brought about by conventional acid-catalysed hydration. This is because, in the presence of acids, the aldehyde group gets protonated in preference to the double bond, and is followed by an intramolecular cyclisation and

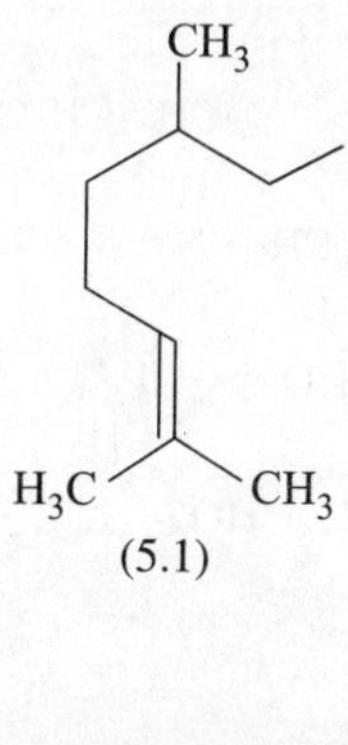

(5.1)

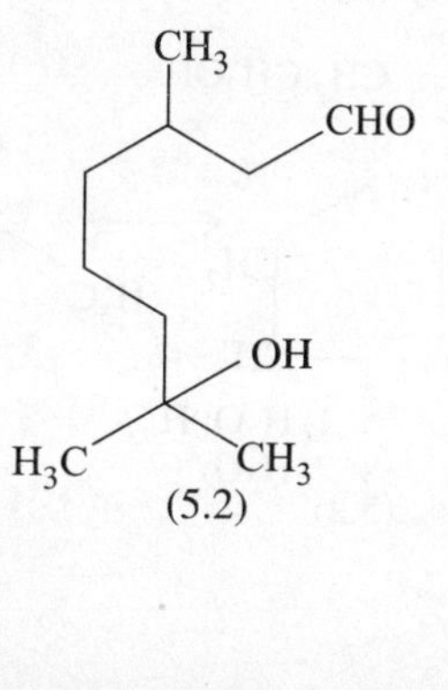

(5.2)

hydroxylation as shown in Scheme 5.1. The product does not have any great perfumery value. To avoid such a cyclisation, it is necessary to protect the aldehyde group before bringing about hydration at the double bond; deprotection then yields the desired product.

For a long time the only practical method to protect the aldehyde group was by conversion into the bisulphite adduct. However, the adduct formation is slow and incomplete. The adduct is also not very stable under acidic conditions. Hence, the yield of the final desired product obtained by this method is less than quantitative. In 1974, a group of Japanese workers reported a process in which

Scheme 5.1

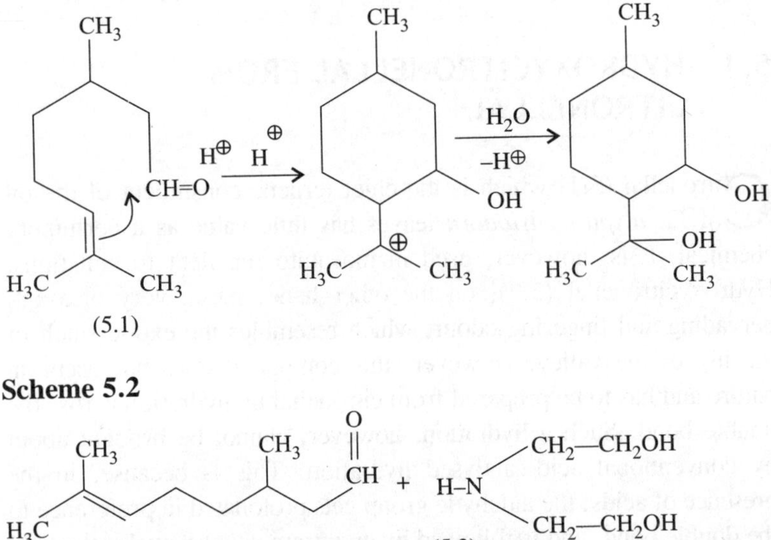

Scheme 5.2

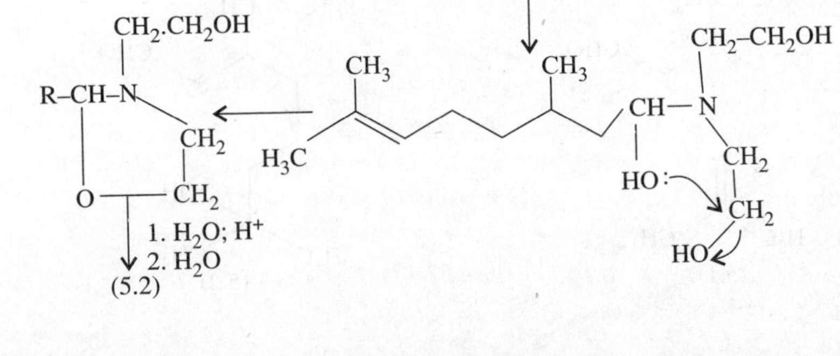

the aldehyde is protected by conversion into an enamine, or related derivative, before hydration and deprotection. The method is fast and efficient and the yield of hydroxycitronellal is almost quantitative. The reactions involved in this process are shown in Scheme 5.2.

PROCEDURE

Pure diethanolamine (5.3; 10.5 g) is added to pure citronellal (15.4 g) taken in a 50 ml beaker cooled in an ice water bath. The amine is added over a period of three minutes, with stirring, maintaining the temperature of the reaction mixture between 15°C and 25°C. The stirring is continued for a further period of 30 minutes. The mixture is thereafter centrifuged to separate out the oily enamine (pyrazoline) layer, which can be used as such for the next stage. It may also be purified by distillation under reduced pressure using an efficient vacuum pump. In the next step, aqueous sulphuric acid (50% v/v; 34 ml) is taken in a 100 ml beaker cooled to 5–7°C in an ice water bath.

The whole of the citronellal–diethanolamine adduct obtained as described above is added drop-wise over a period of 2 minutes, keeping the temperature of the reaction mixture below 30°C. During the addition, the mixture is vigorously stirred. The stirring is continued for 2 more minutes and then the mixture is poured, with stirring, into a 1-litre beaker containing saturated aqueous sodium chloride solution (500 ml), toluene (50 ml), sodium hydroxide (24 g) and crushed ice (200 g). The pH of the solution is then adjusted to 6.5–7.0 by the addition of aqueous sodium bicarbonate or dilute sulphuric acid. The mixture is then transferred to a large separatory funnel and the aqueous layer run off. The toluene layer is kept aside. The aqueous layer is once again extracted with fresh toluene (50 ml) before discarding it. The combined toluene layer is washed thrice with saturated sodium chloride solution (20 ml each time) by shaking in a separatory funnel. The solvent is removed by distillation under reduced pressure. The residual oil is then distilled using an efficient vacuum pump, when pure hydroxycitronellal boils over at 110°C and 5.5 mm pressure. The overall yield of the final product

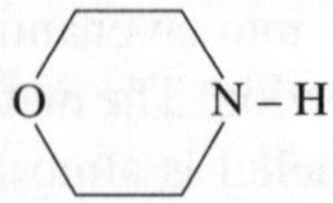 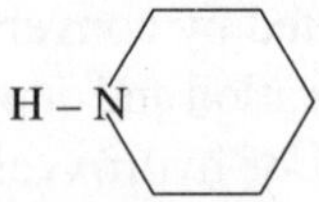

(5.4) (5.5)

is about 90%. In place of diethanolamine, either morpholine (5.4) or piperidine (5.5), in the same molar proportion, can be used for preparing the enamine from citronellal.

5.2 CITRAL (5.6) FROM GERANIOL (5.7)

For the oxidation of primary alcohols to aldehydes, a number of reagents are available. One of the most efficient and specific reagents for this purpose is pyridinium chromate. Organic reagents on solid supports offer several advantages over the conventional solution phase reactions. For instance, the reagent can be filtered off after the reaction, making it easier to separate the desired product. The following procedure describes the oxidation of geraniol to citral using pyridinium chromate deposited on silica gel.

The reagent is prepared by adding silica gel (25 g) to a solution of chromium trioxide (5 g) in water (30 ml). During the addition, and for one hour thereafter, the mixture is mechanically shaken at room temperature. Excess water is then removed at reduced pressure, preferably using a rotary evaporator at 90°C to get the reagent as a yellow-orange free-flowing powder (31.2 g). This material is taken in a 3-necked flask and covered with light petroleum (60 ml). The flask is fitted with a mechanical stirrer, a calcium chloride guard tube, and a dropping funnel through which pyridine (7.9 g) is added in drops, keeping the temperature between 20°C and 24°C. After stirring for one more hour, the mixture is filtered under suction using a Buchner funnel, and the solid washed on the funnel with light petroleum and dried on the funnel itself under suction. The dark brown–coloured oxidising agent (35.8 g) can be stored in a coloured bottle.

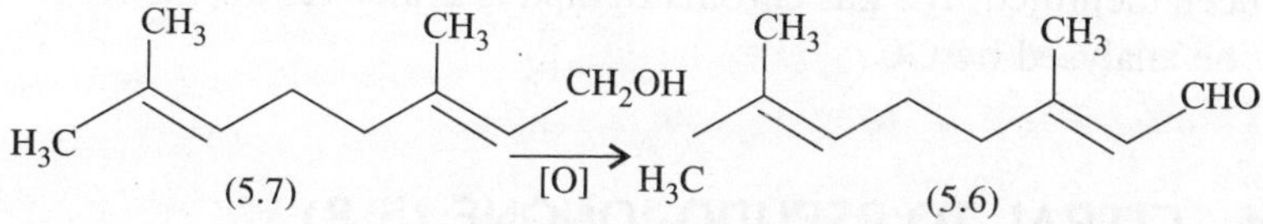

To a solution of geraniol (5.7, 1.54 g) in dichloromethane (15 ml), the oxidising agent (14.4 g) and acetic acid (0.48 g) are added and the mixture shaken for 4 hours at room temperature. Thereafter, diethyl ether (30 ml) is added and the mixture shaken for another 2 minutes and then filtered. The solid is washed with ether and the combined filtrate is transferred to a separatory funnel wherein it is shaken successively with 5% aqueous hydrochloric acid (16 ml), water (10 ml, twice), 5% aqueous sodium bicarbonate (16 ml), water (16 ml, twice) and sodium chloride solution (10 ml). The organic layer is then passed through a small bed (0.8 cm × 4 cm) of alumina (Brockman grade II) which is washed with ether (20 ml). The combined filtrate is then gently distilled from a water bath to remove the solvent. The residue (5.6, 1.35 g) is citral, which can be identified by comparison with a natural sample (see Chapter 4) on a TLC plate.

5.3 SYNTHETIC LIME MIX FROM CITRAL

A solution of citric acid of pH 1.75 is prepared by dissolving powdered anhydrous citric acid (18.0 g) in distilled water (250 ml). Citral (30 g) is added to this solution taken in a 500-ml round-bottomed flask, and the mixture gently refluxed for 2 hours. The flask is then equipped with a water-cooled condenser and a receiver flask cooled in an ice water bath. The mixture is then distilled, when water and an oil distill over and collect in the receiver flask. The distillate is transferred to a separatory funnel and the oil separated from water. The yield of the oil is 22.0 g (73%). It has a very pleasant lime-like odour. The remaining non-distillable residue is resinous and not fragrant. The oil is a mixture of terpene hydrocarbons and oxygen-containing compounds, all of which have not been identified. If a gas chromatograph is available, the mixture may be analysed by GC.

5.4 CITRAL TO PSEUDO-IONONE (5.8)

A solution of pure citral (10 g) in acetone (40 g) is cooled to –5°C to –8°C using an ice–salt cooling bath. A previously cooled solution of metallic sodium (0.46 g) (caution!) in absolute alcohol (10 ml) is slowly added to it with vigorous stirring. The stirring is continued for 3–4 minutes after adding the sodium ethoxide solution, keeping the temperature below –5°C. The reaction mixture is diluted with diethyl ether and the mixture transferred to a separatory funnel, where it is shaken with a solution of tartaric acid (3.0 g) in water (10 ml). After running off the aqueous layer, the ether layer is washed with ice-cold water till the washings are neutral. After removal of the solvent, pseudo-ionone (5.8) is obtained as an oil. It can be further purified as follows.

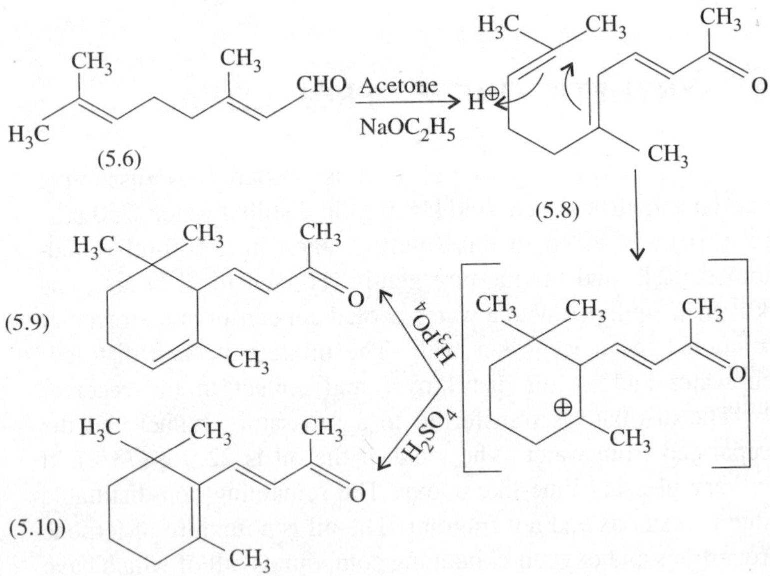

To one part of the crude product, 2 parts of a 35% solution of sodium bisulphite and 1 part of water are added and the mixture refluxed for 5 hours. After cooling the reaction mixture, it is extracted with diethyl ether and transferred to a separatory funnel. The solvent removes impurities, whereas pseudo-ionone remains in the aqueous layer as the bisulphite adduct. To the adduct solution taken in a beaker along with some ether, 10% sodium hydroxide solution is added gradually, with stirring, till no further turbidity is seen on addition of the alkali solution. At the same time, the liberated pseudo-ionone would go into the ether layer. Excess alkali should be avoided as it can cause polymerisation of the ionone. The mixture is then transferred to a separatory funnel, more ether added, and shaken well to complete the extraction. After running off the aqueous layer, the ether layer is repeatedly washed with ice-cold water till the washings are neutral to litmus. Evaporation of the solvent gives pure pseudo-ionone. If sufficient quantity is available it may be purified by distillation using a micro vacuum distillation set under reduced pressure. Pure pseudo-ionone distills over at 145–50°C at 12 mm pressure.

5.5 PSEUDO-IONONE TO α-IONONE (5.9)

Pseudo-ionone (10 g) is added drop-wise, with continuous stirring, to 85% phosphoric acid (75 g), keeping the temperature at 30°C for 30 minutes. The reaction mixture is then poured into cold water (250 ml) and then transferred to a separatory funnel where it is extracted with diethyl ether. After running off the aqueous layer, the ether layer is washed with cold water till the washings are neutral to litmus. After drying the solution over anhydrous sodium sulphate, the solvent is evaporated. The residue is subjected to steam distillation when pure α-ionone (see p.113) distills over, leaving behind resinous impurities. The distillate is extracted with diethyl ether in a separatory funnel. The ether extract is dried over sodium sulphate and evaporated on a water bath. The residue may be further purified by distillation under reduced pressure. α-Ionone boils at 126–131 °C at 12 mm pressure.

The yield is about 7–8 g. UV spectrum (solvent, methanol): absorption maximum at 228.5 nm (ε 14,300).

5.6 β-IONONE (5.10) FROM PSEUDO-IONONE

In a 100 ml beaker placed in an ice bath, a mixture of concentrated sulphuric acid (35 g) and glacial acetic acid (15 g) is taken. After the temperature has dropped below 10 °C, pseudo-ionone (10 g) is added through a dropping funnel with vigorous stirring. During the addition, and for 10 minutes thereafter, the temperature of the reaction mixture is kept below 15 °C. It is then poured with stirring into a mixture of ice water (100 ml) and diethyl ether (25 ml). The mixture is transferred to a separatory funnel and shaken to ensure complete extraction of the product into the ether layer. After running off the aqueous layer, the ether layer is washed in succession with ice water, sodium carbonate solution (1 %) and water, and then dried over anhydrous sodium sulphate. Removal of the solvent yields impure β-ionone which is then purified by steam distillation. The distillate is extracted with diethyl ether and the ether layer dried and evaporated. The residue (5.10, 7.5 g) is a pleasant smelling yellow-coloured liquid.

Distillation using a Claisen flask with a short fractionating column at reduced pressure gives pure β-ionone, b.p. 126–8°C at 12 mm pressure. UV spectrum (solvent, methanol): absorption maximum at 293.5 nm (ε 8,700). The Proton NMR, ^{13}C NMR (off resonance proton decoupled), INEPT and COSY spectra of β-ionone are given at the end of this chapter. (These spectra have been reproduced from *One-dimensional and Two- dimensional NMR Spectra by Modern Pulse Techniques*, edited by Nakanishi, K Kodansha, Tokyo; University Science Books, Mill Valley, California. This book also contains spin decoupling difference spectrum, NOE difference spectrum, selective-population transfer

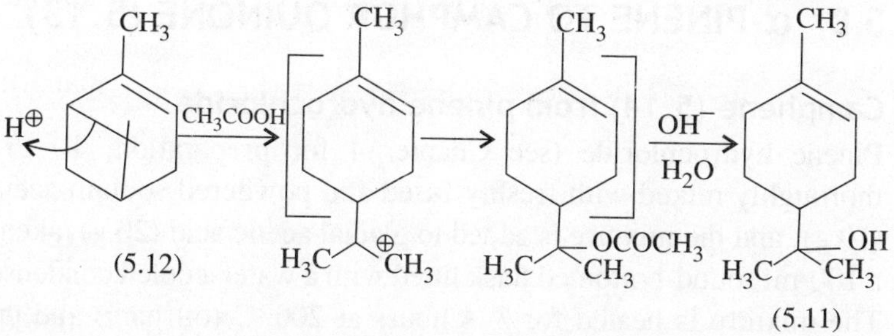

spectrum, broadband proton decoupling ^{13}C NMR spectrum, DEPT, INEPT and DEPT without proton decoupling spectra and NOESY spectrum of β-ionone. For an explanation of the terms and an in-depth understanding of all aspects of NMR spectroscopy, the books recommended at the end of Chapter 2 may be consulted.)

5.7 α-TERPINEOL (5.11) FROM α-PINENE (5.12)

Only an outline of the procedure is given here. Students are advised to experiment and find out, with the help of the supervising teacher, the optimum conditions for obtaining the product. The yield is influenced by variations in the concentration of acetic acid.

A mixture of α-pinene and aqueous acetic acid is refluxed for several hours at 100°C. The duration of the reaction may be determined by periodic TLC monitoring of the reaction which is terminated when all the pinene has reacted by dilution with water. The cooled reaction mixture is then extracted with diethyl ether, the ether layer washed with ice water to free it of acid, dried and distilled. The crude ester is saponified by refluxing with 10% aqueous sodium hydroxide solution for 2 hours. The reaction mixture is then cooled and extracted with diethyl ether. The ether layer is washed free of alkali with cold water, dried and distilled.

The residue is examined by TLC and further purified by distillation, b.p. 219°C (it is a low melting solid, m.p. 35°C). α-Terpineol has a pleasant smell and is used in perfumery.

5.8 α-PINENE TO CAMPHOR QUINONE (5.13)

Camphene (5.14) from pinene hydrochloride

Pinene hydrochloride (see Chapter 4 for preparation, 10 g) is thoroughly mixed with freshly fused and powdered sodium acetate (10 g), and the mixture is added to glacial acetic acid (20 g) taken in a 100-ml round-bottomed flask fitted with a water-cooled condenser. The mixture is heated for 3–4 hours at 200°C (oil bath) and then steam distilled. The distillate is extracted with diethyl ether, the ether layer dried over anhydrous sodium sulphate and evaporated.

The residue is cooled in an ice chest when camphene crystallises out, m.p. 50°C (b.p. 159–60°C).

Isobornyl acetate from camphene

Isobornyl acetate (5.15) is obtained from camphene (10 g) by heating a mixture of it with acetic acid (30 ml) and 50% sulphuric acid (2 ml) for 20 minutes on a steam bath. The reaction mixture is then diluted with water (20 ml), cooled and extracted with diethyl ether. The ether layer is washed in succession with cold water, 5% sodium carbonate solution and cold water, till the washings are neutral. The ether extract is then dried and evaporated. The residue (10 g) is an oil which can be purified by distillation under reduced pressure. Pure isobornyl acetate boils at 105°C at 15 mm pressure.

Isoborneol (5.16) from isoboryl acetate

The above ester (10 g) and potassium hydroxide (5 g) in water, (10 ml) are added to ethanol (30 ml) and the mixture refluxed for 1 hour on a steam bath. It is then cooled and diluted with water, when isoborneol separates out. After cooling, the solid is collected on a Buchner funnel under suction, washed with cold water, and pressed dry on the funnel itself. The yield is 8 g.

Camphor (5.17) from isoborneol

Camphor (5.17) is obtained from isoborneol (5 g) dissolved in acetone (7 ml) to which a solution of chromium trioxide (18 g) in concentrated sulphuric acid (16 ml) is added, followed by the addition of water (30 ml). The mixture is allowed to stand at room

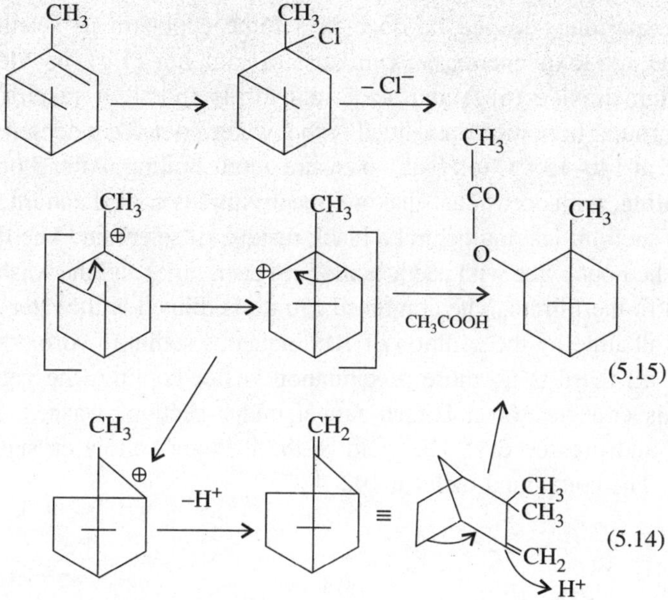

(5.15)

(5.14)

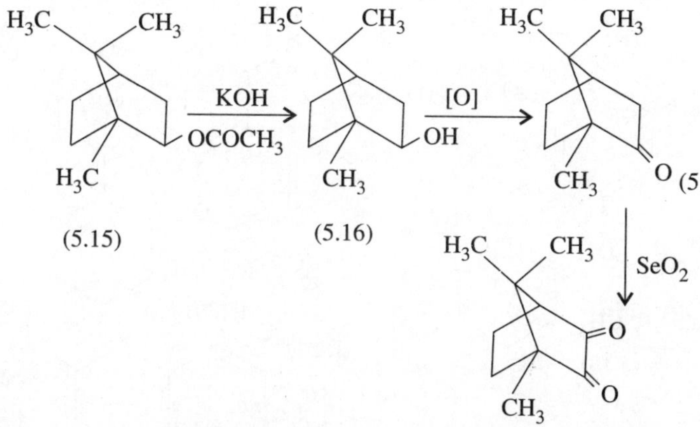

(5.17)

(5.15)

(5.16)

(5.13)

temperature for an hour to complete the oxidation of the alcohol to ketone. Steam distillation of the mixture gives camphor which separates out as a solid in the distillate. It is filtered and washed with water. It can be purified by sublimation, using a micro-sublimation apparatus. Pure camphor has a m.p. of 176°C. The yield is 2 g.

Camphor quinone (5.13) from camphor

This experiment should be done in a fume cupboard as selenium dioxide is a toxic chemical. A mixture of camphor (5 g), powdered selenium dioxide (6 g) and acetic anhydride (5 ml) is taken in a 25 ml round-bottomed flask fitted with a water-cooled condenser and heated at 140–150°C (oil bath) to ensure gentle boiling. After 3 hours of heating, with occasional shaking, the mixture is cooled and filtered under suction, leaving behind a black residue of selenium. The flask is washed out twice with acetic acid (5 ml each time) and the washing added to the filtrate. The combined filtrate is diluted with water and made alkaline by the addition of 10% aqueous sodium hydroxide in drops till there is no more precipitation. After cooling, the yellow solid is collected on a Hirsch funnel under suction, washed with water and pressed dry. The yield of the brilliant yellow crystals is 7.5 g. The compound melts at 192–4°C.

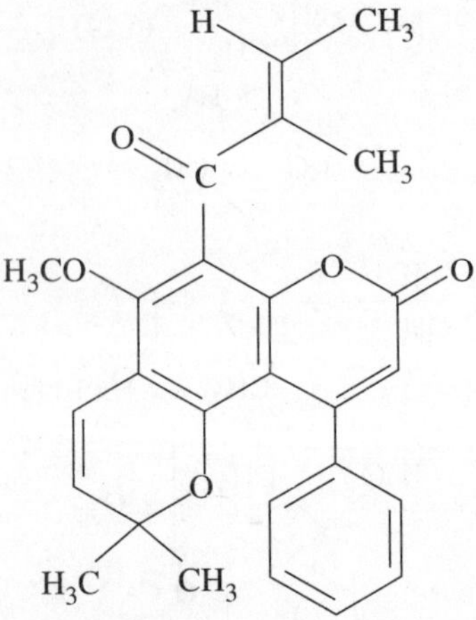

(5.18)

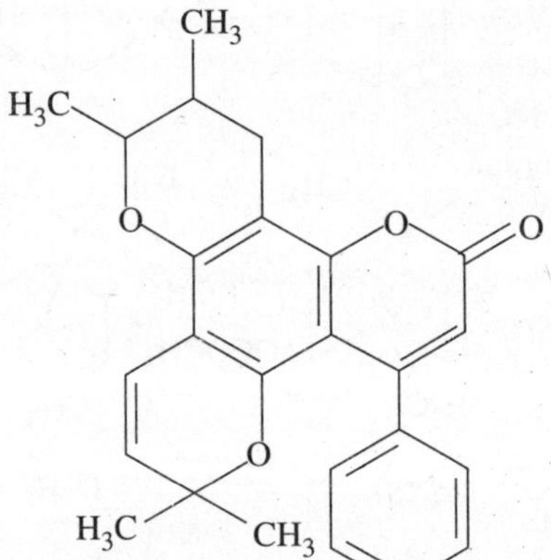

(5.20)

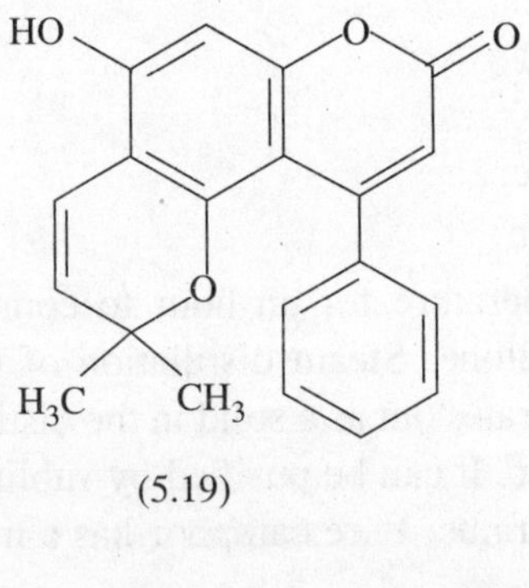

(5.19)

It is dried in a desiccator and re-crystallised from light petroleum (caution!). This is done by dissolving it in minimum amount of solvent and quickly filtering the solution through a fluted filter paper in a pre-heated funnel. On cooling the solution, pure camphor quinone crystallises out, m.p. 196–97°C (yield: 2.8 g).

5.9 CALOPHYLLOLIDE (5.18) TO 2,2,-DIMETHYL-5-HYDROXY-7,8-(4'-PHENYL-α-PYRENO) CHROMAN (5.19)

Calophyllolide (5.18) and the related inophyllolide (5.20) are complex 4-phenylcoumarins occurring in the seed oil of *Calophyllum inophyllum*. They were the first members of the neoflavonoid class of compounds to be isolated from a natural source. Calophyllolide has been reported to possess anti-coagulant as well as anti-inflammatory activities. The seed oil is commercially available. The seeds can also be easily procured. In the following experiments the isolation of calophyllolide and inophyllolide, and an unusual transformation of calophyllolide to (5.19) under demethylative conditions are described.

ISOLATION OF CALOPHYLLOLIDE

Brownish yellow, ripe seed kernels (100 g) of *Calophyllum inophyllum* are extracted with light petroleum (20 × 200 ml, 24 hours each time) in the cold. The combined extract is concentrated to about 30 ml and kept in the refrigerator, when calophyllolide starts crystallising out after 10 days. The crystals are collected on a small Hirsch funnel, washed with ice-cold light petroleum and dried. Yield: 600 mg, m.p. 159–60°C. It can be recrystallised from benzene–light petroleum.

From the mother liquor, on further cooling for 15 days, inophyllolide is obtained as a crystalline solid, 150 mg, m.p. 186–88°C. It is recrystallised from ethanol.

Conversion of calophyllolide into 2,2,-dimethyl-5-hydroxy-7,8-(4'-phenyl-α-pyreno) chroman (5.19)

A mixture of calophyllolide (0.53 g), hydriodic acid (57%, *d*, 1.7; 12 ml) and red phosphorus (0.1 g) is taken in a two-necked round-bottomed flask fitted with an air condenser and a gas inlet tube, and is heated at 145–50°C for 2 hours in an oil·bath. Through the inlet tube carbon dioxide gas is passed in throughout the duration of the reaction. The reaction mixture is then cooled and diluted with water. The solid that separates out is collected by filtration on a small funnel and macerated with cold diethyl ether. The ether insoluble residue is extracted with boiling absolute ethanol and filtered to remove the phosphorous.

The filtrate is concentrated and cooled, when the product (5.19) separates out as a solid (0.2 g) which does not melt below 300°C. Its UV absorption spectrum in ethanol shows maxima at 260 and 337 nm. Its acetate, prepared by treatment with acetic anhydride–pyridine at room temperature (24 hrs) crystallises from ethanol as colourless cubes, m.p. 142-44°C.

5.10 CONVERSION OF METHYL ESTERS OF TIGLIC ACID AND ANGELIC ACID INTO THEIR EPOXY DERIVATIVES

Tiglic acid or trans-2-methylcrotonic acid (systematic name: E-2-methyl-2-butenoic acid; 5.21) occurs in croton oil and is one of the factors responsible for the skin irritant action of croton oil. Along with its *cis* (Z) isomer, angelic acid (5.22), it occurs fairly widespread in a number of plants, in the form of esters. The other component may be an alkaloid, as in the case of cevadilla seeds or sesquiterpene lactones, as for example, the case of the essential oil of Roman chamomile. Tiglic acid has also been found to be a chemical constituent of the defensive secretions of several carabid beetles (for example, *Pterostichus californicas*). Both tiglic and angelic acids are commercially available. They are easily converted into their methyl esters using ethereal diazomethane.

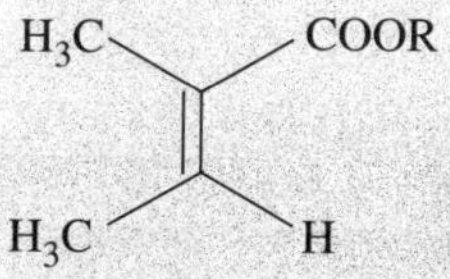

(5.21) : R = H
(5.24) : R = CH_3

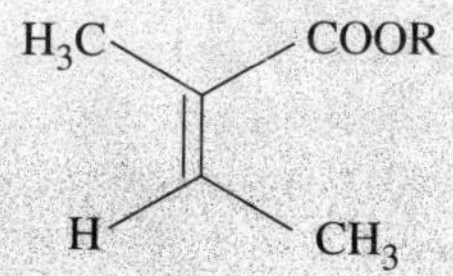

(5.22) : R = H
(5.23) : R = CH_3

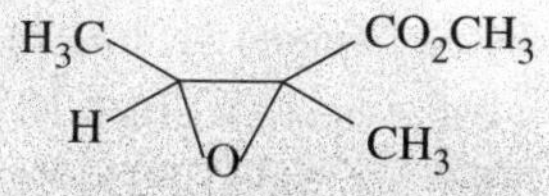

(5.25)

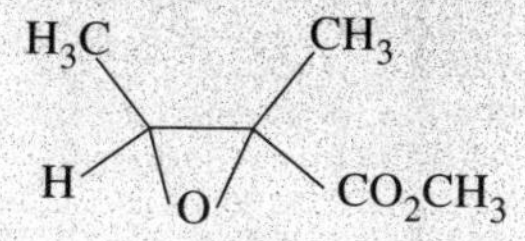

(5.26)

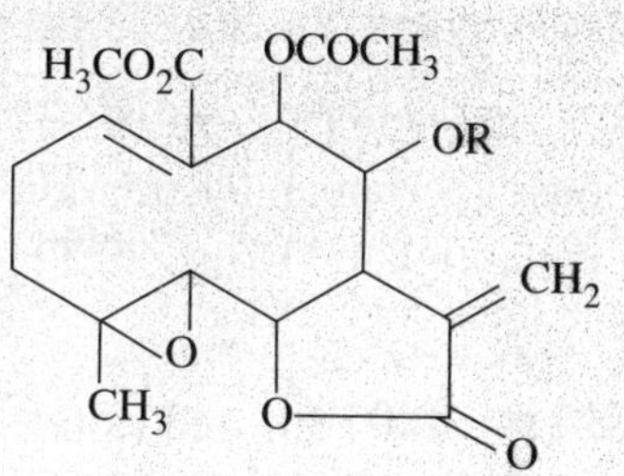

(5.27)

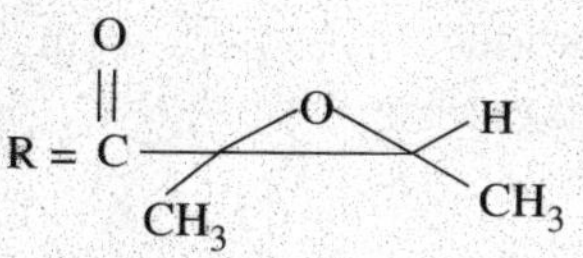

In the following procedures, the conversion of methyl angelate (5.23) and methyl tiglate (5.24) to the corresponding epoxy derivatives—(5.25) and (5.26)—are described. Epoxytiglic acid is a constituent of the sesquiterpene lactone, enhydrin (5.27), from which methyl epoxytiglate is obtained by methanolysis.

METHYL EPOXYANGELATE

To a cooled solution of methyl angelate (5.23, 1.4 g) in chloroform (25 ml) a cold solution of *m*-chloroperbenzoic acid (2.3 g) in chloroform is added. The mixture is stirred for 30 minutes while being cooled in an ice bath and then left in a refrigerator to stand for 12 hours. Excess perbenzoic acid is destroyed by the cautious addition of aqueous sodium sulphite (5%) to the mixture; the addition is continued until the chloroform layer gives no positive test with starch–iodide paper.

The chloroform layer is then repeatedly extracted with aqueous sodium bicarbonate (10%), washed with water, and dried (Na_2SO_4). Removal of the solvent at room temperature yields a liquid which is distilled to obtain methyl epoxyangelate (1.1g, 70%), b.p. (at 9 mm pressure) 60–65°C.

IR ν_{max} (neat): 1725 (s), 1575 (w), 1352 (s), 1265 (s), 1225 (s), 1165 (s), 1150 (s), 1075 (s), 1040 (s), 985 (s), 910 (m), 845 (s), 800 (m) and 763 (s) cm^{-1}.

PMR (CCl_4): δ1.25 (3H, d, *J* = 5.5 Hz), 1.48 (3H, s), 2.88 (1H, q, *J* = 5.5 Hz) and 3.70 (3H, s).

METHYL EPOXYTIGLATE

This ester is prepared by the epoxidation of methyl tiglate (5.24, 2.0 g) using perbenzoic acid as in the previous experiment. Distillation of the crude product gives pure methyl epoxytiglate (1.6 g, 70%), b.p. (at 11 mm pressure) 84–86°C.

IR ν_{max}(neat): 1735 (s), 1580 (w), 1330 (s), 1205 (m), 1115 (s), 1060 (w), 980 (m), 910 (m), 865 (m), 805 (w) and 745 (s) cm^{-1}.

PMR (CCl_4): δ 1.29 (3H, d, *J* = 5.5 Hz), 1.42 (3H, s), 3.18 (1H, q, *J* = 5.5 Hz) and 3.65 (3H, s).

5.11 NITRATION AND OTHER REACTIONS OF OSTHOL (5.28)

Osthol, 7-methoxy-8-isopentenylcoumarin, is a naturally occurring coumarin found in a number of plants belonging to the family Umbelliferae (Apiaceae). It can be isolated from *Prangos pabularia* and other species of the genus Prangos. *Prangos pabularia* is a perennial plant indigenous to Kashmir and is widely used in the Ayurvedic system of medicine. In China, the plant material used for

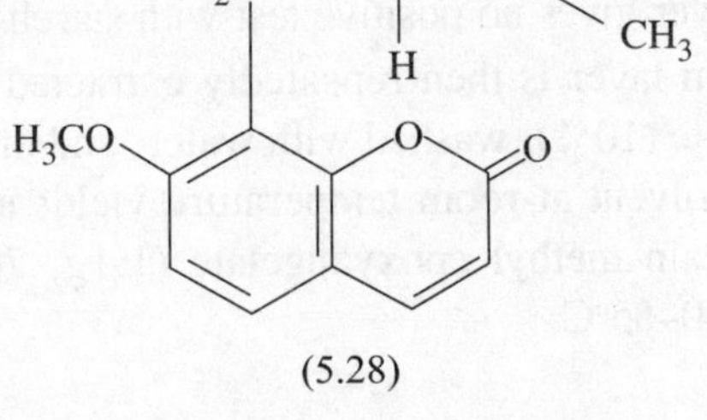

(5.28)

the isolation of osthol is *Cnidium monnieri*. Species of Australian Flindersia, such as *F. bennettiana*, also contain this coumarin along with related compounds.

Pure osthol has been reported to possess a number of pharmacological properties such as respiratory and cardiac stimulant action, bactericidal and anti-fungal activities. In a recent study, it has been shown that this coumarin derivative is capable of protecting plants against mildew attack. In the following procedures the isolation of osthol from the dried fruits of *Cnidium monnieri* (L.) Cusson, the bark of *Flindersia bennetiana* and the roots of *Prangos pabularia* and the products obtained from it on nitration under different conditions and bromination with N-bromosuccinimide are described.

ISOLATION OF OSTHOL FROM *CNIDIUM MONNIERI*

Coarsely powdered dried fruits (300 g) of *Cnidium monnieri* (L.) Cusson are extracted by boiling with 95% ethanol in a Soxhlet extractor till the extract is colourless. The extract is then distilled under reduced pressure, preferably using a rotary evaporator. The dark brown residue thus obtained is dissolved in the minimum amount of ethyl acetate and chromatographed over a column of silica gel. The column is developed using *n*-hexane ethyl acetate as the gradient eluting solvent with increasing amount of ethyl acetate. On evaporation of the solvent from the hexane (6)-ethyl acetate (1) eluates, a solid is obtained which is further purified by chromatography over a short column of silica gel. From hexane (10)–ethyl acetate (1) eluates, osthol (1.6 g) is obtained after the removal of the solvent. It is recrystallised from light petroleum. Pure osthol melts at 83°C.

Proton NMR (500 MHz, $CDCl_3$): δ1.69 (3H, s), 1.86 (3H, s), 3.55 (2H, d, J = 7.3 Hz), 3.94 (3H, s), 5.25 (1H, t, J = 7.3 Hz), 6.20 (1H, d, J = 9.5 Hz), 6.80 (1H, d, J = 8 Hz), 7.30 (1H, d, J = 8 Hz), 7.60 (1H, d, J = 9.5 Hz).

^{13}*C NMR* (125 MHz, $CDCl_3$): δ 18.34, 22.34, 26.20, 56.46, 107.78, 113.34, 113.39, 118.32, 121.67, 126.66, 133.00, 144.19, 153.22, 160.64 and 161.78.

EI-MS: 244 (M^+, 100%), 229 (78%) m/z.

Its infrared spectrum has a strong absorption band at 1717 cm^{-1} due to the lactone carbonyl group.

ISOLATION OF OSTHOL FROM *FLINDERSIA BENNETTIANA* F. MUELL

Air-dried, powdered bark of *Flindersia bennettiana* (2.6 kg) is exhaustively extracted with light petroleum followed by ether. The extracts are combined and the solvents removed by evaporation. The residue is dissolved in diethyl ether, the extract transferred to a separatory funnel and washed in succession with dilute hydrochloric acid, water, (0.4%) sodium hydroxide solution and water. The ether layer is then dried over anhydrous sodium sulphate, filtered and evaporated. The residue is dissolved in light petroleum and cooled in the refrigerator. After a few days, osthol crystallises out. Total yield: 2.4 g.

ISOLATION OF OSTHOL FROM *PRANGOS PABULARIA* LINDL

Air-dried and powdered *Prangos pabularia* roots (100 g) are extracted in a Soxhlet extractor with light petroleum. The extract is concentrated and cooled. The residue obtained is a mixture of three compounds as shown by TLC examination using silica gel and *n*-hexane–ethyl acetate (7:3) as the solvent. The spots exhibit blue fluorescence under UV light. It is purified by chromatography over a column of silica gel or acid (acetic acid) washed alumina. Light petroleum–benzene (4:1) eluates yield pure osthol on removal of the solvent. Yield: 3.2 g, m.p. 83–84°C.

NITRATION OF OSTHOL

The following two procedures describe the nitration of osthol under two different conditions, in the first of which the nitration is carried out using nitric acid–acetic acid–urea mixture. Two products are obtained: a mononitro acetate (5.29) and a dinitro compound (5.30). In the second procedure, the nitrating agent used is benzoyl nitrate in acetonitrile. In this case the product obtained is (5.31), as a result of nitration and a Ritter reaction involving the solvent.

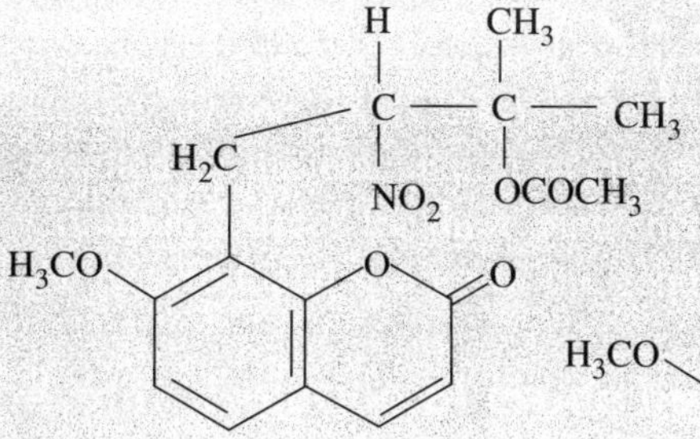

(5.29)

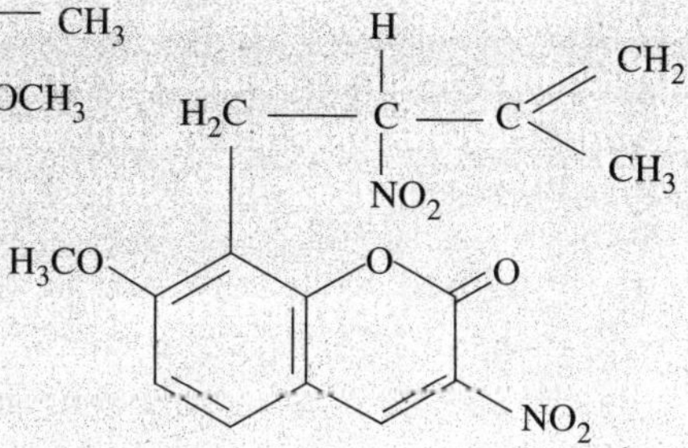

(5.30)

Nitration with nitric acid–acetic acid–urea

To a solution of osthol (1.2 g) in acetic anhydride (20 ml) taken in a 100 ml beaker, an ice-cold mixture of glacial acetic acid (10 ml), concentrated nitric acid (10 ml) and urea (100 mg) is added drop wise with stirring, maintaining the temperature of the reaction mixture at 25–30°C. After allowing the mixture to stand for an hour at room temperature, it is poured into ice-cold water (50 ml). The yellow solid that precipitates out is collected on a small funnel, washed with ice water and dried. A TLC examination on a silica gel coated plate using light petroleum–ethyl acetate (2:3) as the irrigating solvent shows the presence of two compounds.

The solid is dissolved in minimum quantity of ethyl acetate and the solution applied to the top of a column (1.5 cm × 60 cm) of silica gel (75 g). The column is developed using light petroleum and light petroleum–ethyl acetate mixture. From the light petroleum–ethyl acetate (7:3) eluates, compound (5.29) separates out as a colourless solid (430 mg), on removal of the solvent. It can be recrystallised from methanol–chloroform. The pure compound melts at 152–54°C.

Its UV absorption spectrum in methanol shows absorption maxima at 215, 225, 246 and 318 nm. Its emission spectrum shows an emission maximum at 433 nm. Its IR spectrum in KBr has absorption maxima at 1735 and 1710 cm^{-1} due to the acetate and lactone carbonyl groups.

Proton NMR spectrum (90 MHz, $CDCl_3$): δ 1.70 (3H, s), 1.80 (3H, s), 2.02 (3H, s), 3.97 (3H, s), 3.40 (2H, d, J = 7 Hz),

5.50 (1H, t, J = 7 Hz), 6.30 (1H, d, J =9.5 Hz), 6.95 (1H, d, J = 8.5 Hz), 7.62 (1H, d, J = 8.5 Hz) and 7.76 (1H, d, J = 9.5 Hz).

Mass spectrum : m/z (%): M^+ 349 (5), 243 (100).

From the light petroleum–ethyl acetate (3:2) eluates, a yellow compound (290 mg) is obtained after removal of the solvent. It is recrystallised from ethyl acetate-acetone. The pure compound (5.30) melts at 197–99°C.

Its UV spectrum in methanol has absorption maxima at 223, 238, 260 and 365 nm. Its emission spectrum shows maximum at 503 nm.

In its IR spectrum (KBr), the strong absorption band at 1705 cm^{-1} is due to the lactone carbonyl group.

Proton NMR spectrum (90 MHz, DMSOd6): 1.82 (3H, s), 3.70 (2H, d, J = 7 Hz), 3.99 (3H, s), 4.99 (2H, s), 5.26 (1H, t, J = 7 Hz), 7.25 (1H, d, J = 8.5 Hz), 7.95 (1H, d, J = 8.5 Hz) and 9.21 (1H, s).

In the mass spectrum, the base peak appears at m/z 288. The relative intensity of the molecular ion peak at m/z 334 is 15%.

Nitration with benzoyl nitrate

To an ice-cold solution of osthol (600 mg), and silver nitrate (850 mg) in acetonitrile (20 ml), pure benzoyl chloride (2 ml) is added slowly, keeping the temperature of the reaction mixture at 15–20°C. After an hour at room temperature it is diluted with crushed ice. The precipitate is collected by filtration and purified

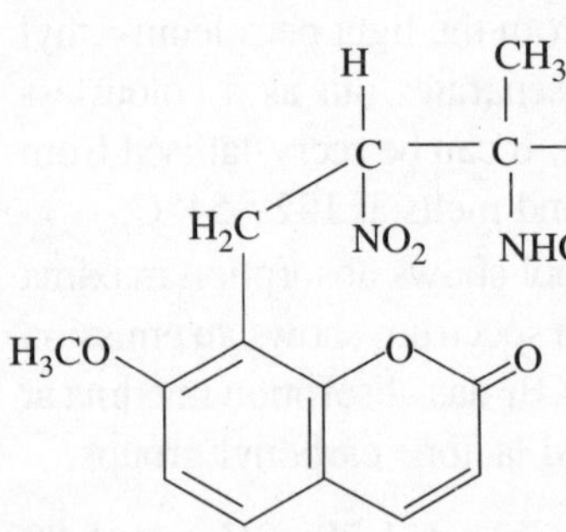

(5.31)

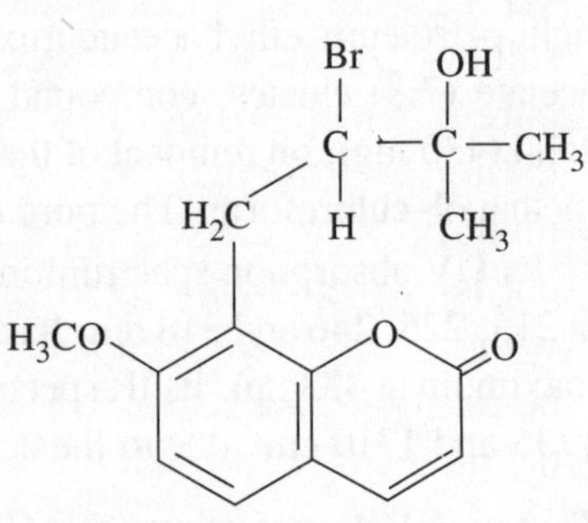

(5.32)

by chromatography over a short column of silica gel (30 g), Elution with light petroleum–ethyl acetate (3:2) gives an eluate from which a cream-coloured crystalline solid (360 mg) is obtained after removing the solvent. Pure (5.31) melts at 213–15°C.

Its UV spectrum in methanol has absorption maxima at 209 and 320 nm. In its emission spectrum the maximum is seen at 391 nm.

IR spectrum (KBr): 3300, 1730, 1705, 1650, 1550, 1390 cm^{-1}

Proton NMR spectrum (90 *MHz,* $CDCl_3$): δ 1.64 (6H, s), 1.96 (3H, s), 3.33 (1H, m), 3.64 (2H, d), 3.98 (3H, s), 5.57 (1H, m), 6.63 (1H, d, J = 9.5 Hz), 6.80 (1H, d, J = 8.5 Hz), 7.34 (1H, d, J = 8.5 Hz) and 7.73 (1H, d, J = 9.5 Hz).

Mass spectrum: m/z M^+ 302 (15%), 243 (100%).

Reaction of Osthol with *N*-Bromosuccinimide in Dimethyl Sulphoxide

N-Bromosuccinimide is a convenient reagent for bringing about bromination at allylic and benzylic positions, under free radical conditions. It can also be used to bring about addition of elements of HOBr across a double bond. The following procedure describes such a reaction for the preparation of the bromohydrin (5.32) from osthol.

Preparation of *N*-bromosuccinimide

To a mixture of crushed ice (20 g) and 16% sodium hydroxide solution (20 ml) taken in a 100 ml beaker, and cooled in an ice bath, pure succinimide (8 g) is gradually added with stirring. As soon as the imide dissolves, bromine (4.3 ml) is added in one lot and the mixture stirred for 15 minutes. The crystalline solid that separates out is collected on a small Buchner or Hirsch funnel, and washed with ice-cold water till the washings are free from bromine. It can be recrystallised from the minimum amount of hot water. Yield of the pure colourless *N*-bromosuccinimide is 9.2 g, m.p. 181–82°C.

Reaction of osthol with NBS

To a solution of osthol (240 mg) in dimethyl sulphoxide (15 ml), containing water (1 ml), *N*-bromosuccinimide (350 mg) is added with stirring at the room temperature. After a few hours, crystals separate out. These are collected on a small funnel and dried. Yield: 180 mg. Melting point: 152–54°C.
Its UV absorption spectrum in methanol has maxima at 215, 240 and 324 nm. Emission maximum: 465 nm.

IR spectrum (KBr): 3420 (broad), 1710, 1600, 1590, 1460, 1285, 1240 cm^{-1}.

Proton NMR spectrum (90 MHz, $CDCl_3$): 1.47 (6H, s), 2.99 (1H, s), 3.47 (2H, d), 3.90 (3H, s), 4.44 (1H, m), 6.19 (1H, d, J = 9.5 Hz), 6.80 (1H, d, J = 8.5 Hz), 7.33 (1H, d, J = 8.5 Hz) and 7.55 (1H, d, J = 9.5 Hz).

Mass spectrum (%): m/z 342 (28), 340 (M+) (28), 327 (10), 325 (10), 284 (52), 282 (54), 203 (base peak).

Recommended reading

1. Gupta BK, Wali BK, Vishwapaul and Handa KL, *Indian J. Chem,* 1964, 2, 464–66 (for isolation of osthol from *Prangos pabularia*).
2. Buckles RE, Mock GV and Locatell L, Jr., *Chem. Rev.*, 55: 659–77, 1955 (for a review of angelic and tiglic acids and their derivatives).
3. Chou S-Y, Hsu C-S, Wang K-T, Wang M-C and Wang C-C, *Phytotherapy Res.*, 21: 226–30, 2007 (for isolation of osthol from *Cnidium monnieri*).
4. Galbraith MN, Ritchie E and Taylor WC, *Aust. J. Chem.*, 13: 427–29, 1960. (for isolation of osthol from *Flindersia bennettiana*).
5. Hibbert H and Cannon LT, *J. Am. Chem. Soc.*, 46: 123,127, 1924 (for the ionones).
6. Ikan R, *Natural Products—A Laboratory Guide,* 2nd Edition, Academic Press, London, 1991 (for the conversion of pinene into camphor).

7. Ishino R and Kumanotani J, *J. Org. Chem.*, 34: 105, 1974 and references therein (for the preparation of hydroxycitronellal).
8. Kaul SK, Dhar KK and Atal AK, *Ind. J. Chem.*, 18B: 410,1979 (for nitration of osthol).
9. Krishnaswamy NR and Vijayan KK, *Ind. J. Chem.*, 28B: 664–66, 1989 (for bromination of osthol).
10. Mann FG and Saunders BC, *Practical Organic Chemistry*, 4th Edition, Longman, Oxford, 1960 (for camphor quinone).
11. Polonsky J, *Bull. Soc. Chim.* Fr., 1957, 1079 (for isolation and reactions of calophyllolide).
12. Sukh Dev, *Tetrahedron*, 35: 1789, 1970 (for the oxidation of geraniol).
13. Thakur RS, Rao PS and Krishnaswamy *NR, Ind. J. Chem.*, 13B: 750, 1975 (for nitration of osthol).
14. Torrence-valencia JM, Cerdia-Garcia-Rojos CM and Nathan PJ, *Tetrahedron:Asymmetry*, 9: 757–64, 1998 (for enantioselective synthesis of epoxytiglic and epoxyangelic acids).
15. Torrey S, (Ed.), Fragrance and Flavors—Recent Developments, *Chemical Technological Review*, No.156, Noyes Data Corporation, NJ, 1980 (for synthetic lime).

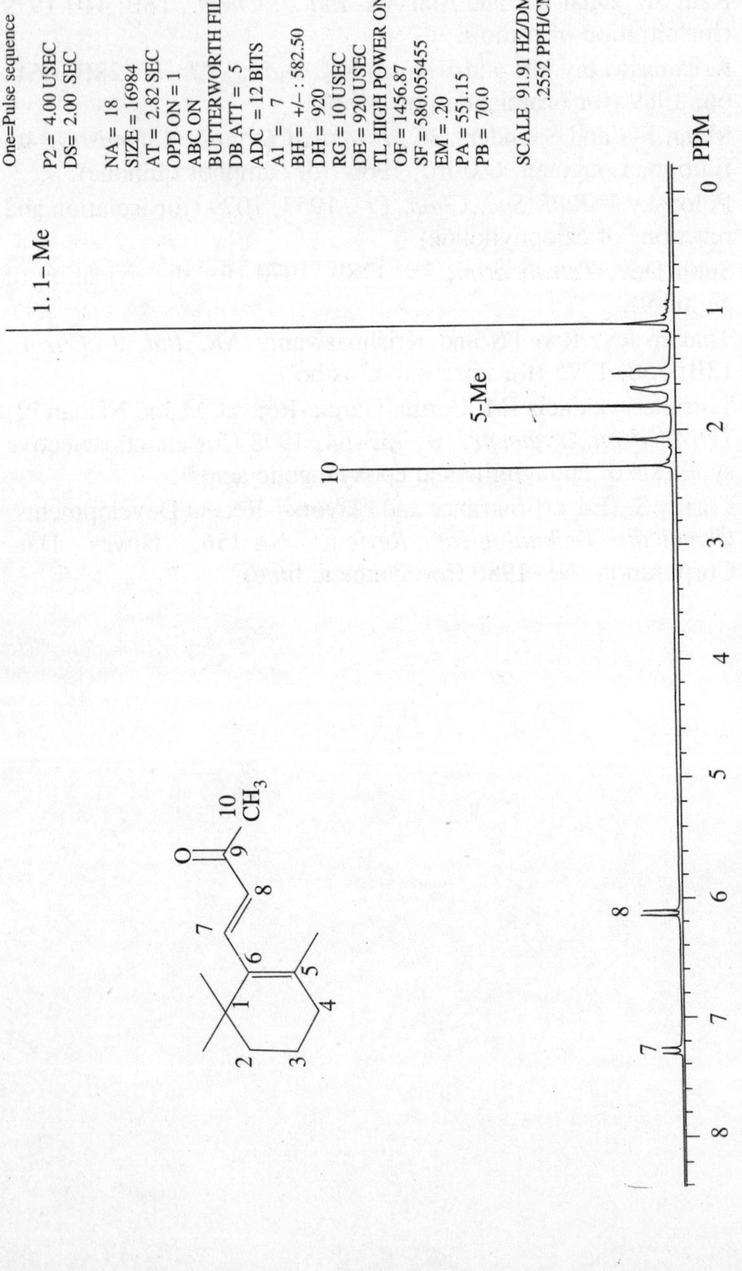

Normal ^{1}H-NMR spectrum of β-ionone (360 MHz, $CDCl_3$) [TI]

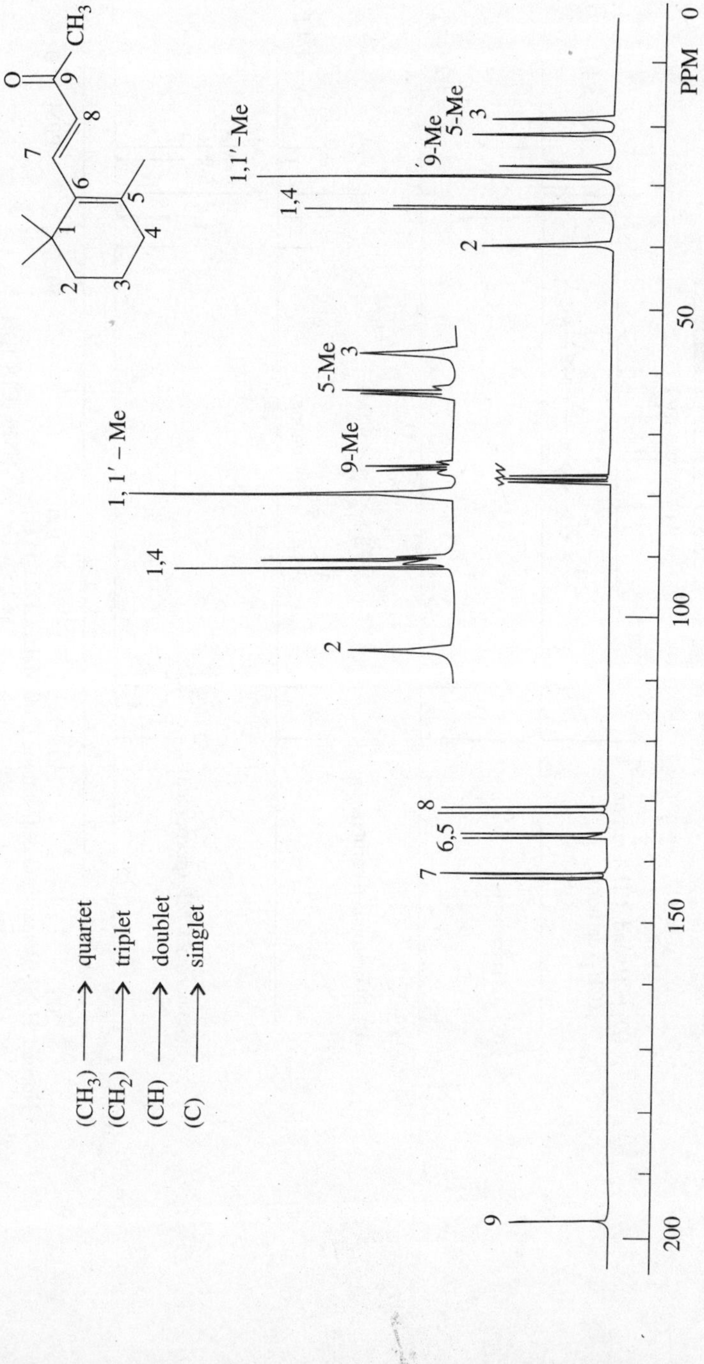

Off - resonance proton decoupling spectrum of β-lonone [62.5 MHz ^{13}C–NMB $(CDCl_3)_2$]

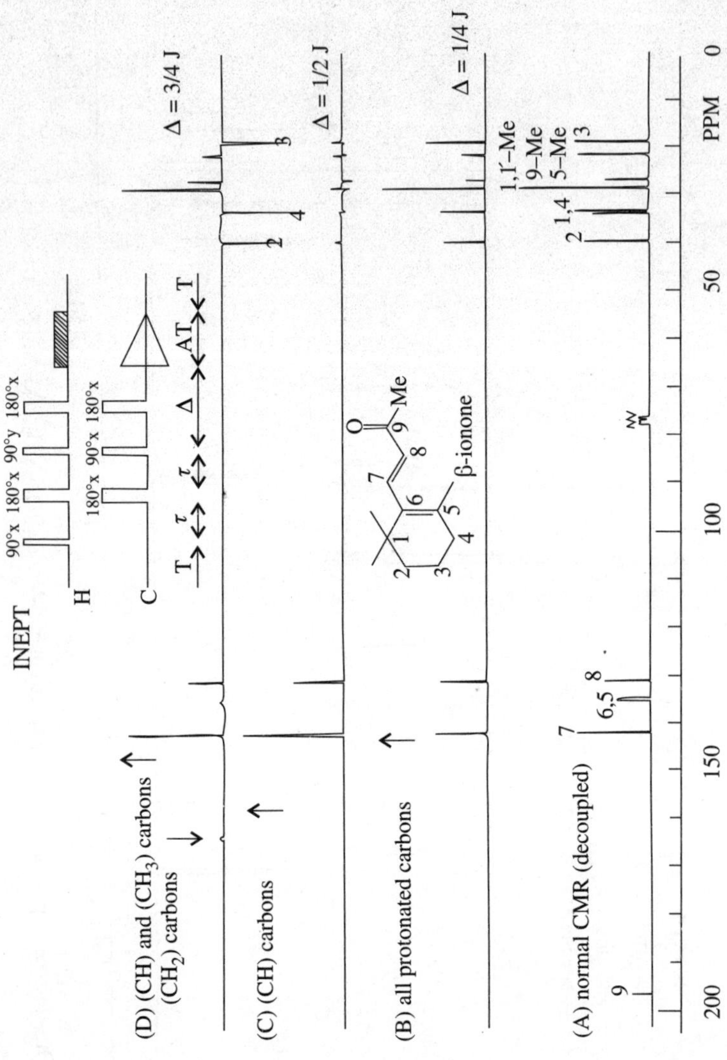

[62.5 MHz ^{13}C-NMR (CDCl$_3$)[3]]

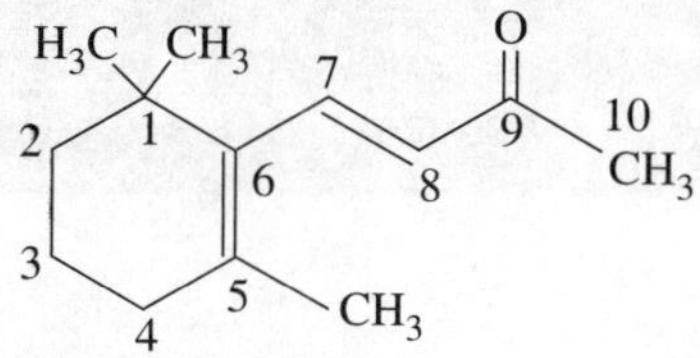

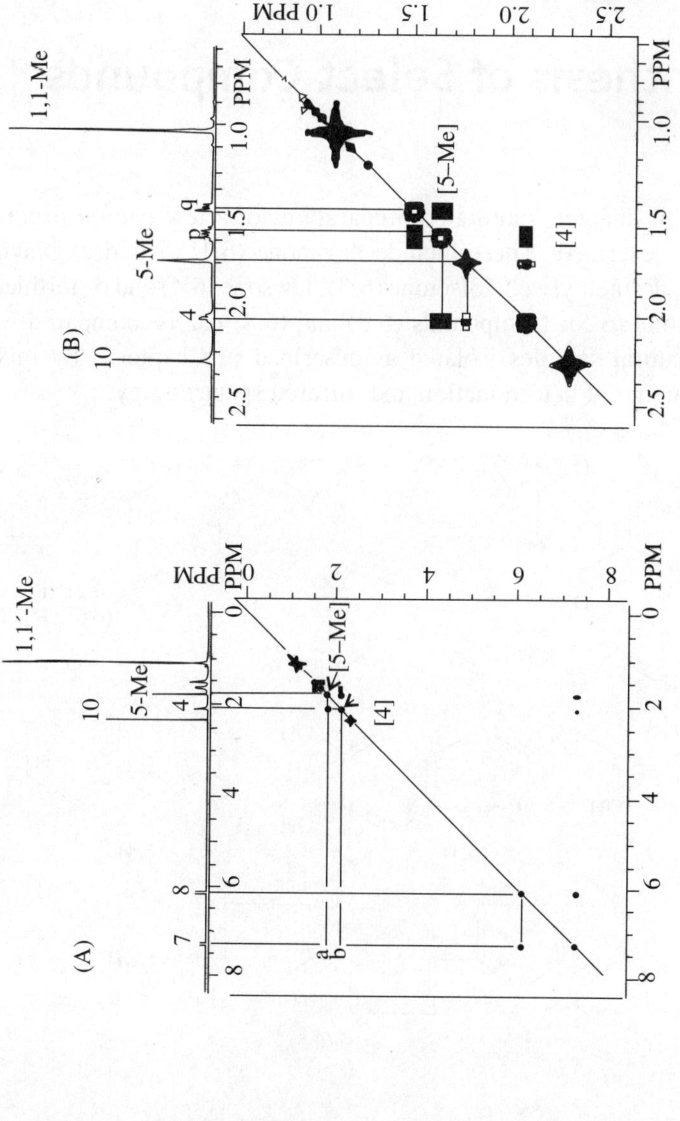

360 MHz ^{1}H-NMR $(CDCl_3)$ [T1]

CHAPTER 6

Synthesis of Select Compounds

In this chapter, multi-step preparations of a few natural products are described. These include flavanone (6.1), 7-hydroxyflavone (6.2), desmethylwedelolactone (6.3), lawsone (6.4) and α–terthienyl methanol (6.5). Compounds (6.3) and (6.4) can be compared with the natural samples isolated as described in Chapter 3 by mixed melting point determination and infrared spectroscopy.

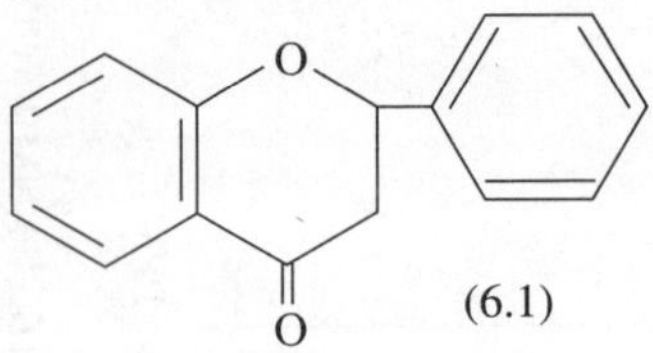

(6.1)

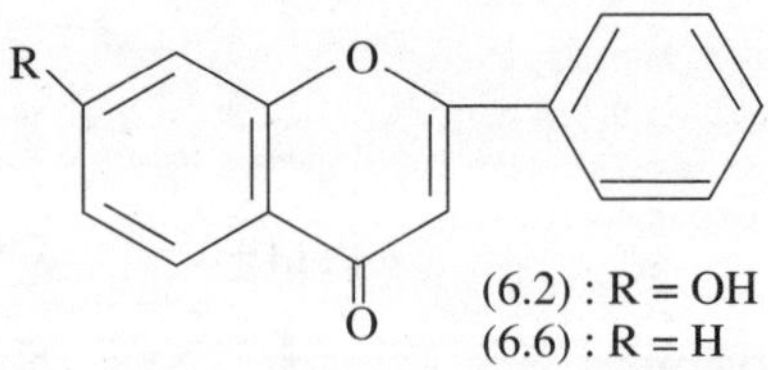

(6.2) : R = OH
(6.6) : R = H

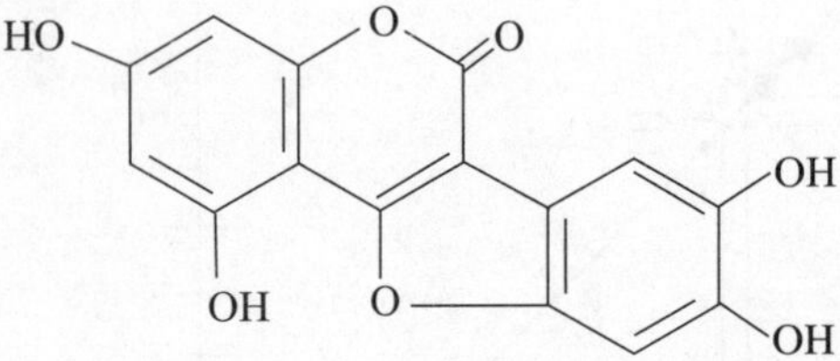

(6.3)

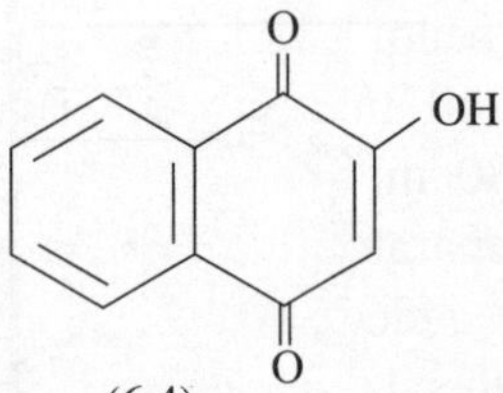

(6.4)

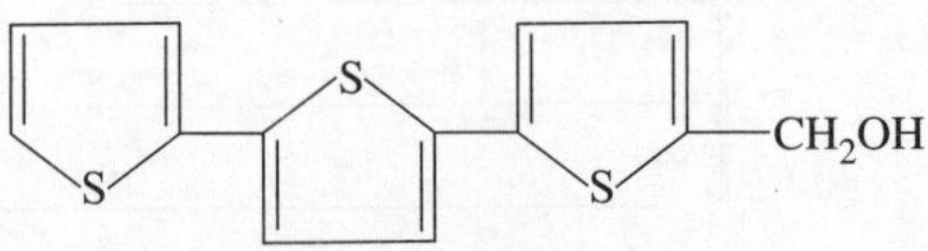

(6.5)

6.1 FLAVANONE

Flavanone does not occur in nature, but flavone (6.6) does. This compound occurs as dust on the stalks and leaves of plants of the genus Primula. Flavanone is obtained by cyclisation of the chalcone (6.7), which itself is prepared from *o*-hydroxyacetophenone (6.8), for which the starting material is phenyl acetate (6.9); the latter on Fries rearrangement yields (6.8) and its *p*-isomer (6.10).

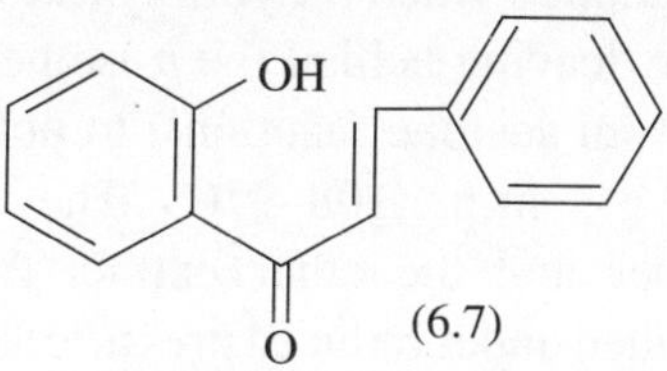
(6.7)

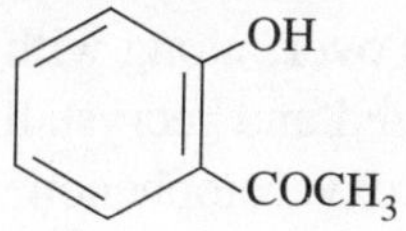
(6.8)

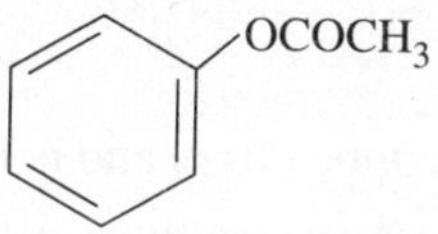
(6.9)

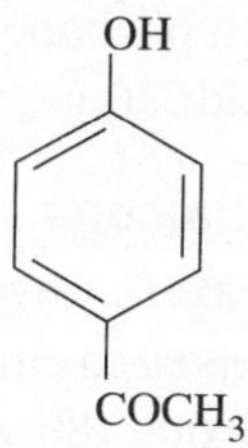
(6.10)

PROCEDURE

Phenyl acetate

Phenol (23.5 g) is dissolved in 10% sodium hydroxide solution (160 ml). Ice is added to cool the solution. Acetic anhydride (30 ml) is then added and the mixture shaken vigorously in a separatory funnel for about 5 minutes. Thereafter, diethyl ether is added, and shaken again to extract the phenyl acetate into the ether layer, which is separated and washed with saturated sodium bicarbonate solution and water. After drying over anhydrous sodium sulphate, the solvent is evaporated from the ether extract and the residue distilled. Phenyl acetate boils over at 180–85°C. The yield is 35 g.

Pure *o*-hydroxyacetophenone

In a 100-ml double-necked round-bottomed flask, anhydrous aluminium chloride (30 g) is taken and phenyl acetate (30 g) is added through a dropping funnel attached to one of the necks of the flask. The mixture is then heated at 110°C in an oil bath until the evolution of hydrogen chloride gas ceases (about 30 minutes). After cooling the semisolid mass, dilute hydrochloric acid is added to decompose the aluminium complex and the mixture allowed to stand overnight. It is then subjected to steam distillation when *o*-hydroxyacetophenone distills over, along with water, leaving behind the *p*-isomer, which is filtered and recrystallised from acetone (caution!) to obtain pure *p*-hydroxyacetophenone (12 g), m.p. 108–9°C. The distillate is extracted with diethyl ether and the ether extract dried and evaporated. The residue is distilled under reduced pressure to get pure *o*-hydroxyacetophenone, which boils over at 107–8°C at 20 mm pressure. Yield: 10 g.

2-Hydroxychalcone

In a 250 ml beaker, *o*-hydroxyacetophenone (10 g) and benzaldehyde (8 g) are dissolved in ethanol (30 ml). To this solution, 40% aqueous sodium hydroxide (80 ml) is added with stirring until the mixture turns into a solid mass. The reaction mixture is then acidified by the cautious addition of concentrated hydrochloric acid and the bright yellow precipitate collected on a Buchner funnel under suction. The solid is washed with water, dried and recrystallised from ethanol.

The pure chalcone (yield 12 –13 g) melts at 86–88°C. Its proton NMR spectrum has signals at δ 6.6 (1H, d, J=15 Hz) and 7.8 (1H, d, J= 15 Hz), characteristic of the conjugated olefinic moiety present in the compound.

Flavanone

A solution of 2’-hydroxychalcone (10 g) in ethanol (30 ml) is taken in a 250-ml conical flask to which a 1.5% aqueous sodium hydroxide solution (150 ml) is added with stirring, which is continued for 3 hours. After leaving it overnight, the reaction mixture is acidified with concentrated hydrochloric acid added in drops. The colourless precipitate is filtered, washed with water and recrystallised from ethanol. The pure compound (quantitative yield) melts at 76°C.

The proton NMR spectrum does not have the signals due to olefinic hydrogens but instead has signals at δ 2.9 (2H, m) and 5.4 (1H, dd). Its infrared spectrum has a strong absorption band at 1680 cm^{-1}.

6.2 7-HYDROXYFLAVONE (6.2, see p. 136)

Hydroxylated flavones are widespread in nature. Several methods have been developed for their synthesis. One of them is the Baker–Venkataraman reaction which involves rearrangement. A typical example is the preparation of 7-hydroxyflavone from 2,4-dihydroxyacetophenone (6.11).

Procedure

2,4-Dihydroxyacetophenone (6.11)

In a 100 ml beaker, freshly fused and powdered zinc chloride (10 g) is dissolved in glacial acetic acid (16 ml). After adding fused and powdered resorcinol, the mixture is heated to about 140°C and kept at that temperature for about 10–15 minutes. It is then cooled and poured into ice-cold dilute hydrochloric acid. The solid separating out is collected on a Buchner funnel under suction, washed with water and dried. It is recrystallised from hot water saturated with sulphur dioxide. Yield is 10 g. The pure ketone (resacetophenone) melts at 144–45°C.

Diketone (6.12)

To a solution of resacetophenone (6 g) in acetone (300 ml) taken in a 500-ml round-bottomed flask, benzoyl chloride (15 ml) and anhydrous potassium carbonate (25 g) are added, and the mixture refluxed on a water bath for 20 hours. The mixture is filtered hot and the potassium salts washed with warm acetone. The filtrate is distilled to remove the solvent, and the residue treated with water.

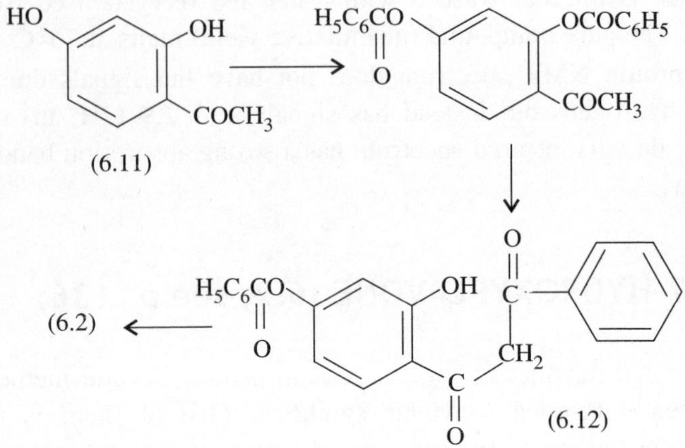

The diketone separating out is filtered, washed with water, dried and recrystallised from ethanol. The yield of the product which melts at 167°C is 13 g.

7-Hydroxyflavone

In a 250-ml round-bottomed flask fitted with a water-cooled condenser, the diketone (12 g), acetic acid (50 ml) and concentrated hydrochloric acid (50 ml) are taken and the mixture refluxed for 2 hours. After cooling, the mixture is poured into water and the solid separating out is filtered, washed first with 5% sodium bicarbonate solution and then with water. After drying it is recrystallised from ethanol. 7-Hydroxyflavone (6.5 g) thus obtained melts at 240°C.

6.3 DESMETHYLWEDELOLACTONE

The isolation of this coumestan (6.3, see p. 136) was described in Chapter 4. It can be prepared by the oxidative coupling of 4,5,7-trihydroxycoumarin (6.13) with catechol (6.14) in the presence of potassium ferricyanide; this reaction was first used by Wanzlick and co-workers (*Chem.Ber.*, 96: 305, 1963).

PROCEDURE

4,5,7-Trihydroxycoumarin

A rapid stream of hydrogen chloride gas is passed through a solution of dry phloroglucinol (10 g) and freshly distilled ethyl cyanoacetate (10 ml) in dry diethyl ether (15 ml), and cooled in an ice–salt bath

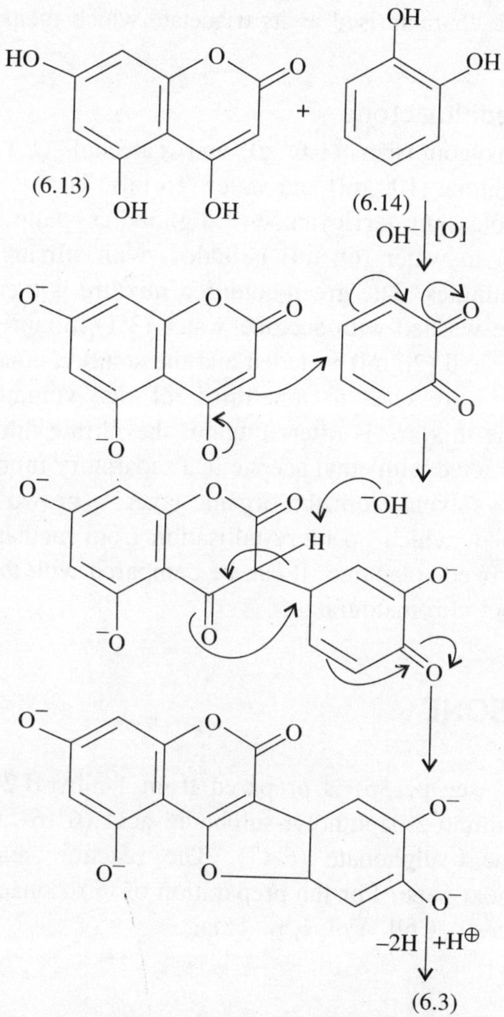

(6.3)

in a fume cupboard. After 2 hours, a reddish solid starts separating. The passage of hydrogen chloride gas is continued for 4 more hours and the mixture kept overnight in an ice chest. The solid ketimide (9 g) is collected on a Buchner funnel and washed with ether. This compound (8 g) is refluxed with 30% w/v dilute hydrochloric acid (250 ml) for 2 hours. On cooling the solution, a yellow solid separates out and is collected by filtration and recrystallised from water. The compound has a very high melting point (above 320°C) and is therefore characterised as its triacetate which melts at 193–94°C.

Desmethylwedelolactone

4,5,7-Trihydroxycoumarin (1.6 g) and catechol (1.1 g) are dissolved in acetone (100 ml) and water (15 ml). To this solution, a solution of potassium ferricyanide (8.8 g) and crystalline sodium acetate (7.7 g) in water (68 ml) is added, with stirring, over a period of 90 minutes. The green-coloured mixture is then filtered and the residue washed with acetone–water (3:1) mixture. To the filtrate, formic acid (20 ml) is added and the solution concentrated under reduced pressure to one-third of its volume. After 90 minutes, the mixture is filtered again, the filtrate diluted with water, and extracted with ethyl acetate in a separatory funnel. After removal of the solvent from the organic layer, a brown-coloured solid is obtained, which on recrystallisation from methanol gives pure desmethylwedelolactone. It can be compared with the natural sample on paper chromatograms.

6.4 LAWSONE

Lawsone (6.4, see p.136) is prepared from 1-nitroso-2-naphthol (6.15) via 1-amino-2-naphthol-4-sulphonic acid (6.16) and 1, 2-naphthoquinone-4-sulphonate (6.17). The reaction sequence is given on the next page. For the preparation of nitrosonaphthol see *Organic Synthesis*, Coll. Vol. I, p. 411).

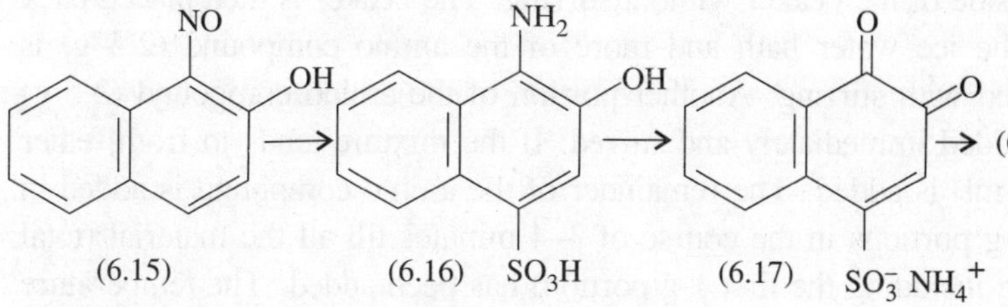 (6.4)

(6.15) (6.16) (6.17)

PROCEDURE

1-Amino-2-naphthol-4-sulphonic acid

1-Nitroso-2-naphthol (from 30 g of 2-naphthol) is added to a solution of sodium bisulphite (60 g) in 6N sodium hydroxide (10 ml) and water (200 ml) in a 1-litre beaker and stirred well. More water (400 to 450 ml) is added until the nitrosonaphthol dissolves completely. The dark solution is filtered through a Buchner funnel under suction to remove the small amount of tarry substance present. The whole operation should be done as quickly as possible to prevent oxidation of the amine. To the filtrate, more water (about 50–90 ml) is added till the total volume of the solution is 700 ml. To this solution, concentrated sulphuric acid (40 ml) is slowly added with stirring and the beaker placed in a hood protected from light. The temperature rises from 20–25°C to 35-40°C at once, and then to about 50°C in the course of two hours. After allowing the mixture to stand for another 3–4 hours, the precipitate is filtered and washed with water, followed by alcohol, till the washings are no longer coloured deep-red. It is then dried by washing with diethyl ether on the funnel itself. Further drying is done by heating the compound to 60–80°C. The yield of the greyish white product is about 37–38 g.

Ammonium 1, 2-naphthoquinone-4-sulphonate

A 1-gram portion of 1-amino-2-naphthol-4-sulphonic acid is stirred into a mixture of nitric acid (14.5 ml) and water (40 ml) in a large beaker, previously cooled to 30°C in an ice-water bath. After the addition, the beaker is taken out of the cooling bath and allowed to stand undisturbed. If the mixture does not turn yellow within 2 minutes, a little (about 0.2 ml) concentrated nitric acid is added down the side of the beaker without stirring. The beaker is then placed back in the ice water bath and more of the amino compound (2.5 g) is added with stirring. Another portion of the amino compound (2.5 g) is added immediately and stirred. If the mixture tends to froth, ether (10 ml) is added. The remainder of the amino compound is added in 2.5 g portions in the course of 3–4 minutes till all the material (total 35 g including the first 1-g portion) has been added. The temperature is kept at 25–30°C with stirring. The thick mass is then stirred until the temperature drops to 5–1°C. A saturated solution of ammonium chloride (17.5 ml) is then added and the mixture cooled to 0°C when ammonium 1, 2-naphthoquinone-4-sulphonate separates out. It is collected on a Buchner funnel and the solid washed with a cold mixture of saturated ammonium chloride (15 ml) and water (10 ml), followed by alcohol and ether. It is pressed dry on the funnel under suction.

2-Hydroxy-1, 4-naphthoquinone (Lawsone)

To a mixture of absolute methanol (100 ml) and concentrated sulphuric acid (8 ml) taken in a 250-ml round-bottomed flask cooled to 0°C in an ice–salt bath, the above-mentioned ammonium salt (25.5 g) is added and made into an even paste by shaking. After standing for 30 minutes, when the temperature rises to 15–20°C, the flask is heated on a steam bath with continuous shaking, and swirling, so that the solution reaches its boiling point in about 15 minutes. The solution becomes red, accompanied by evolution of sulphur dioxide gas, and the product starts separating out.

After about 15 minutes of gentle heating and shaking, the reaction mixture turns into a stiff mass when more methanol (25 ml) is added and the heating and rotating are continued for an additional 15–20 minutes. It is then cooled and diluted with water and ice when a dark-red solid precipitates out. It is collected on a Buchner funnel under suction and washed with ice-cold water. The moist material is then added to a solution of sodium hydroxide (3 g) in water (150 ml) in a 250-ml beaker, and the mixture is rapidly heated to boiling point. The resulting deep-red solution is filtered hot, and acidified while still hot, by the addition of 6N hydrochloric acid (13 ml), with stirring. The yellow suspension of lawsone is then cooled to 0°C and allowed to stand for 2 hours before collecting it on a funnel under suction. It is washed on the funnel with ice-cold water and dried overnight at room temperature. The yield is 10-11 g. The compound melts at 188–89°C. It can be recrystallised from acetic acid, when it separates out as yellow prisms, m.p. 195–96°C.

6.5 TERTHIENYLMETHANOL

This compound (6.5, see p.136) was first isolated from the leaves of the Indian medicinal plant, *Eclipta alba*. It is prepared from α-terthienyl (6.18) by Vislmier–Haack formylation and reduction of the aldehyde (6.19) thus obtained. α–Terthienyl itself was first isolated from the flowers of African marigold, *Tagetes erecta,* by Zechmeister and Sease (*J. Amer. Chem. Soc.*, 69: 273, 1947) who also synthesised it from iodothiophene (6.20). Thiophene derivatives occur in a number of plants belonging to the family Compositae, wherein they are biosynthetically derived from the corresponding polyacetylenic compounds.

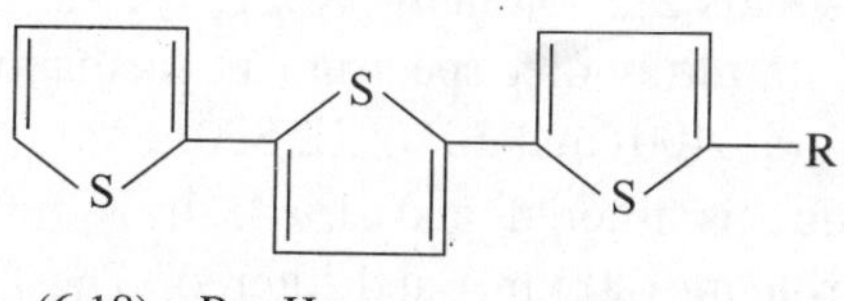

(6.18) : R = H
(6.19) : R = CHO

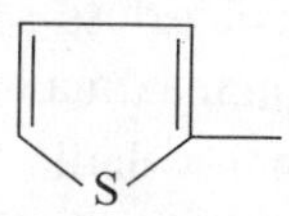

(6.20)

PROCEDURE

Iodothiophene

In a glass-stoppered wide-mouthed bottle, thiophene (35 g) and petroleum (60–80°C, 50 ml) are taken and the bottle cooled in ice water. With constant shaking and cooling when necessary, yellow mercuric oxide (75 g) and iodine (109 g) are added alternately in small amounts during a period of 15–20 minutes. The yellow mercuric oxide changes to crimson mercuric iodide. The mixture is filtered and the residue washed with three 25-ml portions of diethyl ether. The combined filtrate is shaken in a separatory funnel with a dilute solution of sodium thiosulphate and dried over calcium chloride (5 g). After filtering off the drying agent, the solvents are removed on a water bath. The residue is fractionally distilled under reduced pressure. 2-Iodothiophene distills over at 90–94°C at 34–38 mm pressure. The yield is 65 g.

Terthienyl

To iodothiophene (40 g) in a 500-ml conical flask, copper bronze (41 g) is added and the two mixed into a paste which is heated in an oil bath at 185–90°C. The mixture is maintained at this temperature until an exothermic reaction sets in. The flask is immediately removed from the oil bath and the mixture vigorously stirred with a stout glass rod. The long neck of the flask effectively prevents any iodothiophene escaping as vapour. After the reaction subsides (about 15 minutes), the flask is held at the oil bath temperature (190°C) for 5 more minutes with vigorous stirring. The contents of the flask are then extracted with acetone in a Soxhlet apparatus, the extract concentrated on a water bath and the residue steam distilled. The distillate on cooling yields 2,2'-bithienyl (6.21, 6 g) as a low melting colourless solid. Its ultraviolet spectrum in methanol has absorption maxima at 246 (ε 6400) and 301(ε 12,800) nm.

The non-volatile residue is filtered and dried. It is refluxed for 1 hour with light petroleum (200 ml) and filtered. The filtrate after concentration is passed through a column of alumina built in petroleum. Elution is carried out with petroleum. From the initial fractions, a small amount (0.8 g) of 2,2'-bithienyl is obtained. Later fractions give terthienyl (2.8 g) which crystallises from petroleum as needles (m.p. 94–95°C).

Its ultraviolet spectrum has absorption maxima at 251 (ε 9200) and 350 (ε 24,500) nm. Further elution of the column with petroleum–benzene mixture yields quaterthienyl (6.22, 0.48 g) [UV maxima at 251 (ε 17,700) and 385 (ε 32,000) nm] and pentathienyl (6.23) (0.14 g).

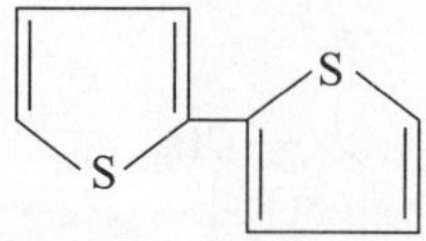

(6.21)

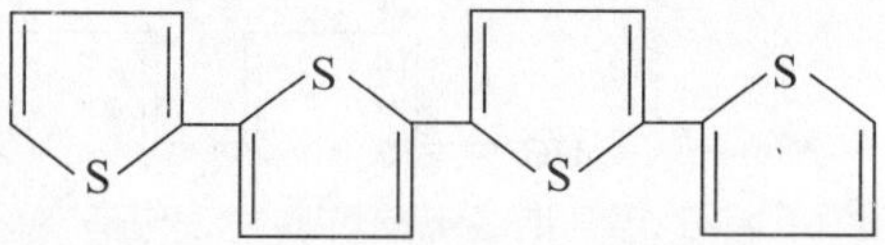

(6.22)

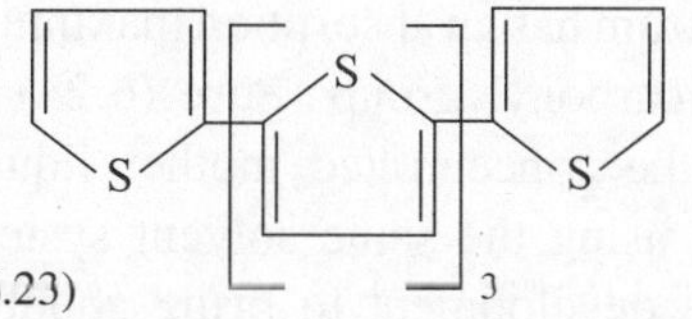

(6.23)

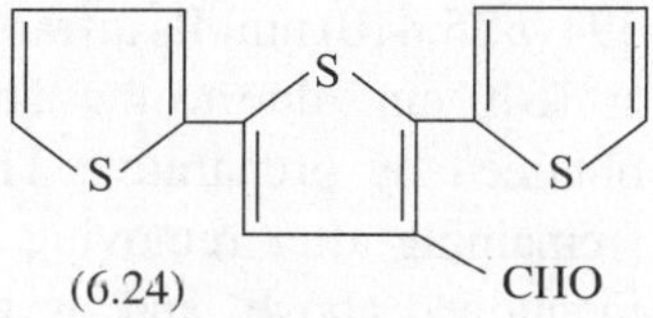

(6.24)

5-Formyl-2, 2', 5', 2''-terthienyl

To a cooled mixture of terthienyl (2.48 g) and dimethylformamide (0.73 g), phosphorus oxychloride (1.7 g) is added and the mixture stirred and heated gradually to the temperature of a steam bath, when an exothermic reaction takes place. The dark-red mass is kept at this temperature for 5 minutes, with stirring, then cooled and diluted with a solution of sodium acetate (15 g) in water (40 ml). The mixture is thoroughly mixed and heated on a steam bath for 30 minutes to liberate the aldehyde which separates out as an orange-yellow solid. It is filtered, washed with water and dried (2.7 g). It is dissolved in warm benzene (100 ml), and the solution concentrated to 75 ml. Alumina (10 g) is added to it and the mixture evaporated on a water bath in a fume cupboard, with stirring, to remove the solvent. The residue is dried in a desiccator and then packed over a column of alumina (200 g). The column is developed with petroleum, which elutes out a small amount of unchanged terthienyl (0.13 g).

Subsequent elution with petroleum–benzene (3:2) mixture removes 5-formyl-2, 2', 5', 2''-terthienyl (2.2g, 6.19), along with a small quantity of an isomer (6.24) as shown by TLC (solvent, petroleum–benzene, 3:2) which gives two spots with R_f values 0.3 (due to 6.19) and 0.4 (due to 6.24). Recrystallisation from benzene yields pure (6.19) leaving (6.24) behind in the mother liquor. Pure (6.19) (yield, 2.2 g) melts at 139°C. Its ultraviolet spectrum in methanol has maxima at 239 (ε 7415), 266 (ε 6014) and

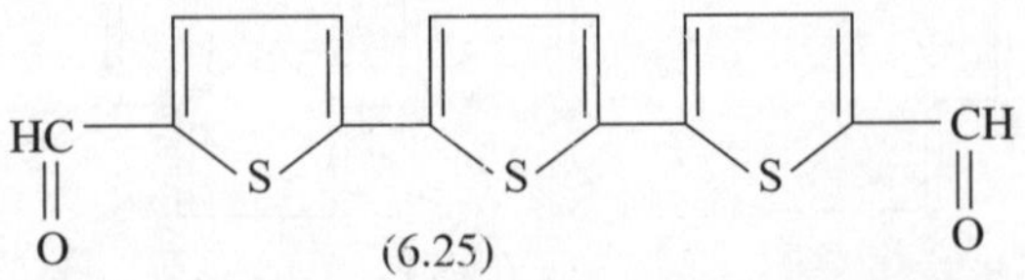

(6.25)

394 (ε 35,410) nm. Its infrared spectrum has an absorption maximum at 1640 cm^{-1} due to the aldehyde carbonyl group. Pure (6.24) is obtained by preparative TLC of the concentrated mother liquor [remaining after removing (6.19)] using the same solvent system mentioned above, and by multiple development to bring about a better resolution. The yield is just 0.03 g. It melts at 75–77°C.

Its UV spectrum has maxima at 208 (ε 5466), 256 (ε 4748) and 365 (ε 5245) nm. In its IR spectrum the carbonyl group frequency is seen at 1640 cm^{-1}. Its proton NMR spectrum has signals at δ 6.9–7.5 (7H, m) and 10.12 (1H, s). Its mass spectrum shows the molecular ion signal at m/z 276 (100%).

From the original alumina column, benzene elutes out another compound, which is the dialdehyde (6.25). Its yield is 0.23 g and it melts at 218–20°C. Its UV spectrum has maxima at 251 (ε 6518), 176 (ε 7410) and 406 (ε 30,410) nm and its IR spectrum shows a single carbonyl stretching frequency at 1650 cm^{-1}.

Terthienylmethanol

To a cooled solution of the aldehyde (6.19) (1.4 g) in tetrahydrofuran (50 ml), sodium borohydride (0.8 g) is added followed by water (5 ml). The reaction mixture is left overnight at room temperature in the dark and then concentrated under reduced pressure. The excess reducing agent is destroyed by the cautious addition of 0.1N hydrochloric acid. The precipitated terthienylmethanol is filtered on a small funnel, washed free of acid with water and dried. It is carefully recrystallised from petroleum–benzene. The pure compound (yield, 1.3 g) melts at 151–52°.

Its ultraviolet spectrum in methanol has absorption maxima at 250 and 350 nm.

ADDENDUM

Alternate procedure for the preparation of α-terthienyl

For the preparation of α-terthienyl and other oligothiophenes, better methods than the one described on page 145 are now available. These procedures have been developed, not only for the preparation of these compounds in the laboratory, but also for their large-scale production, as they are used as building blocks in the formation of one type of conducting polymers. In the following procedure, the Grignard reagent, 2-thienylmagnesium bromide, prepared from 2-bromothiophene (6.26) is coupled with 2,5-dibromothiophene (6.27) in the presence of the catalyst Ni(DPPE)Cl_2, prepared from nickel chloride and the ligand, 1, 2-bis(diphenylphosphino)ethane (DPPE) (6.28). Another commercially available ligand, 1, 2-bis (diphenylphosphino)benzene (DPPbenz; 6.29) can also be used, instead of DPPE, for the preparation of the nickel catalyst.

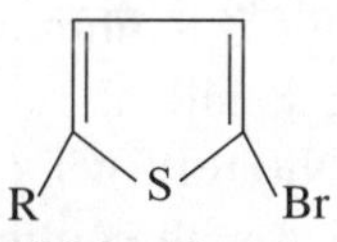

(6.26) : R = H
(6.27) : R = Br

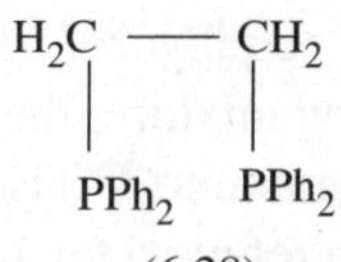

(6.28)

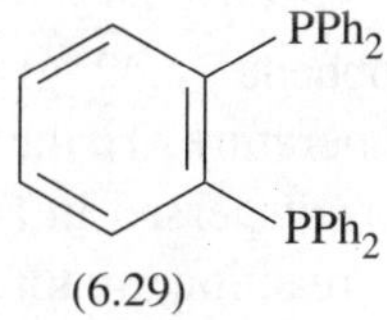

(6.29)

PROCEDURE

Preparation of the catalyst

Preparation of the ligand, 1, 2-bis(diphenylphosphino) ethane To 1.06 g of finely cut and purified lithium metal taken in a 100-litre round-bottomed flask, a solution of triphenylphosphine (20 g) in dry tetrahydrofuran (THF) is added, with stirring, until the lithium dissolves completely. This may take about 90 minutes. To the resulting dark red-coloured solution, 1, 2-dichloroethane (6 ml) dissolved in THF (10 ml) is added in drops, and the mixture refluxed for 20 minutes. After cooling, the reaction mixture is diluted with methanol (150 ml). The white solid that precipitates is filtered. Further dilution of the filtrate with water gives more of the solid. It is recrystallised from isopropanol to obtain feathery, colourless crystals of the ligand, m.p. 143–44°C.

Preparation of Ni(DPPE)Cl_2 To a solution of the ligand (0.502 g) in warm isopropanol (50 ml) taken in a 250-ml beaker, a solution of nickel chloride hexahydrate ($NiCl_2.6H_2O$; 0.319 g) in a mixture of isopropanol and methanol (2:1) (30 ml) is added with stirring. The orange-coloured crystalline solid that separates out is collected on a small funnel, washed with diethyl ether and dried. Yield: 0.621 g.

Preparation of α-terthienyl 2-Bromothiophene (3.26 g) is slowly added, with stirring, to a slurry of magnesium metal turnings (480 mg) in dry THF (15 ml) at the reflux temperature of the solvent. After all the bromothiophene has been added, the mixture is refluxed for 1 hour. The Grignard reagent is filtered to remove excess magnesium and kept under a blanket of argon before use in the next step.

The Grignard reagent is added to a solution of 2,5-dibromothiophene (2.42 g) in dry tetrahydrofuran (THF; 8 ml) at room temperature. To the resulting mixture, the catalyst Ni(DPPE)Cl_2 (20 mg), dispersed in a small amount of THF, is added with cooling. The reaction mixture is then refluxed for 16 hours. It is diluted with a saturated aqueous solution of ammonium chloride and extracted with diethyl ether in a separatory funnel. The ether layer is evaporated to obtain α-terthienyl as a bright yellow solid. Yield: 2.24 g, m.p. 94–95°C.

The proton NMR spectrum has signals at δ 7.01 (2H, s), 7.06 (2H, s), 7.11 (2H, s) and 7.20 (2H, s). ^{13}C NMR spectrum: δ 124.26, 127.84, 136.14 and 137.07.

6.6 NORDALBERGIN (6.30)

Nordalbergin or desmethyldalbergin or 6,7-dihydroxy-4-phenylcoumarin (6.30) is one of the simpler members of the

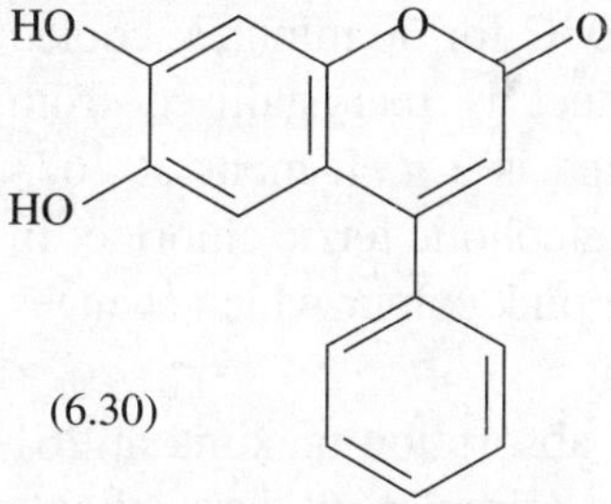

(6.30)

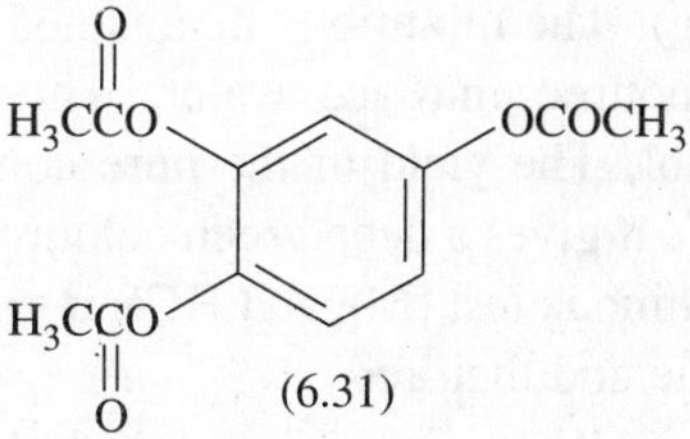

(6.31)

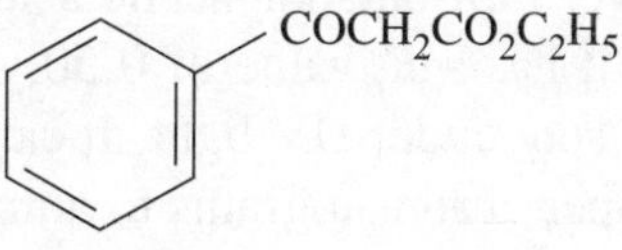

(6.32)

neoflavonoid group of naturally occurring polyphenolic compounds. It is one of the chemical constituents of the heartwood of the durable wood, *Dalbergia sissoo*. The procedure for its synthesis from hydroxyhydroquinone triacetate (6.31) and ethyl benzoylacetate (6.32) is described below.

Procedure

Hydroxyhydroquinone triacetate

Powdered *p*-benzoquinone (10g) is added with stirring during a period of 15 minutes to acetic anhydride (30 ml) containing concentrated sulphuric acid (2 ml) taken in a 100-ml beaker, maintaining the temperature between 40°C and 50°C. The clear solution is then poured into crushed ice and the precipitate collected by filtration. After washing with cold water it is dried and recrystallised from 95% ethanol. Hydroxyhydroquinone triacetate is obtained as colourless cubes (20 g), m.p. 96–97°C.

Nordalbergin

Sulphuric acid (75%) (4 ml) is added to a mixture of hydroxyhydroquinone triacetate (5.5 g) and ethyl benzoylacetate

(4.2 g). The mixture is maintained at 80°C for 30 minutes, cooled and poured into ice water. The product is recrystallised from ethanol. The yield of the pure compound is 3 g. It melts at 267–68°C. It gives a deep green colour with alcoholic ferric chloride. In the Shinoda test (Mg and HCl) it gives a pink colour which changes to blue and then red.

The UV spectrum in ethanol shows absorption maxima at 261 and 303 nm. On paper chromatograms (circular or descending), using the lower layer of *n*-butanol–acetic acid–water (4:1:5) as the irrigating solvent, it has a R_f value of 0.50; it can be viewed as a fluorescent ring or spot under UV light. It can also be made visible by exposing the paper chromatograms to ammonia vapours.

6.7 2-HYDROXY-4-METHOXYBENZALDEHYDE

2-Hydroxy-4-methoxybenzaldehyde or 4-methoxysalicyladehyde (6.33) occurs in the roots of *Hemidesmus indicus* and *Decalepis hamiltonii* (Asclepiadaceae) and also in *Mondia whytei* Skals (also of Asclepiadaceae). It has been reported to possess tyrosinase inhibitory activity, taste modifying properties as well as anti-fungal and anti-bacterial activities. It is a good food preservative. The roots of *Hemidesmus indicus* are used in the Ayurvedic system of medicine for the treatment of bowel complaints and also as a blood purifier. The fresh roots of *Decalepis hamiltonii* are widely used in South India for the preparation of pickles to which 2-hydroxy-4-methoxybenzaldehyde adds a sweet, aromatic fragrance and a characteristic taste.

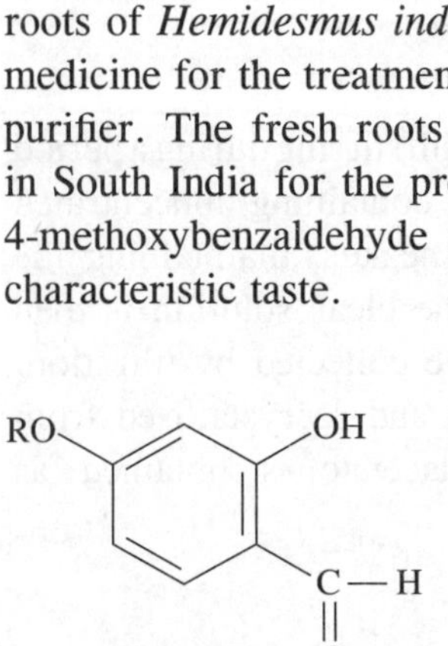

(6.33) : R = CH_3
(6.35) : R = H

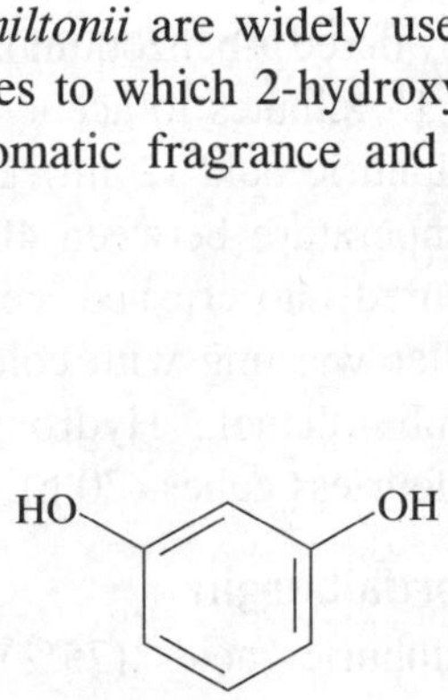

(6.34)

The following procedure describes a convenient method for its preparation from resorcinol (6.34) via resorcylic aldehyde (2,4-dihydroxybenzaldehyde; 6.35).

PROCEDURE

2,4-Dihydroxybenzaldehyde

It can be prepared from resorcinol by the Gattermann reaction, the Reimer–Tiemann reaction, or the Vilsmeier–Haack reaction. The Vilsmeier reaction is more convenient and is described below.

Resorcinol (11 g) and pure dimethylformamide (20 ml) are placed in a 100-ml double-necked round-bottomed flask. (Resorcinol can be freed from water as follows. The compound is heated in a China dish and the molten liquid poured into a mortar. After it solidifies, it is powdered with the help of a pestle.) To one neck of the flask a dropping funnel containing phosphorus oxychloride (16 ml) is attached. The flask is cooled in an ice-water bath and the phosphorus oxychloride added in drops while shaking the flask. During the addition the temperature of the reaction mixture should not exceed 25°C. When all the $POCl_3$ has been added, the reaction flask is transferred to a water bath, a reflux condenser attached to the other neck and the reaction mixture gently heated for two hours, Thereafter, the flask is cooled and the contents poured into a 250-ml beaker. The mixture is neutralised to Congo red by the cautious addition of sodium acetate solution (100 g in 175 ml of water), and allowed to stand till the product crystallises out. The yield is 9.5 to 10 g. The compound can be recrystallised from the minimum amount of hot water. Pure 2, 4-dihydroxybenzaldehyde melts at 135–37°C.

2-Hydroxy-4-methoxybenzaldehyde

A solution of 2,4-dihydroxybenzaldehyde (13.8 g) in anhydrous acetone (75-ml) is taken in a 250-ml round-bottomed flask fitted with a water-cooled reflux condenser. To this solution, pure dimethyl sulphate (13.8 g; 10.4 ml) is added (Caution: dimethyl sulphate should be handled with extreme care), followed by freshly ignited anhydrous potassium carbonate (26.5 g). The mixture is gently refluxed on a water bath for 6 to 8 hours. It is cooled, the potassium salts are filtered off on a Buchner funnel (the residue is washed with a small amount of hot acetone), and the combined filtrate concentrated and diluted with water. The product that separates out is purified by steam distillation, when 2-hydroxy-4-methoxybenzaldehyde collects in the distillate as a colourless crystalline solid. It can be further purified by recrystallisation from ethanol. The yield is noted. The pure compound melts at 41°C.

For comparison, the natural specimen is isolated from *Decalepis hamiltonii* roots.

Isolation of 2-hydroxy-4-methoxybenzaldehyde from *Decalepis hamiltonii* roots

Fresh roots of *Decalepis hamiltonii* (250g) are washed free of mud particles, etc., and the inner fibrous matter manually removed. The clean roots are then cut into small pieces and transferred to a 1-litre double-necked round-bottomed flask along with some water. To the middle neck a distillation head is attached, which in turn is attached to a water-cooled condenser. Through the other neck steam is let in from a steam generator. To the other end of the condenser a receiver joint is attached to collect the distillate in a large conical flask. The distillate is extracted with dichloromethane in a separatory funnel. The organic layer is separated and dried over anhydrous sodium sulphate. After filtering off the drying agent, the filtrate is distilled on a water bath to remove the solvent. The residue is recrystallised either from light petroleum or ethanol, when colourless needles (2 g) are obtained, m.p. 41°C.

Its 1H NMR spectrum in $CDCl_3$ shows signals at δ 3.9 (s, 3H), 6.5 (d, J = 2 Hz, 1H), 6.6 (dd, J = 2, 9 Hz, 1H), 7.5 (d, J = 9 Hz, 1H), 9.7 (s, 1H) and 14.6 (s, 1H).

6.8 UMBELLIFERONE, HERNIARIN AND 7-METHOXY-8-ALLYLCOUMARIN

Umbelliferone is the trivial name for 7-hydroxycoumarin (6.36). This compound is the most well known member of the coumarin

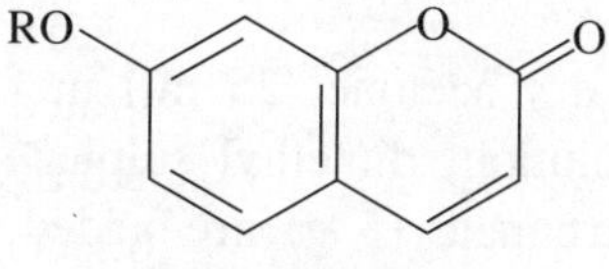

(6.36) : R = H
(6.37) : R = CH_3
(6.39) : R = $-CH_2-CH=CH_2$

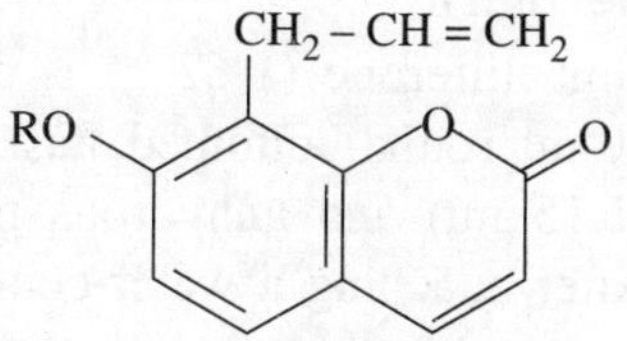

(6.38) : R = CH_3
(6.40) : R = H

family and occurs in a number of plants, particularly in those belonging to the Umbelliferae family. It exhibits a bright blue fluorescence and is used as an optical whitener in textiles and also as a sun-screen agent. It is used as an intermediate in the preparation of some laser dyes. It is conveniently prepared in the laboratory using the Pechmann reaction. The procedural details are given below. Its *O*-methyl ether (6.37) is commonly known as herniarin. It has been reported that it acts as a phytoalexin in the leaves of *Apeum graveolens*. It also has anti-fungal and anti-bacterial properties.

Umbelliferone can also be used as the starting material for the preparation of 7-methoxy-8-allylcoumarin (6.38), via 7-allyloxycoumarin (6.39) and 7-hydroxy-8-allylcoumarin (6.40).

Procedure

Umbelliferone

To an intimate mixture of resorcinol (3 g) and malic acid (2.5 g) taken in a 100-ml beaker, a mixture of concentrated sulphuric acid and acetic acid in the ratio 4:1 (12.5 ml) is added with stirring, The mixture is then heated at 120°C till a clear solution is obtained. The fluorescent solution is cooled and poured over crushed ice in another beaker, when umbelliferone separates out as a solid. It is collected on a small Buchner or Hirsch funnel, washed free of acid with ice water, dried and recrystallised from ethanol using activated charcoal as a decolorising agent. Pure umbelliferone separates out as pale yellow needles (2.5 g), m.p. 224–25°C (decomposes at 234°C).

Its UV spectrum in ethanol exhibits absorption maxima at 300, 305 and 325 nm.

Herniarin

Umbelliferone (1.62 g) is dissolved in dry acetone (25 ml) in a 50-ml round-bottomed flask. To this solution, dimethyl sulphate (1.15 ml) and anhydrous potassium carbonate (5 g) are added. After attaching a water-cooled condenser with a calcium chloride guard tube at the top, the flask is heated on a water bath for 6 hours. The potassium salts are then filtered, washed with hot acetone and the combined filtrate distilled to remove the solvent. The residue is macerated with dilute (5%) sodium hydroxide solution to remove any unreacted umbelliferone and then filtered. After washing the residue free of alkali with ice-cold water, the compound is dried and recrystallised from ethanol or methanol. Pure herniarin melts at 119-21°C.

7-Allyloxycoumarin

Umbelliferone (2 g) is dissolved in dry acetone (50 ml) in a 100-ml round-bottomed flask fitted with a reflux condenser. To the solution freshly ignited potassium carbonate (10 g) and allyl bromide (3 g) are added, and the mixture refluxed over a water bath for 6 hours. The hot mixture is filtered, the potassium salts washed with hot acetone and the filtrate distilled to remove the solvent. The residue is macerated with 5% sodium hydroxide solution, to remove any umbelliferone remaining unreacted, and then filtered. The residue is repeatedly washed with ice-cold water to free it of alkali and then dried. It is recrystallised from methanol. 7-Allyloxycoumarin separates out as colourless needles (3.5 g), m.p., 79–81°C.

7-Hydroxy-8-allylcoumarin

A solution of 7-allyloxycoumarin (2 g) in redistilled *N, N*-dimethylaniline (15 ml) taken in a 50-ml round-bottomed flask is refluxed at 185°C for 90 minutes. The reaction mixture is cooled and poured into ice-cold 2N hydrochloric acid (100 ml). The precipitate is collected by filtration and dissolved in 50 ml of 2N sodium hydroxide solution. The alkaline solution is then acidified by the cautious addition of concentrated hydrochloric acid. The solid that separates out is filtered, washed free of acid with ice-cold water and dried. It is recrystallised from methanol. The yield of the colourless crystalline 7-hydroxy-8-allylcoumarin is 1.8 g. It melts at 164°C.

The above experiment may be repeated using ethylene glycol instead of *N, N*-dimethylaniline and the results recorded. (In this case, besides 7-hydroxy-8-allylcoumarin, the isomeric 7-hydroxy-6-allylcoumarin, m.p. 157–59°C, is also obtained as a minor product).

7-Methoxy-8-allylcoumarin

A mixture of 7-hydroxy-8-allylcoumarin (1.8 g), dimethyl sulphate (0.95 ml) and anhydrous potassium carbonate (4 g) in dry acetone (50 ml) is taken in a 100-ml round-bottomed flask, refluxed over a water bath for 6 hours and worked up as described under the preparation of herniarin. The product separates out as colourless crystals when recrystallised from methanol. The yield is quantitative. It melts at 136°C.

6.9 ω-METHOXY-2,4-DIHYDROXYACETOPHENONE (6.41) AND ω-METHOXY-2,4,6-TRIHYDROXYACETOPHENONE (6.42)

The above two compounds are important intermediates in the synthesis of flavonols by the Allan–Robinson reaction. This reaction is one of the synthetic routes to flavones, flavonols and isoflavones. The reaction involves the condensation of a 2-hydroxyacetophenone with the anhydride of an aromatic acid, in the presence of the sodium salt of the same acid, which acts as a base catalyst.

Procedure

Methoxyacetonitrile

A solution of sodium cyanide (26 g) in water (75 ml) is taken in a 500-ml conical flask and cooled to 0°C in a freezing mixture. It is then treated with an aqueous solution of formaldehyde

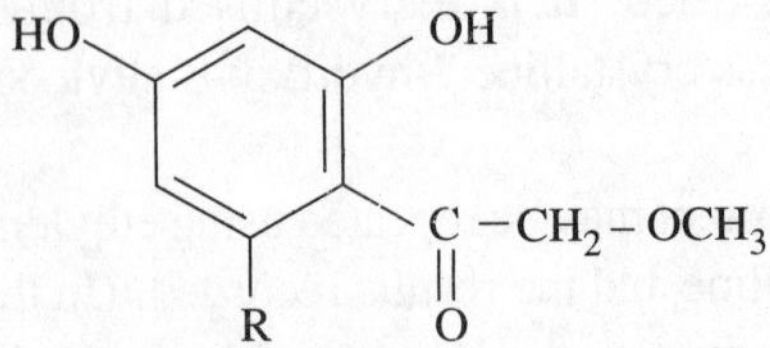

(6.41) : R = H
(6.42) : R = OH

(35 ml of 40% formalin and 35 ml of water) which is added in small lots, taking care to keep the temperature of the mixture below 0°C (a thermometer is inserted in the flask to watch the temperature). After all the formaldehyde solution has been added (about 30 minutes), the reaction mixture is left in the cooling bath for an hour with shaking at intervals. Thereafter, dimethyl sulphate (50 ml) is added to the mixture in one lot. The flask is then taken out of the ice bath and allowed to reach room temperature. A vigorous reaction sets in at about 25°C, as is evident by the sudden rise in the temperature of the reaction mixture. By judicious use of the cooling bath, the temperature of the reaction mixture is not allowed to rise more than 10°C above the room temperature.

The completion of the reaction is indicated by the disappearance of the dimethyl sulphate layer at the bottom of the flask and the separation at the top of a pleasant-smelling colourless oil. The mixture is then transferred to a large separatory funnel and the oily layer extracted with diethyl ether. The ether extract is dried over anhydrous sodium sulphate, filtered and evaporated on a water bath. The residual liquid is distilled and the fraction boiling between 115°C and 125°C is collected. It is redistilled over phosphorus pentoxide at 118–20°C. Yield of pure methoxyacetonitrile is 10 g.

ω-Methoxy-2,4-dihydroxyacetophenone

Dry resorcinol (molten, powdered and dried in a desiccator; 15 g) and methoxyacetonitrile (15 ml) are dissolved in sodium-dried diethyl ether (200 ml) in a 500-ml conical flask cooled in a freezing bath. Dry hydrogen chloride gas generated in a separate set-up is led into the conical flask, until the solution gets saturated with the gas (about 2 hours). The flask is then left in the cooling bath, overnight, when the ketimine hydrochloride separates out as a crystalline solid. After decanting the ether, the solid is washed with cold ether and then dissolved in hot water (200 ml). The solution is heated on a water bath at 80°C for one hour to effect the hydrolysis of the ketimine hydrochloride. The solution gradually turns a deep orange, and on cooling deposits ω-methoxy-2,4-dihydroxyacetophenone as an almost colourless crystalline solid. It is recrystallised from hot water. Yield: 19–20 g. The pure compound melts at 136°C.

ω-Methoxy-2,4,6-trihydroxyacetophenone

To a solution of dry phloroglucinol (15 g) and methoxyacetonitrile (10 ml) in dry diethyl ether (150 ml) taken in a 250-ml conical flask, cooled in an ice bath, freshly fused zinc chloride (2.5 g) (zinc chloride is melted in a China dish—if a nickel dish is available, it is preferred—poured into a mortar, and powdered with the help of a pestle) is added. The mixture is saturated with hydrogen chloride gas, as described under the above experiment, during a period of 4 hours. The ketimine hydrochloride separates out as a brown solid. After allowing the mixture to stand overnight in the cooling bath, the ether is decanted, the residue washed with ether and then dissolved in warm water (100 ml). To effect hydrolysis of the ketimine hydrochloride the solution is heated on a water bath at 80°C for 30 minutes. On cooling in a refrigerator, the red-coloured solution deposits a cream-coloured crystalline solid which is collected on a Buchner funnel by filtration, washed with ice-cold water and dried. Yield: 16 g. It is recrystallised from aqueous ethanol. The pure compound melts at 192°C.

Recommended reading

1. Ahluwalia VK and Seshadri TR, *J. Chem. Soc.*, 971, 1957 (for nordalbergin).
2. Bhargava KK, Krishnaswamy NR and Seshadri TR, *Ind. J. Chem.*, 8: 664, 1970.
3. Feuerstein W and Kostanecki V, *Chem. Ber.*, 31: 710, 1898.
4. Jain AC, Mathur SK and Seshadri TR, *J. Sci. Ind. Res.*, 21B: 214, 1962.

5. Krishnaswamy B and Seshadri TR, *Proc. Ind. Acad. Sci.*, 13A: 43, 1941 (for the preparation of umbelliferone).
6. Krishnaswamy NR and Prasanna S, *Ind. J. Chem.*, 8: 2828, 1970.
7. Krishnaswamy NR, Seshadri TR and Sharma BR, *Tetrahedron Letters*, 4227, 1966; *Current Science*, 35: 542, 1966.
8. Lowenbein A, *Chem. Ber.*, 1924, 57: 1515.
9. Nagarajan S and Mohan Rao LJ, J. *AOAC Int.*, 86: 564–67, 2003 (for the isolation of 2-hydroxy-4-methoxynenzaldehyde).
10. *Organic Syntheses*, Coll. Vol. II.
11. *Organic Syntheses*, Coll. Vol. III.
12. Robinson R and Venkataraman K, *J. Chem. Soc.*, 63, 1929 (for ω-methoxyphloracetophenone).
13. Robinson R and Shah RC, *J. Chem. Soc.*, 1494, 1934.
14. Scarrow JA and Allen CFH, *Organic Syntheses*, Coll. Vol. II, 387, 1943; 1933, 13, 56 (for the preparation of methoxyacetonitrile).
15. Slater WK and Stephen H, *J. Chem. Soc.*, 312, 1920 (for ω-methoxyresacetophenone).
16. Smeets JJ, Meijer RH, Meuldijk J, Vekemans AJM and Hulshof LA, *Organic Process Research & Development,* 7: 10–16, 2003. (for the alternative method of synthesis of ω-terthienyl).
17. Sonn A., *Chem. Ber.*, 2: 1292, 1917.

CHAPTER 7

Metabolism of Natural Products

The increasing interest in natural products as therapeutic agents has made it necessary to study their metabolism in experimental animals as an essential component of a comprehensive investigation before they can emerge as effective drugs. The effectiveness of a chemical as a drug is determined not only by its pharmacological properties but also by other factors, such as toxicity, the onset and duration of action, metabolic fate and the rate of its elimination of metabolites from the body.

Metabolic transformation of a foreign chemical takes place primarily in the liver, to make the compound more polar and easier to eliminate from the body through urine or the faeces. In the process, a toxic chemical usually gets detoxified, though in several cases the metabolites could be more toxic than the substrates. The metabolites are excreted either in the free form or as conjugates, which are more polar, being predominantly either glucuronides or sulphates.

Biotransformation of an organic compound is a two-phase reaction. In the first phase, the compound undergoes transformations which may involve oxidation, such as introduction of one or more hydroxyl groups, reduction (for example, elimination of one or more hydroxyl groups), and hydrolysis. These reactions are catalysed by enzymes located in the endoplasmic reticulum of the liver (microsomal) or at other sites (non-microsomal). In the second phase, the metabolites thus formed get conjugated with glucuronic acid or other endogenous conjugating entities such as sulphuric acid, amino acids or an alkylating agent.

The metabolic profile of a compound is determined by several factors which may be genetic, physiological or environmental in nature. Genetic factors include not only differences in species but also differences in strains within a species. Age, sex, nutritional state and condition of health are some of the physiological factors that affect the metabolism of a drug.

7.1 EXPERIMENTAL METHODS USED IN STUDIES ON DRUG METABOLISM

Both in vitro and in vivo procedures are available for the systematic study of metabolism as well as absorption, distribution and excretion; the entire package is termed as ADME. Currently, in vitro methods are preferred, as they are more efficient than the traditional in vivo techniques. One of the most popular and widely used in vitro procedures makes use of hepatic microsomes. These microsomal preparations retain the enzymatic activity of the intact endoplasmic reticulum. The enzymes involved are cytochrome P 450 (CYP), flavin monooxygenase and glucuronyltransferase.

In another in vitro technique, isolated hepatocytes which retain a broader range of enzymes, not only of the reticular system but also those of cytosolic and mitochondrial systems, are utilised. The use of liver slices is also becoming increasingly popular. Purified enzyme preparations of the appropriate type are also available for conducting test tube reactions.

Another important technique which can be employed in any chemical laboratory is the use of immobilised enzymes. In this method, purified or partially purified enzymes, such as cytochrome P 450, UDP glucuronyltransferases, glutathione *S*-transferases, *S*-methyltransferases and *N*-acetyltransferases are attached to a solid support, such as sepharose, agarose, cellulose or polyacrylamide. The attachment may be achieved by adsorption, covalent bonding or entrapment techniques. Such preparations offer several advantages over other in vitro methods, such as increased storage stability, easier separation of the products from the incubates, and recovery and reuse of the enzyme catalyst.

The procedure described in this chapter is an in vivo technique. There are two reasons for this choice.

1. The majority of recent publications on drug metabolism, which can be readily accessed, describe only in vitro methods. Details of in vivo procedures can be obtained only from older publications, which are difficult to access online. The procedure described here is a traditional one.
2. Collaboration with a pharmacological laboratory, with animal house facilities, would be necessary, and thus a student of chemistry gets exposure to traditional pharmacological methods as well.

A natural product chemist can no longer work in isolation; she or he has to establish active collaboration with biologists to understand and appreciate the role of naturally occurring organic compounds in nature as well as their pharmacological potentials.

In the experimental part, the metabolism of mangiferin (7.1), 7-hydroxy-4-phenylcoumarin (7.2) and 7-methoxy-4-phenylcoumari (7.3) are described. The isolation of mangiferin is described in Chapter 4.

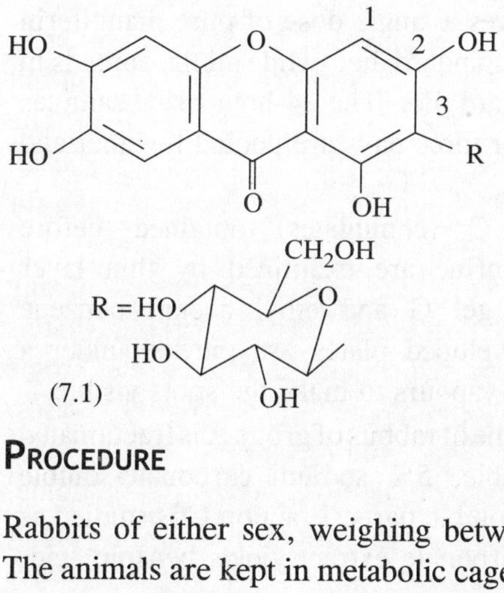

(7.1)

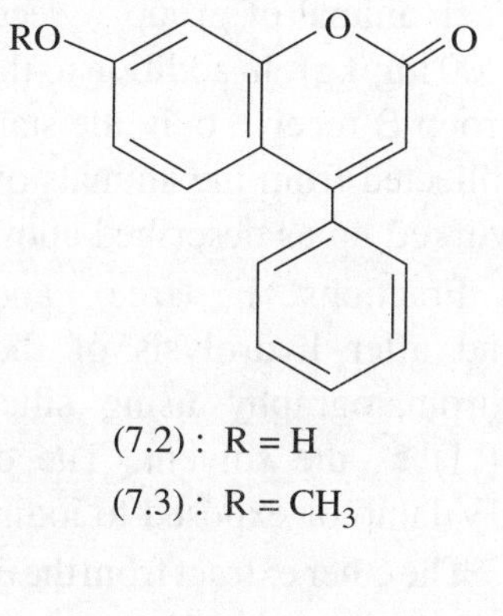

(7.2) : R = H

(7.3) : R = CH_3

PROCEDURE

Rabbits of either sex, weighing between 1.5 to 2.0 kg, are used. The animals are kept in metabolic cages designed to permit separate collection of urine and faeces. The animals are fed cabbage and grams during the experimental period and are allowed free access to water. The compound under study is administered orally by stomach tube, as an emulsion in Tween 80 and water at 200 mg/kg dose level. The urine collected at 24-hour intervals is acidified with dilute sulphuric acid and exhaustively extracted with diethyl ether (or dichloromethane) in a liquid–liquid extractor. The ether extract is fractionated into aqueous sodium bicarbonate–soluble and –insoluble parts, which are then separately examined for any unchanged test compounds and their metabolites.

For examining the conjugates, the acidified urine, after removal of the ether soluble, is subsequently refluxed with sulphuric acid (18%) to effect hydrolysis of any conjugates present. This is followed by extraction with diethyl ether. Glucuronides are detected by the red colour produced with naphthoresorcinol reagent [prepared by dissolving naphthoresorcinol (0.35g) in dilute sulphuric acid (0.1%;100 ml)]. The solution is filtered and stored at 0°C in the dark. It is stable for about a week.

Metabolism of mangiferin

Six rabbits are given the standard diet for one week. At the end of this period the animals are divided into two groups, A and B. Each animal of group A receives a single dose of pure mangiferin (200 mg/kg), in addition to the standard diet, while all the animals in group B receive only the standard diet. The 24-hour urine samples collected from the animals over three days are pooled together and worked up as described above.

Fractions F (free) and C (conjugates) obtained before and after hydrolysis of the urine are examined by thin layer chromatography using silica gel G and ethyl acetate–benzene (1:1) as the solvent. The developed plates are viewed under a UV lamp or exposed to iodine vapours to make the spots visible.

The ether extract from the urine of rabbits of group A is fractionated into sodium bicarbonate–soluble, 5% sodium carbonate-soluble and 0.4% sodium hydroxide–soluble parts. Fraction C is studied as such. Acidification of the bicarbonate extract yields benzoic acid, m.p. 120–21 °C. Neutralisation of the sodium hydroxide extract yields a yellow solid (30 mg). TLC reveals that it is a mixture of three compounds. On crystallisation from methanol, lemon yellow needles separate out, m.p. 242-43 °C.

Its ultraviolet absorption spectrum in ethanol shows maxima at 235, 260, 285 and 315 nm. These data correspond with those of euxanthone (7.4). Fraction C is a single compound identical with euxanthone. The results of a typical experiment are given below.

Animal weight	Dose	Benzoic acid	Euxanthone (free)	Euxanthone (as conjugates)
1.5 kg	300 mg	30.72 mg	28.80 mg	32.32 mg

For an account of naturally occurring 4-phenylcoumarins, also classified as neoflavonloids, see Chapter 1, *Chemistry of Natural*

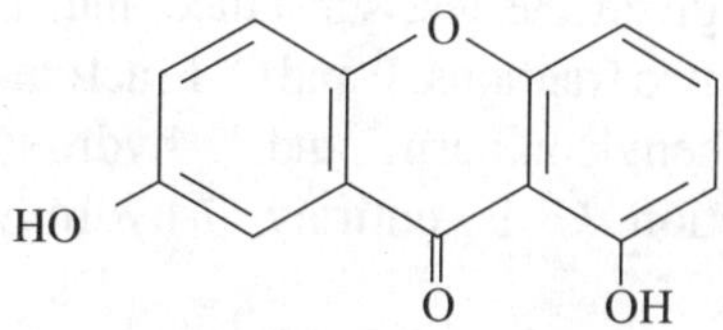

(7.4)

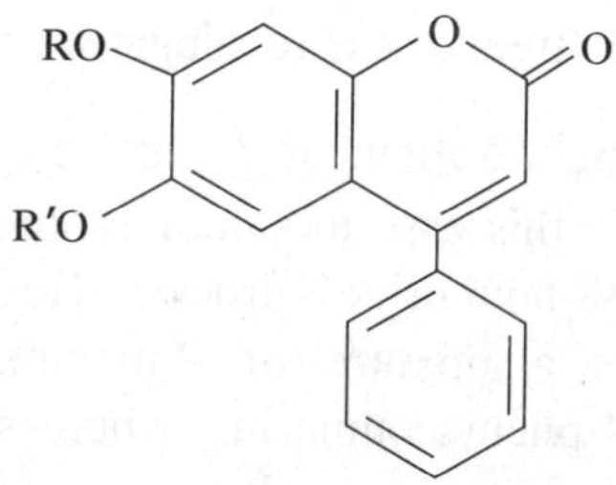

(7.5) : R = CH_3; R′ = H

(7.6) : R = R′ = H

Products: A Unified Approach, 2nd edition, Universities Press, 2010. Typical examples are dalbergin (7.5) and nordalbergin (7.6). In this section the metabolism of two simpler members of this group, namely, 7-hydroxy-4-phenylcoumarin (7.2) and its *O*-methyl ether (7.3) are described.

Preparation of 7-hydroxy-4-phenylcoumarin

To a mixture of resorcinol (5 g) in ethyl benzoylacetate (5 ml), dilute sulphuric acid (78%, 50 ml) is added with vigorous stirring.

The reaction mixture is maintained at 80°C for 30 minutes and thereafter poured into water. The precipitated solid is filtered and recrystallised from ethanol, when 7-hydroxy-4-phenylcoumarin separates out as colourless leaflets, m.p. 242-44°C. Yield: 4 g.

Preparation of 7-methoxy-4-phenylcoumarin

To a solution of 7-hydroxy-4-phenylcoumarin (2 g) in dry acetone (80 ml), dimethyl sulphate (1.5 ml) and freshly ignited potassium carbonate (6 g) are added, and the mixture gently refluxed for 6 hours. After filtering the potassium salts, which are washed with hot acetone, the filtrate is distilled to remove the solvent. The residue is recrystallised from ethanol, when 7-methoxy-4-phenylcoumarin is obtained as colourless needles, m.p. 116–18°C. Yield: 1.8 g.

Metabolism of 7-hydroxy-4-phenylcoumarin

Four rabbits (1.4 to 1.6 kg body weight) are given a total dose of 1.2 g (200 mg/kg) of 7-hydroxy-4-phenylcoumarin. The 48-hour urine is then worked up as described under mangiferin. Both fractions, F (free) and C (conjugates), yield only the starting material.

Metabolism of 7-methoxy-4-phenylcoumarin

In this case too, four rabbits are given the test substance and the 48-hour urine is processed to obtain two fractions, F and C. Fraction F is a mixture of 7-methoxy-4-phenylcoumarin and 7-hydroxy-4-phenylcoumarin, whereas fraction C is entirely 7-hydroxy-4-phenylcoumarin.

7.2 BIOCHEMICAL TRANSFORMATIONS OF NATURAL PRODUCTS

Closely allied to metabolic studies are chemical transformations of organic compounds, brought about using microorganisms, cellular extracts and enzymes. They have several advantages over conventional laboratory reactions involving chemical reagents and catalysts. They show substrate selectivity of a high order, and take place at room temperature under mild conditions.

The yields of the desired products are often quantitative. As most of these reactions are conducted in aqueous or predominantly aqueous media, the use of toxic solvents can be avoided. This is a distinct advantage from the environmental point of view. A major restricting factor is the poor solubility in water of a large number of organic compounds. However, this can be overcome to a certain extent by the addition of small amounts of an organic solvent—miscible with water—to the aqueous medium, and by converting the substrate to a more polar derivative.

The biochemical agents used in such reactions are microorganisms, such as the fungus *Aspergillus niger*, and cell-free or purified enzymes, which include several types of oxidases and hydrolyases. The reactions that can thus be brought about are different types of oxidations, reductions, hydrolytic reactions and condensation reactions.

For example, using *Aspergillus niger*, the monoterpene α-pinene (7.7) has been converted into a mixture of verbenol (7.8), verbenone (7.9) and trans-sobrerol (7.10). The same microorganism has also been used to convert citronellol acetate (7.11) into citronellol

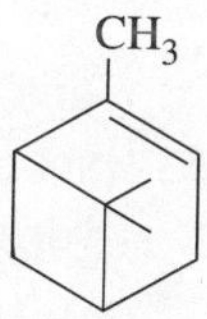

(7.7)

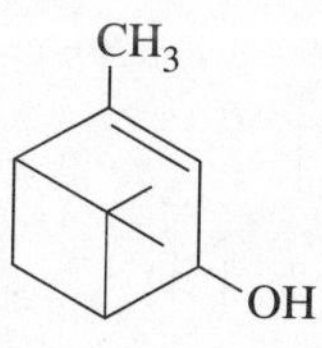

(7.8)

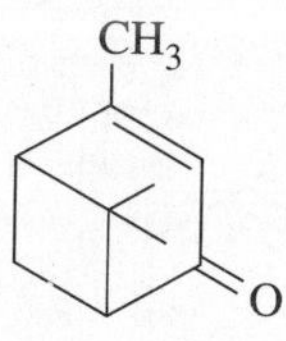

(7.9)

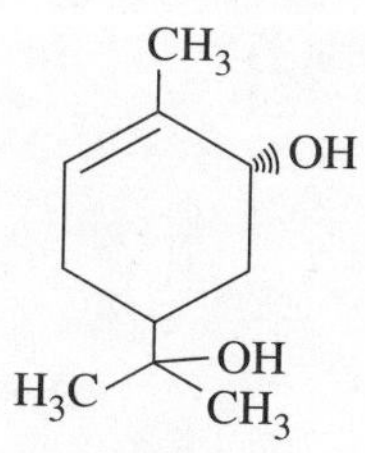

(7.10)

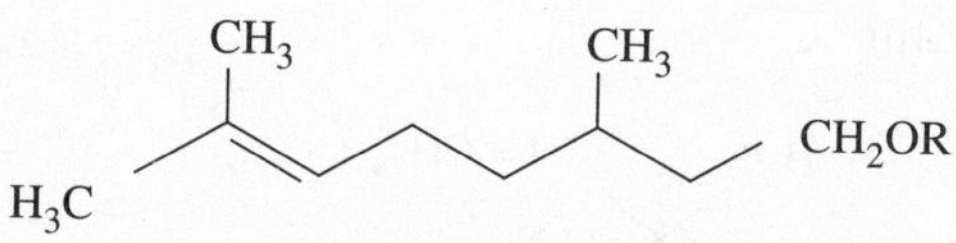

(7.11) : R = $COCH_3$

(7.12) : R = H

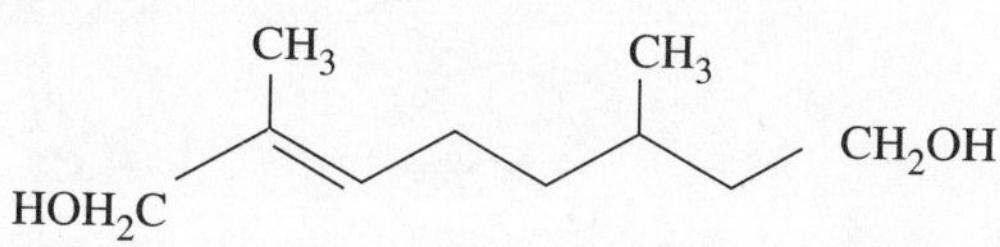

(7.13)

(7.12) and the hydroxyl derivative (7.13) of the latter. Thus, in this case, this fungus has oxidative as well as hydrolytic activities.

In the experiment described below, the acetate (7.15) of the phenolic monoterpene, bakuchiol (7.14), is used as the substrate. Bakuchiol is a chemical constituent of the seeds of *Psoralea corylifolia*. The compound has been reported to exhibit in vitro anti-bacterial activity, against oral microorganisms, as well as anti-oxidant activity.

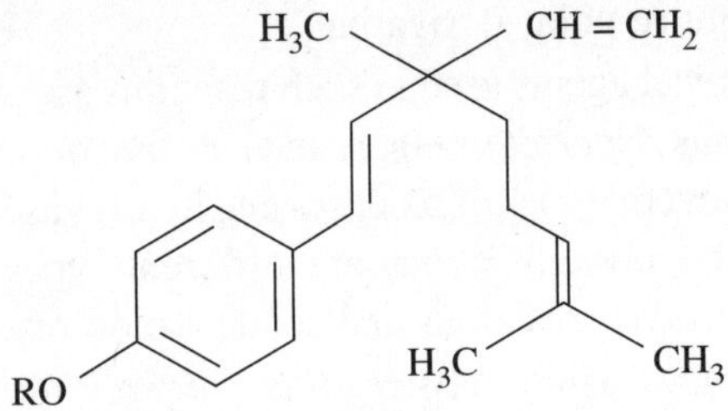

(7.14) : R = H

(7.15) : R = $COCH_3$

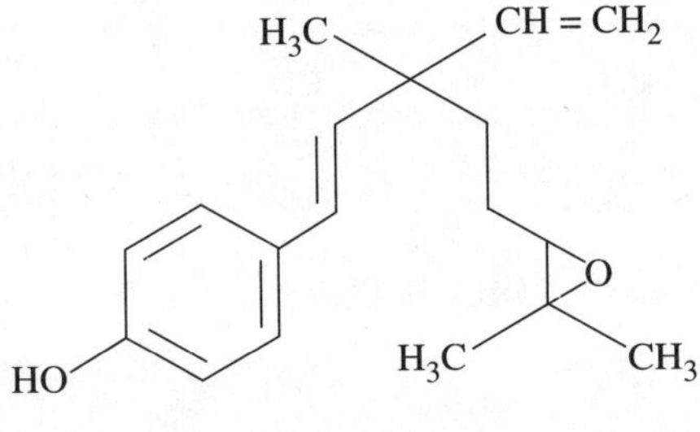

(7.16)

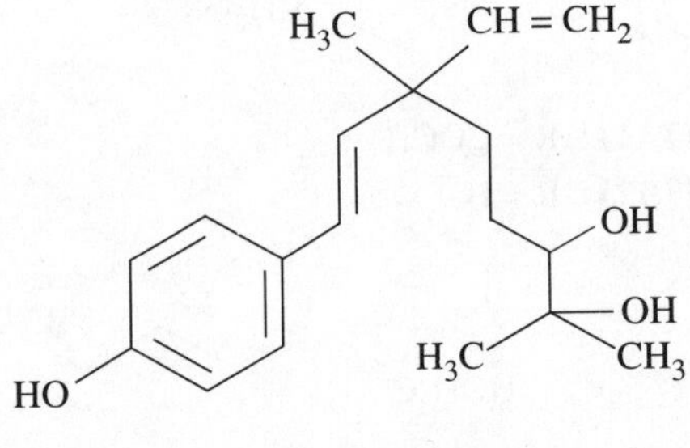

(7.17)

7.2.1 Isolation of bakuchiol

Procedure 1

Powdered seeds (1 kg) of *Psoralea corylifolia* are extracted in a Soxhlet extractor with light petroleum or hexane (1 litre). The extract is concentrated to a small volume, when the crude bakuchiol separates out as a solid (22 g). It is purified by chromatography over a column of silica gel (60–120 mesh) using chloroform–methanol as the eluting solvent. Yield of pure bakuchiol, which is a colourless liquid, is 6 g.

The UV absorption spectrum in methanol shows a single absorption maximum at 254 nm.

Procedure 2

Whole seeds (1 kg) of *Psoralea corylifolia* are percolated in a percolator with diethyl ether (5 l) at room temperature. On removal of the solvent from the total extract, a dark brown gummy material (30 g) is obtained. This is dissolved in diethyl ether (200 ml), washed free of acidic compounds using 1 % sodium hydroxide solution, washed with water, and then dried over anhydrous sodium sulphate. Evaporation of the solvent results in a bakuchiol-rich residue (20 g), which can be further purified by column chromatography over silica gel as described above. Yield of pure bakuchiol is 8 g.

Bakuchiol acetate

To a solution of bakuchiol (0.5 g) in acetic anhydride (0.9 ml), dry pyridine (0.8 ml) is added. The mixture is gently warmed and kept at room temperature for 24 hours. It is then poured into cold water and extracted with chloroform. The organic layer is separated using a separatory funnel. It is washed with water, salt solution and dried over anhydrous sodium sulphate. On removal of the solvent, bakuchiol acetate is obtained as a liquid (0.75 g). It is purified by column chromatography over a short column of silica gel using hexane–ethyl acetate as the eluting solvent.

Its proton NMR spectrum in $CDCl_3$ has the following signals: δ 1.24 (3H, s), 1.54 (2H, m), 1.62 (3H, s), 1.71 (3H, s), 2.0 (2H, m), 2.31 (3H, s), 5.07 (1H, d, *J* = 17.2 Hz), 5.09 (1H, d, *J* = 10.8 Hz), 5.15 (1H, t), 5.92 (1H, dd, *J* = 17.2, 10.8 Hz), 6.19 (1H, d, *J* = 16.2 Hz), 6.34 (1 H, d, *J* = 16.2 Hz), 7.05 (2H, d, *J* = 8.6 Hz) and 7.4 (2H, d, *J* = 8.6 Hz).

Bakuchiol epoxide (7.16)

To a solution of bakuchiol (2 g) in dichloromethane (10 ml) taken in a 25-ml conical flask, *m*-chloroperbenzoic acid (1.97 g) dissolved in dichloromethane (5 ml) is added in drops, maintaining the temperature of the reaction mixture at 0°C by cooling the flask in a ice bath. After stirring the mixture for 30 minutes, it is diluted with ice water and transferred to a separatory funnel. The organic layer is separated and washed in succession with 10% aqueous sodium bicarbonate, water and salt solution. It is dried over anhydrous sodium sulphate, filtered and distilled to remove the solvent. The residual liquid (2.5 g) may be further purified by chromatography over a short column of silica gel, as described under bakuchiol acetate.

Bakuchiol diol (7.17)

To a stirred solution of bakuchiol epoxide (0.4 g) in 75% aqueous dimethyl sulphoxide (5 ml), 0.2N sulphuric acid (2 ml) is added in drops, with stirring, at the room temperature. After diluting with water, the reaction mixture is extracted, in a separatory funnel with ethyl acetate. The organic layer is separated, washed with ice-cold water and dried over anhydrous sulphate. After filtering the drying agent, the solvent is evaporated, when bakuchiol diol separates out as a solid (0.2 g), m.p. 115–17°C.

Its proton NMR spectrum in $CDCl_3$ has the following signals: δ 1.17 (3H, s), 1,20 (3H, s), 1.29 (3H, s), 1.48 (2H, m), 2.09 (2 H, m), 2.66 (1H, t), 4.95 (1H, d, *J* = 10Hz), 5.02 (1H, d, *J* = 17.2 Hz), 5.80 (1H, dd, *J* = 17.2, 10 Hz), 6.02 (1H, d, *J* = 16.2 Hz), 6.26 (1H, d, *J* = 16.2 Hz), 6.77 (2H, d, *J* = 8.6 Hz) and 7.23 (2H, d, *J* = 8.6 Hz).

Biochemical oxidation of bakuchiol acetate

The microorganism used is a strain (MTCC 961) of *Aspergillus niger*. The culture medium for the fungus contains the following substances, per litre: D-glucose (20 g), hydrolysed casein (2.5 g), yeast extract (0.2 g), potassium dihydrogen phosphate (0.6 g) and calcium chloride (0.15 g). Sodium citrate (100 M, pH 6) is used as the buffer.

Cultures of the fungus are incubated in a 250 ml Erlenmeyer flask containing 100 ml of the culture medium at 30°C and shaken for 48 hours. After the incubation period, bakuchiol acetate–ß-cyclodextrin complex is added at a concentration of 0.5 mg/ml. (The complex is prepared by dissolving equivalent amounts of bakuchiol acetate and ß-cyclodextrin in methanol. After evaporating the solvent, the residue is dried in a vacuum desiccator to constant weight). After 10 days, the mycelium is removed by filtration through Whatman No. 3 filter paper. The clear filtrate is extracted with ethyl acetate; dried mycelium is also extracted with the same solvent. The combined extract is dried over anhydrous sodium sulphate, filtered and distilled. The residue (0.15 mg, m.p. 115-17°C) is found to be identical with backuchiol diol.

Recommended reading

1. Arora RB, Krishnaswamy NR, Seshadri TR and Tahir PJ, *Ind. J. Exp. Biol.*, 9: 458–61, 1971 (for metabolism of mangiferin).
2. Dulik DM and Fenselau C, *FASEB J.*, 2: 2235-40, 1988 (for use of immobilized enzymes in drug metabolism).
3. Jiangning G, Xin Zchu W, Zou W, Qinghua L and Kaishun B, *Food Chem.*, 91: 287–92, 2005 (for isolation of bakuchiol).
4. Lennard MS and Stachulski AV, *J. Chem. Ed.*, 77: 349, 2000.
5. Mehta G, Nayak UR and Dev S, *Tetrahedron*, 45: 3009–13, 1973.
6. Thomas F.Woolf, *Handbook of Drug Metabolism*, Marcel Dekker, New York, 1999.

7. Vani Rao, Ph.D. Thesis, Bangalore University, Isolation of anti-microbial natural products and their structure–activity relationship through synthetic and biotransformations, 2007–2009.
8. Zhang D, Zhu M and Humphreys WG, (Eds), *Drug Metabolism in Drug Design and Development*, Wiley, 2008.

CHAPTER 8

Suggested Projects

8.1 ANALYSIS OF CITRAL CONTENT IN DIFFERENT SAMPLES OF LEMON GRASS (*CYMBOPOGON CITRATUS*)

Citral, an inseparable mixture of geranial (8.1) and neral (8.2), is an important perfumery chemical, and is used as an intermediate in the synthesis of α-, β-, and γ-ionones (8.3, 8.4, 8.5) and vitamin A (8.6).

Its isolation and preparation are described in Chapters 4 and 5, respectively.

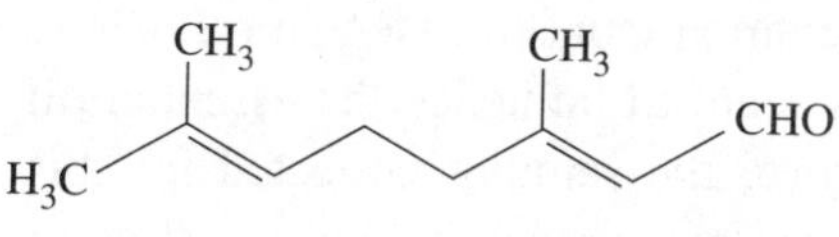

(8.1)

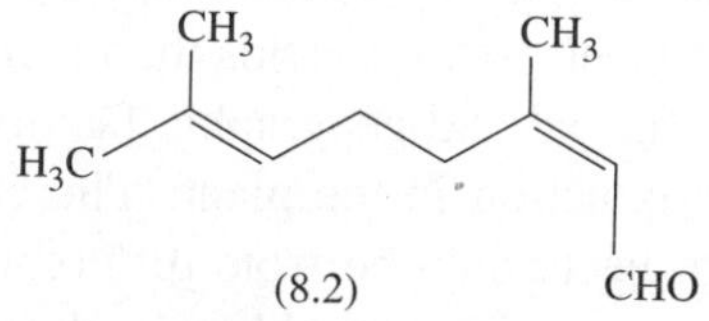

(8.2)

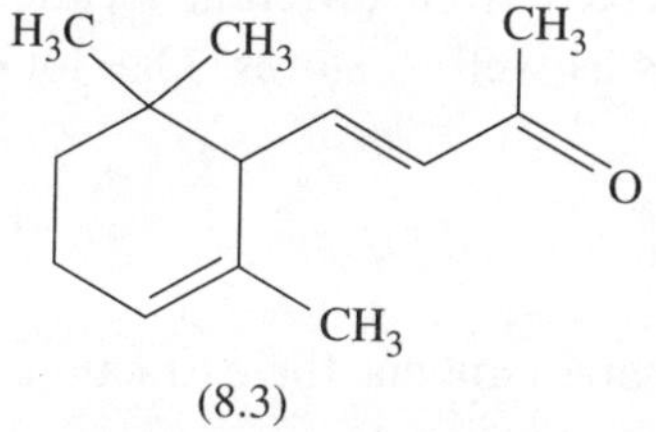

(8.3)

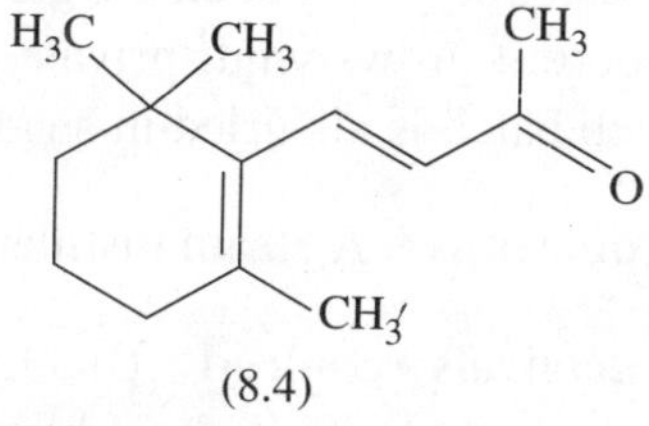

(8.4)

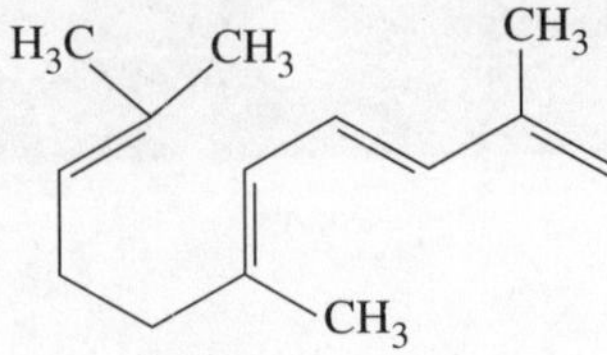

(8.5)

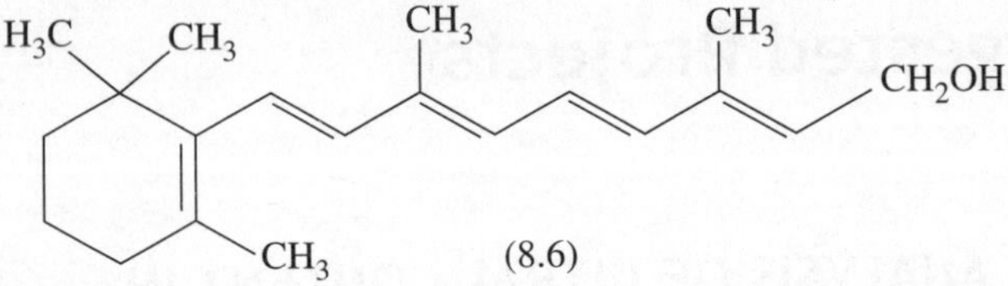

(8.6)

Several varieties of lemon grass have been developed for the isolation of citral on a large scale. The wild variety of lemon grass grows profusely in several parts of India, and in particular, on the slopes of the Western Ghats in South India. The following project is designed to estimate the amount of citral present in different varieties of lemon grass, both wild and cultivated. The effect of drying on the citral content can also be studied by comparing the citral content of fresh and dried samples of the same variety. It has been noted, during a study conducted in the Philippines, that lemon grass growing along hill slopes gives a better yield of the oil than the plant growing in lowlands. Further, the grass collected during the dry, hot season yields the maximum amount of essential oil. Thus, seasonal and geographic factors seem to influence the essential oil production in the plant. Therefore, the samples collected for this project could be from different regions as well as during different seasons. This would make the project more comprehensive.

Materials Fresh lemon grass collected from different locations where it grows wild, private gardens as well as stores. One lot of each batch is air-dried in shade.

Apparatus A steam distillation unit

Chemicals required Dichloromethane (solvent for extraction of the essential oil), sodium bisulphite.

METHOD

A weighed quantity of lemon grass is taken in a 500-ml two-necked flask fitted with a distillation head connected to a water-cooled condenser and a dropping funnel. To the material 250 ml of water are added and the flask heated in an electric mantle. When distillation begins, more water from the dropping funnel is added to maintain the water level in the flask. The distillate is collected in a receiver flask cooled in a water bath. When no more oil is seen in the distillate, the distillation is stopped and the distillate extracted with dichloromethane in a separatory funnel. The dichloromethane extract is dried over anhydrous magnesium sulphate and then distilled to completely remove the solvent. The residue is then transferred to a vacuum desiccator in which wax shavings are kept to remove the remaining traces of the solvent. The dry, solvent-free residue is weighed. To the oil thus obtained, 35% aqueous sodium bisulphite solution is added, with stirring, till no more precipitate appears. The solid citral–bisulphite adduct is collected by filtration, washed with a little light petroleum, dried in a desiccator and weighed.

The above experiment is repeated with different samples of lemon grass, fresh and air-dried separately, and the results tabulated and compared.

In one experiment, the oil obtained is examined by thin layer chromatography using light petroleum as the irrigating solvent. After development the TLC plate is sprayed with a solution of 2,4-dinitrophenylhydrazine. If a UV absorption spectrophotometer is available, the UV spectrum of the oil in methanol can be recorded and the intensity of the absorption maximum at 238 nm measured. A pure sample of citral is used as the reference. If possible, an IR spectrum can also be recorded, and the percentage transmission of the following absorptions bands measured to find out the approximate percentages of geranial, and neral in the sample. The band at 1615 cm^{-1} is due to geranial and those at 1165 and 845 cm^{-1} are given by neral. If the proton NMR spectrum can be recorded, the peak areas under δ 10 (due to the aldehydic proton in geranial) and 9.88 (given by the corresponding proton in neral) can be measured and compared.

8.2 ANALYSIS OF CARVONE CONTENT IN DIFFERENT SAMPLES OF CARAWAY

Carvone is the major component of the essential oil of caraway (*Carvum carvi*) seeds, where it occurs to the extent of 50%–70%. There are two enantiomers of the compound. S (+) carvone (8.7) is obtained from caraway oil, whereas the R (–) isomer (8.8) is present in the oil of spearmint (*Mentha spicata*). S (+) Carvone is used in the Netherlands for the prevention of premature sprouting of stored potatoes. R (–) Carvone is used as a mosquito repellent and in air-freshener compositions. The isolation of S (+) carvone from caraway seeds is described in Chapter 4.

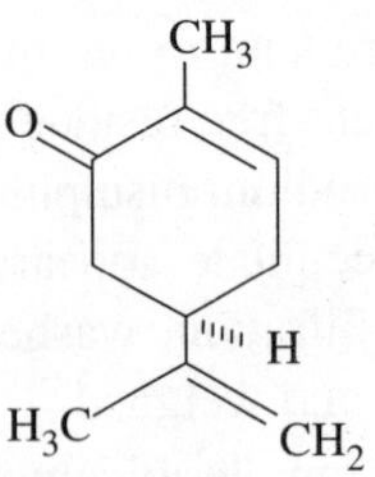

(8.7)

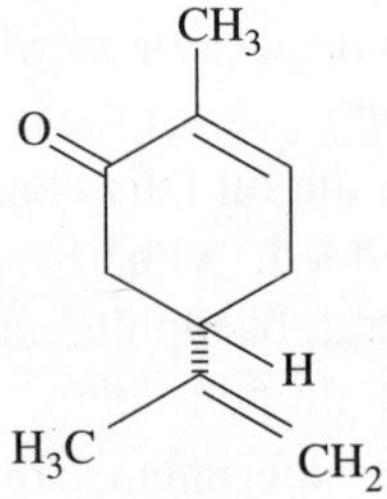

(8.8)

Materials Different brands of caraway obtained from stores.

METHOD

It is the same as described under Project 8.1. In this case, 25 g of coarsely powdered caraway seeds are taken, along with 250 ml of water, in a double-necked flask. The final oil obtained is examined by TLC. The developed plates are sprayed with a solution of 2,4-dinitrophenylhydrazine to make the spot visible. Its UV spectrum can also be recorded and the intensities of the two absorption maxima at 235 and 318 nm measured.

To the oil dissolved in the minimum quantity of ethanol, a hot solution of hydroxylamine hydrochloride in water (1 g in 1 ml) is added with shaking. To the clear liquid, a warm solution of 1 g KOH in 8 ml of water, is added at once. After filtering the potassium chloride which precipitates out, the filtrate is poured into cold water, when carvone oxime crystallises out. It is filtered, washed with a small quantity of ice-cold water, dried and weighed. The results from the different samples of caraway seeds are tabulated and compared.

Instead of caraway seeds, dill seed oil (*Anethum graveolens*) can also be used for the isolation of S (+) carvone. The same method can also be used for the analysis of spearmint oil. If a polarimeter is available, the specific rotation may be recorded as $\pm 61^{\circ}$.

For comparison, pure samples of the two enantiomers can be procured from Aldrich or any other manufacturer.

UV and IR spectra may also be recorded and interpreted.

8.3 STUDY OF ANTIFUNGAL ACTIVITIES OF PLANT EXTRACTS AND SOME ISOLATED COMPOUNDS

There is an increased awareness among agriculturists and horticulturists that synthetic manures, pesticides and herbicides have harmful effects in the long run. Therefore, organic farming has become a key word. One of the harmful effects of excessive and continuous use of synthetic fungicides is the development of resistance to them by the fungi against which they are used. These compounds also result in ecological imbalances which are harmful to the environment. The advantage of using organic compounds of natural origin is that they are biodegradable.

A couple of examples will be cited before describing the methodology to be used in this project. The napthoquinone pigment juglone (8.9) and its precursor (8.10) in the black walnut tree, *Juglans nigra*, have been reported to be responsible for the resistance of walnut to the fungus *Gnemonia lepostyla*. Young tomato plants kept in a solution of catechol (8.11; 50 ppm) for 48 hours, before being transferred to the soil, were found to be resistant to the fungus *Fusarium oxysporum*, whereas untreated tomato plants were infected by this fungus.

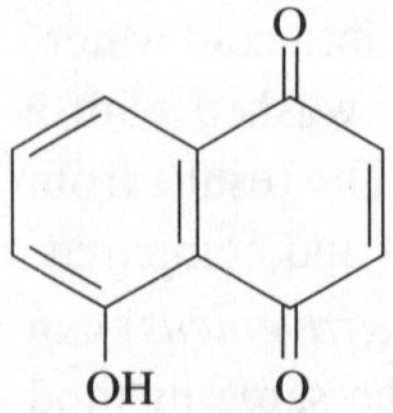

(8.9)

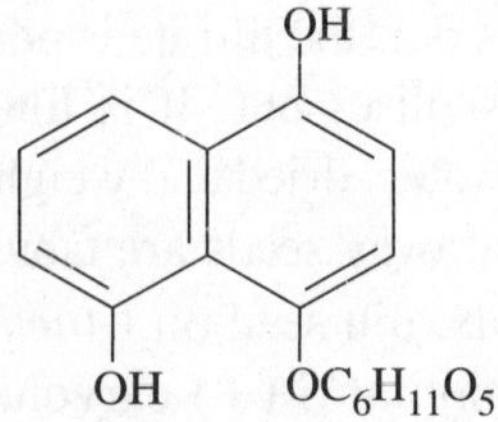

(8.10)

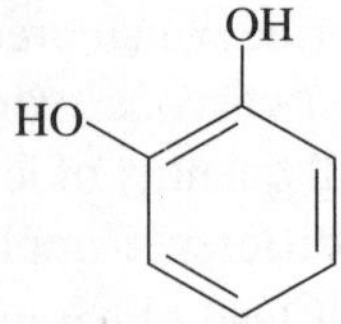

(8.11)

METHOD

The antifungal activities of plant extractives can be conveniently evaluated using the turbidity method developed by Robinson et al. In this method, the extent of inhibition of fungal growth is determined spectroscopically by measuring the percentage transmission at 660 nm. This is inversely proportional to the turbidity caused by fungal growth.

In a test tube containing 5 ml of a sterilised fungal medium, 0.1 ml of the test solution (pure isolated compounds or plant extractives such as essential oils or residues obtained from extracts, after completely removing the solvents) at a concentration of 200 µg in dimethyl formamide is added, followed by the addition of 3 to 4 drops of a 48-hour-old culture. The test tube is shaken well and incubated for 48 hours at 31°C. The commercially available fungicide, bavistin, [methyl *N*-(1H-benzimidazol-2yl) carbamate] can be used as the standard.

Preparation of the medium (Horne and Mitters medium)

The following compounds, in the quantities mentioned against them, are dissolved in double distilled water and the volume made up to 1 litre.

Potassium nitrate 2 g
Potassium dihydrogen phosphate 1.25 g
Magnesium sulphate 75 g
Dextrose 2 g
Soluble starch 10 g

The pH of the solution is adjusted to 4 to 5 by the cautious addition of a 25% solution of lactic acid in distilled water. Streptopenicillin (30 μg) is added to prevent bacterial growth. The medium is then asceptically inoculated with the fungus and incubated at 31°C for 48 hours.

After 48 hours the test solution is examined for percentage transmission at 660 nm using a spectrophotometer.

The fungi that can be used are: *Aspergillus flavus, Aspergillus niger, Fusarium solani, Fusarium oxysporum* and *Alternaria alternata*.

The various compounds described in Chapter 4, as well as any other plant extractive, can be used as the test materials. For example, the extractives of the leaves of *Phyllanthus niruri,* or the berries of *P. emblicus* can be evaluated. Dried gooseberries can also be purchased

Extraction

The leaves or berries, washed free of dust and mud particles, are cut into small pieces, air-dried in the shade and extracted in succession with the following solvents: light petroleum, dichloromethane and ethanol. Each extract is concentrated to dryness, preferably using a rotary evaporator at as low a temperature as possible, and dried in a vacuum desiccator. The residue, free from water, is weighed, dissolved in a small amount of the solvent to be used (for example, dimethyl formamide), transferred to a 10-ml volumetric flask, and the volume made up to the mark using more of the solvent.

Alternative methods of evaluation of antifungal activities have been given by RC Jagessar et al and SV Shobha and RD Kale.

8.4 CHROMATOGRAPHIC STUDY OF ANTHOCYANIN PIGMENTS IN TULIP FLOWERS

Anthocyanin pigments are responsible for the wide spectrum of floral colours ranging from orange to blue with a variety of shades. A brief account of these compounds is given in Chapter 4 of this book.

Species of the genus Tulipa belonging to the Liliaceae family are well known for their attractive cup-shaped brightly coloured flowers. Many cultivars have been developed. In this project, the anthocyanin pigments of the different varieties of tulip flowers will be examined with the help of paper chromatography and visible spectroscopy.

METHOD

Fresh flowers cut into small pieces are soaked in a beaker containing 1% methanolic hydrochloric acid at room temperature for 24 hours. After removing the bleached flowers, the extract is filtered and treated with basic lead acetate. The anthocyanins get precipitated and the solid is collected on a funnel by filtration under suction. The filtrate is kept aside if it is still coloured (indicating that all the anthocyanins have not been precipitated out). The lead salt is dried at room temperature and macerated with methanol containing 2% (v/v) of concentrated hydrochloric acid. The precipitated lead chloride is filtered off. The filtrate is freed of any remaining lead by treatment with hydrogen sulphide. The lead-free methanolic solution of the anthocyanins is then evaporated to dryness at 40°C (or below). The residue is re-dissolved in the minimum amount of methanol. On addition of dry diethyl ether to this solution, the anthocyanins precipitate out. After keeping the mixture in a refrigerator for three days, the solid is filtered and kept in a vacuum desiccator over phosphorus pentoxide.

For paper chromatographic examination, the solid is dissolved in methanol and spotted on Whatman No. 1 filter paper. Both circular and descending (or ascending) modes of chromatography can be used.

The following solvents can be used as irrigating solvents: The upper phase of *n*-butanol–acetic acid–water (4:1:5), 15% acetic acid, isopropanol–2N HCl (1:1 by volume), formic acid–12N HCl–water (5:2:3 by volume) and phenol–water (73:27).

For circular chromatography, a Petri dish (with a glass cover) is convenient. For ascending and descending chromatography a measuring cylinder or a jar can be used.

The R_f values are measured and compared with those recorded for the common anthocyanin pigments.

For visible spectroscopy, a dilute solution of the anthocyanin hydrochloride in methanol is used. Pelargonidin glycosides absorb near about 520 nm, cyanidin glycosides absorb at about 540 nm, whereas delphinidin glycosides give rise to absorption near 550 nm.

For preparative chromatography and identification of the individual anthocyanins, Whatman No. 3 paper is used. After developing the chromatogram by the ascending or descending mode, the bands are cut out separately and the pigment eluted out with 50% aqueous methanol.

A part of the concentrated anthocyanin extract is hyrolysed with 2N hydrochloric acid (equal volumes of the extract and the acid) by heating under reflux for 30 minutes. It is cooled and extracted with a small amount of *n*-amyl alcohol to separate out the anthocyanidins from the sugars which remain in the aqueous layer. The aqueous layer is freed from acid by treatment with a weak anion exchange resin and then concentrated to a small volume for paper chromatographic examination, following the procedure described under nepitrin in Chapter 4. The sugars are detected by spraying the chromatogram with aniline hydrogen phthalate.

The *n*-amyl alcoholic layer is used for the chromatographic examination of the anthocyanidins.

Instead of tulip flowers, poinsettia bracts, *Hibiscus rosa-sinensis* flowers, chrysanthemum flowers (various hybrids) or jacaranda flowers can also be examined.

ALTERNATIVE METHOD OF EXTRACTION OF ANTHOCYANINS

Fresh flower petals are soaked in acetone for 15 minutes. After filtering off the bleached petals, the acetone extract is treated with a few drops of concentrated hydrochloric acid. The resulting solution is diluted with distilled water and extracted with diethyl ether and then with ethyl acetate in a separatory funnel to remove any flavonoid compounds present. The aqueous layer, containing the anthocyanin pigments, is then worked up as described above (precipitation with basic lead acetate).

8.5 CHROMATOGRAPHIC STUDY OF SOME MARINE ALGAE

Marine algae serve as a source for the simple, as well as complex, organic molecules needed by all forms of marine animals. The different kinds of marine algae have evolved as a result of complex ecological interactions, the nature of which varies from environment to environment. Unlike terrestrial plants, the collection of sufficient quantities of marine flora for the isolation of organic compounds by conventional methods is not easy. Chromatographic methods, particularly HPLC, are more suitable for the examination of the extractives from small amounts of a marine alga. Thin layer chromatography is also useful to get ample information regarding the chemical nature of the compounds present in an extractive. Preparative TLC can be used for separation of the components of an extractive.

India has a long coastline. The lagoons surrounding the Lakshadweep islands can provide algae such as *Gracillaria edulis, Laurencia papillona* and *Acanthophora specifera* which can be examined in this project.

Before starting the experimental work, a thorough survey of literature should be made. Several species of the genus Laurencia have been examined in the past and a variety of compounds belonging to different chemical types have been isolated and characterised.

These include sesquiterpenoids, such as Laurencin (8.12), obtusenol (8.13) and caspitol (8.14), diterpenoids like obtusadiol (8.15), triterpenes, for example, squalene epoxide (8.16), sterols and several non-terpenoid compounds. Particularly interesting are the indole derivatives, (8.17 and 8.18), and related compounds.

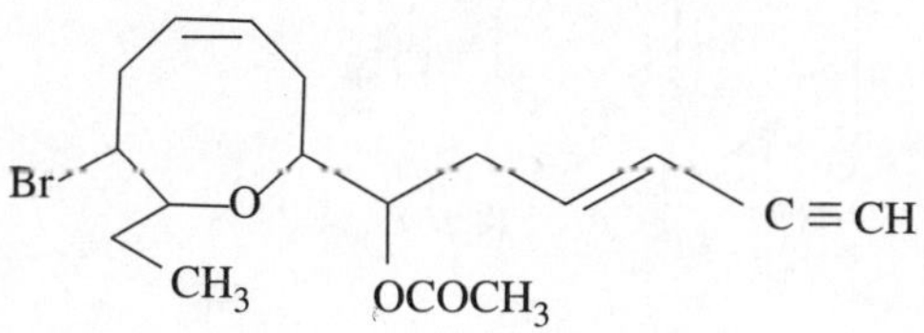

(8.12)

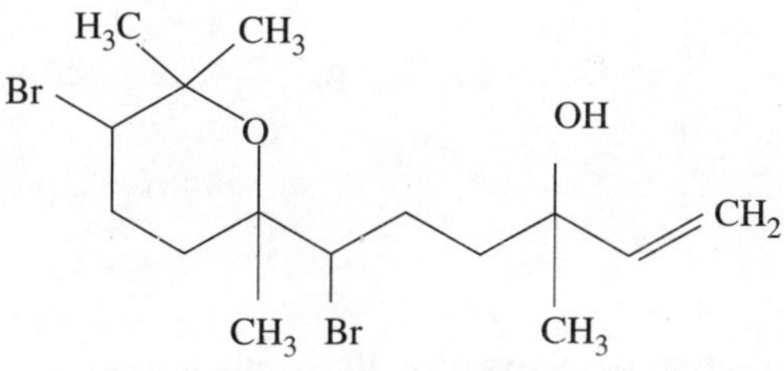

(8.13)

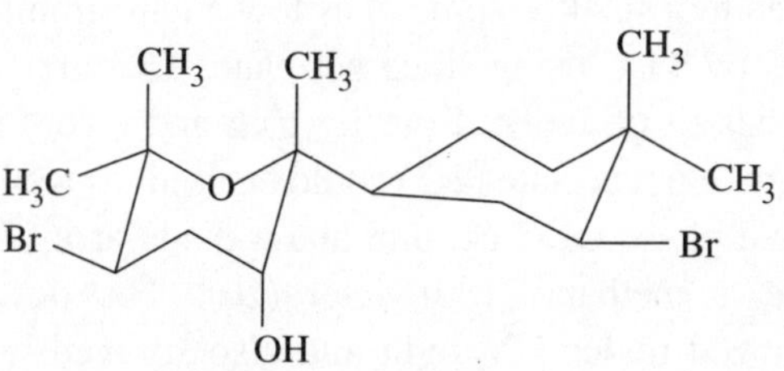

(8.14)

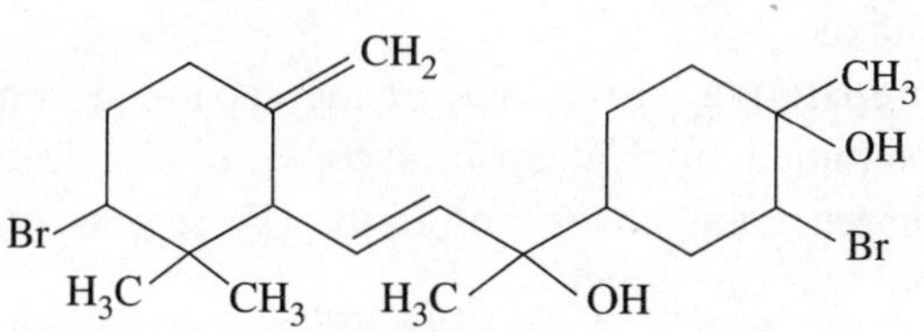

(8.15)

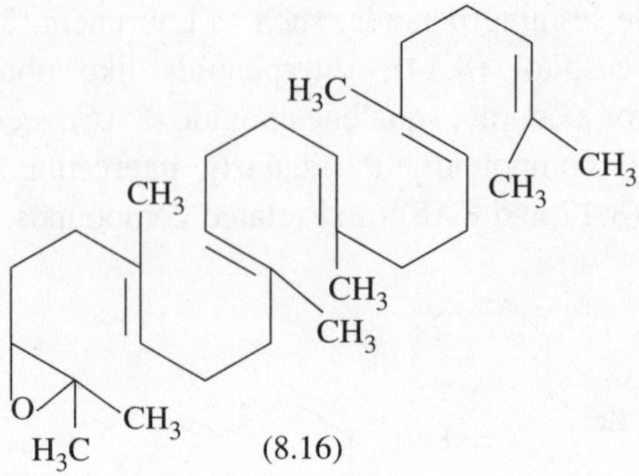

(8.16)

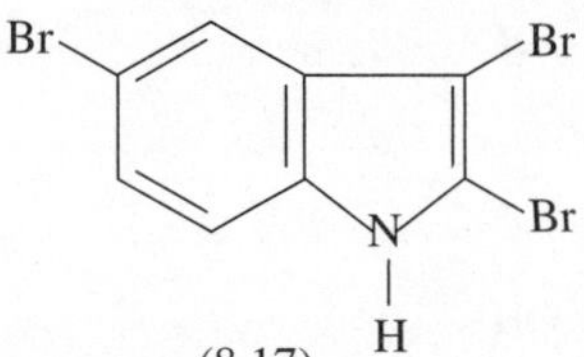

(8.17)

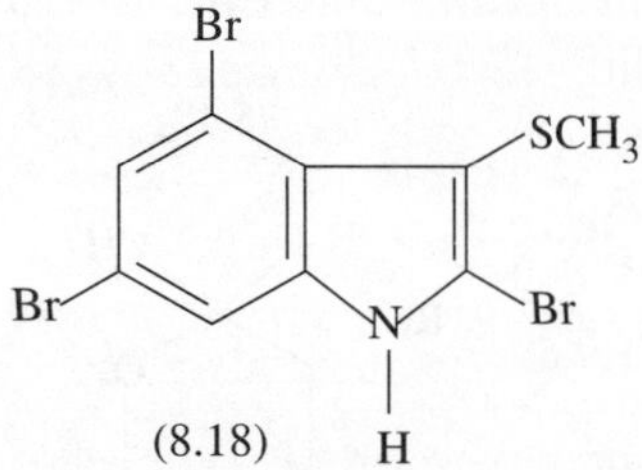

(8.18)

METHOD

The air-dried alga is extracted in a small Soxhlet extractor in succession with dichloromethane and methanol. Each of the extracts is concentrated to a small volume at as low a temperature as possible and examined by TLC using silica gel plates [The irrigating solvent composition has to be worked out by trial and error; for example, light petroleum–ethyl acetate (2:3) could be used] as well as by HPLC using a reverse phase ODS column and a diode-array detector. The mobile phase is methanol (80):water (20). The developed TLC plates are viewed under UV light and also sprayed with a variety of reagents (several plates have to be prepared for this purpose) to elicit as much information as possible about the chemical nature of the compounds.

After preparative TLC, each of the separated components can also be examined by UV spectroscopy. If any fraction exhibits blue fluorescence and absorption in the UV region, the presence of ...les could be suspected.

...method can be used for all the three algae.

8.6 A CHEMOTAXONOMIC STUDY OF SOME SPECIES OF PARMELIA LICHENS

Parmelia is a large genus of lichens and as many as 125 species have been recorded in India alone. They can be found clinging to rock faces, monuments and trees.

A concise account of the special chemical components of lichens can be found in Chapter 1 of *Chemistry of Natural Products: A Unified Approach,* 2nd edition, by this author.

This project involves the comparative study, under identical conditions, of as many species of Parmelia as it is possible to collect. At least three, such as *Parmelia tinctorum*, *P. cirrhatum* and *P. perlata* could do to start with.

METHOD

The method described under Project 8.5 can be used in this case too, though conventional methods of chemical analysis can also be used, as these lichens can be procured in comparatively large amounts. The objective of the project is to evaluate the similarities and differences in the composition of their secondary metabolites among the different species. Paper chromatography and TLC can play a large part in these studies.

As suggested under 8.5, the experimental part of the project should be preceded by a thorough survey of the existing literature. In India, pioneering studies on lichen metabolites were carried out by TR Seshadri and his coworkers.

Other lichens can be similarly examined.

8.7 GAS CHROMATOGRAPHY—MASS SPECTROSCOPIC STUDY (GC—MS) OF SOME SWEET SMELLING WOODS

Several wood species are pleasant smelling. Some examples which come to mind are the different types of cedar woods (species of the genus Cedrus, for example, *C. atlantica* (atlas cedar wood),

C. deodora (Devadar or Himalayan cedar), Lebanon cedar (*C. ibani*) and Cyprus cedar (*C. brevifolia*) as well as several other trees belonging to the genus Juniperus and other genera of the Cupressus family), guaiac wood (*Bulnesia sarmienti*), red sandal wood (*Pterocarpus santalinus*), *P. marsupium*, rose wood (*Aniba rosaeodora*), and the true rose woods belonging to the genus Dalbergia (*D. nigra*, *D. latifolia*, etc.).

Many of the above woods, being hardy, can be extensively used in building construction and furniture making. Therefore, it should not be difficult to collect wood pieces and sawdust of these woods.

METHOD

In this project, small pieces of wood or coarse sawdust or wood shavings of different batches of the four species of Cedrus are subjected to steam distillation, using the usual set up (described at other places in this book). The essential oil thus obtained can be separated from water by extraction with a low boiling solvent, such as diethyl ether or dichloromethane (safer to handle). After completely removing the solvent, the residue is thoroughly dried in a vacuum desiccator and examined using a GC–MS instrument. The results are tabulated and compared. The major components of these oils are mono and sesquiterpenes. The composition varies from species to species. There can also be seasonal and geographic variations. Therefore, samples can be collected from different places at different times and properly labelled.

Alternatively, species of the genus Juniperus, for example, *J. communis* (Juniper), *J. ashei* (mountain or Texas cedar), *J. sabine* (savine), *J. virginiana* (Virginian cedar) and *J. bermudiana* (Bermudas cedar) can be used in this project.

Authentic samples of the terpenes present in these woods can be purchased and their GC–MS spectra recorded for identification. For interesting information regarding these, as well as other essential oils, *The Illustrated Encyclopedia of Essential Oils* by Julia Lawless can be consulted. It is a treasure trove of information on this subject.

8.8 ESSENTIAL OILS FROM CITRUS SPECIES

Essential oils from lime (*Citrus aurantifolia*), lemon (*C. limon*), mandarin orange (*C. reticulata*), oil of petitgrain (obtained from green, unripe oranges, *C. aurantium* var. amara), oil of bergamot (extracted from *C. bergamia* peels), bitter orange (*C. aurantium* var. amara), sweet orange (*C. sinensis*) and grapefruit (*C. x.paradisi*) are extensively used in aromatherapy, in perfume compositions, cosmetics and as flavouring agents. The major component of the oils from bitter orange, sweet orange, grapefruit and lemon is limonene (8.19). Oil of petitgrain and bergamot, on the other hand, contain linalyl acetate (8.20) as the chief constituent.

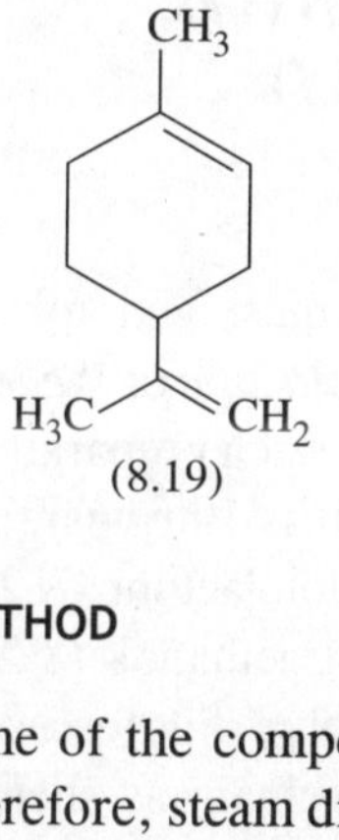

(8.19)

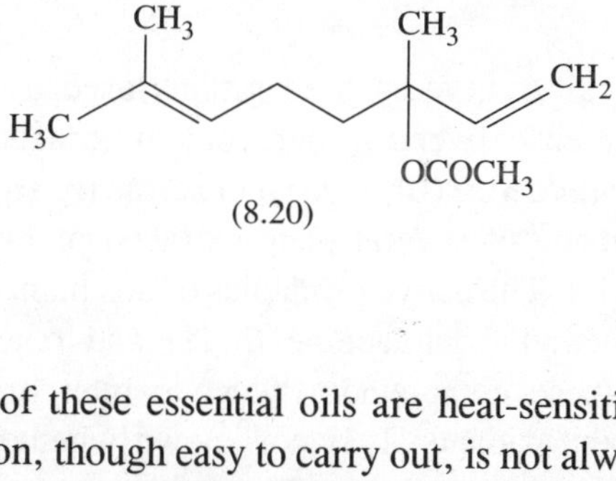

(8.20)

METHOD

Some of the components of these essential oils are heat-sensitive. Therefore, steam distillation, though easy to carry out, is not always the ideal method of extraction of these oils. Other methods are cold expression by manual or mechanical means and supercritical carbon dioxide extraction method. The last mentioned method gives the most satisfactory results, but requires specially designed equipment. One such has been developed in the Department of Chemical Engineering, Indian Institute of Technology Bombay, Mumbai, for the pilot-scale and large-scale isolation of natural extracts.

Laboratory scale models are also available commercially.

In this project, several Citrus species, native and cultivated varieties, can be extracted by all the three methods mentioned above to obtain the essential oils. Percentage yields of the oils from the different samples are noted down and compared. A GC–MS instrument can be used to get further information about the chemical constituents. Qualitative analysis of the oils can be done using TLC. The results are tabulated and compared.

For using the supercritical carbon dioxide extraction method (SC–CO_2), the work of M Bimakr et al and N Thavanapong can be referred to for choosing an appropriate procedure of extraction by this method.

8.9 EXAMINATION OF AYURVEDIC PATENT PREPARATIONS CONTAINING BHRINGRAJ FOR WEDELOLACTONE—DESMETHYL WEDELOLACTONE/α-TERTHIENYL METHANOL CONTENTS

Several Ayurvedic preparations used as hair tonics, and for the treatment of liver disorder, contain extracts of *Eclipta alba* or *Wedelia calendulaceae* (Bhringaraj in Sanskrit). However, such preparations are made of several plant extracts, one of which is Bhringaraj or *E. alba*. The active principles of this plant are wedelolactone (8.21), desmethylwedelolactone (8.22) and α-terthienylmethanol (8.23). All these compounds, which exhibit brilliant blue fluorescence, are antioxidants. It is not known whether they remain as such or undergo some chemical transformation during the preparation of the herbal products which contain extracts of *Eclipta alba*/*Wedelia calendulaceae*. In the two projects suggested herein, the objective is to get an answer to this question.

It will be easier to deal with solid preparations (in the form of pills) than with oils.

Two solid preparations which contain Bhringaraj extracts are Geriforte manufactured by the Himalaya Drug Company and Keshkant produced by Shanker Pharmacy. The former is made of as many as 37 herbal extracts and the latter consists of a dozen constituents.

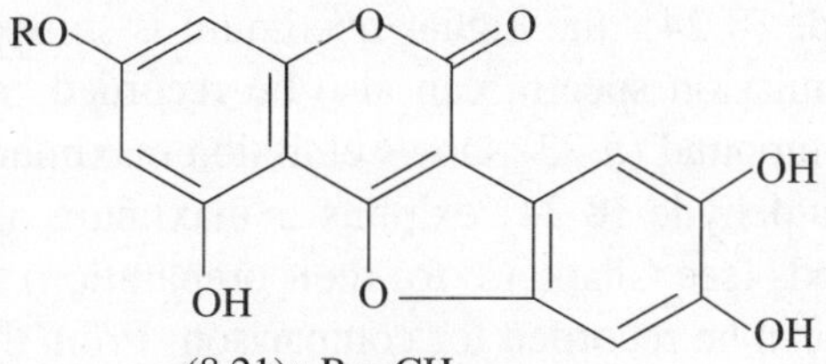

(8.21) : R = CH_3
(8.22) : R = H

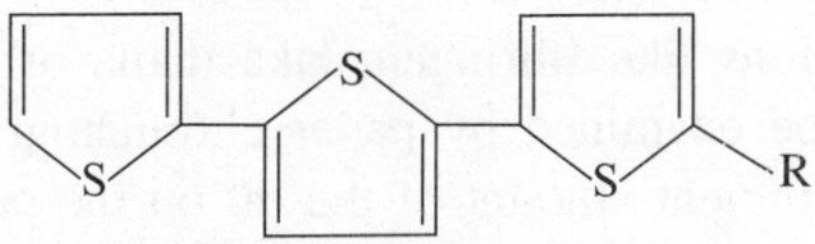

(8.23) : R = CH_2OH
(8.24) : R = CHO

METHOD

For determining the presence of wedelolactone–desmethylwedelolactone and α-terthienylmethanol, the same procedure can be used, and hence these two projects are presented here under one heading.

A sufficient quantity (100 g) of the pills (Geriforte or Keshkant) is reduced to a coarse powder, packed in a thimble and extracted in a Soxhlet extractor with ethyl acetate. If these compounds are present, the extract will exhibit blue fluorescence. After the extraction is complete (after siphoning several times, the last one displaying no colour or fluorescence), the extract is concentrated to a small volume.

For wedelolactone–desmethylwedelolactone, the extract is analysed using paper chromatography and HPLC (see p.106 for details). For α-terthienylmethanol, the analysis is done with the help of TLC. It is possible that compound (8.23) could have undergone oxidation to the corresponding aldehyde (8.24), which exhibits a brilliant yellow fluorescence and has a higher R_f value than compound (8.23). Preparative TLC can be used for isolating these compounds. The UV spectrum of compound (8.23) in methanol shows absorption maxima at 250 and 350 nm. In the case of the aldehyde (8.24), the higher maximum is shifted to 397 nm. If possible, emission spectra can also be recorded. A methanolic solution of compound (8.23) shows emission maximum at 425 nm, whereas the aldehyde (8.24) exhibits a maximum at 525 nm. If pure compounds (see Chapter 6 for their preparation) are available, their spectra, can be recorded for comparison. From the two sets of spectra a quantitative estimation of (8.23) and (8.24), if present, in the test sample can be made out.

Oily preparations like Bhringamalaka thaila or Neelibhringadi thaila can also be examined by paper chromatography and TLC by spotting a sufficient amount of the oil on the paper/TLC plate and developing the chromatograms. The developed plates can be viewed under UV light.

Recommeaded reading

1. Bimakr M, Rahman RA, Taip FS, Chuan LT, Ganjloo A, Selamat J and Hamid A, Supercritical CO_2 (SC-CO_2) extraction of bioactive flavonoid compounds from spearmint (*Mentha spicata* L.) leaves, *Euro. J. Sci. Res.*, 33: 679–90, 2009.
2. Jagessar RC, Mars A and Gomes G, *Nature and Science*, 6 (2), ISSN 1545-0740, 2008.
3. Lawless J, The *Illustrated Encyclopedia of Essential Oils,* Barnes & Noble, New York, 1995.
4. Robinson RCV, Fercoit TN and Robinson HM, *Arch. Dermatol.*, 81: 681, 1960.
5. Shobha SV and Kale RD, *Greenpages*, January 2008.
6. Thavanapong N, The essential oils from peels and flowers of *Citrus maxima*, Thesis submitted for the degree of Master of Pharmacy, Silpakorn University, Thailand, 2006.
7. Zakaria Z, Zakaria S and Ishak MAM, Analysis of major fragrant compounds from *Citrus grandis* flower extracts, *Sains Malaysiana*, 39: 565–69, 2010.

APPENDIX 1

Preparation of Buffers and some Diagnostic Reagents (including some used in forensic chemistry)

Acetate buffer (pH 5)

Sodium acetate (13.6 g) and glacial acetic acid (6 ml) are dissolved in sufficient water to make up I litre.

Ammonia buffer

Ammonium chloride (10.7 g) is dissolved in 5M ammonia solution (40 ml) and diluted with water to I litre.

Borax buffer

Borax (19.07 g) is dissolved in sufficient amount of water to make I litre of solution.

Duquenois–Levine reagent

This reagent is used for detecting the presence of cannabinoids in a test sample. However, it is not specific for these compounds alone. The reagent is prepared by dissolving vanillin (2 g) and acetaldehyde (0.5 to 1 ml) in ethanol (100 ml). The reagent has to be stored in the dark.

In a small test tube containing 10–20 mg of the test substance, 10 drops of the Duquenois reagent are added and shaken well. After adding 10 drops of concentrated hydrochloric acid the test tube is shaken again. If the sample contains cannabinoids a purple colour is seen. To the mixture, 20 drops of chloroform are added and the contents mixed well. The purple colour gets transferred to the lower chloroform layer.

Forrest reagent

Equal volumes of a 0.2% aqueous solution of potassium dichromate, 30% (v/v) of aqueous sulphuric acid, 20% (v/v) of aqueous perchloric acid and 50% nitric acid solution are mixed together. This reagent gives colours ranging from orange, red, pink, blue and violet with phenothiazines.

FPN reagent

This is another reagent used for the detection of phenothiazines, which give a pink or purple colour with it. The reagent is prepared by mixing together 5 ml of aqueous ferric chloride solution (50 g/litre), 45 ml of aqueous perchloric acid (200 g/litre) and 50 ml of 50% nitric acid solution.

Mandelin reagent

This reagent is prepared by dissolving ammonium vanadate (0.5 g) in water (1.5 ml) and diluting to 100 ml with concentrated sulphuric acid. It is filtered through glass wool. Amphetamines give a purple colour with this reagent

Marquis reagent

This reagent which gives a colour ranging from orange (with amphetamines) to deep red (with acetyl salicylic acid) to dark purple (with morphine, codeine and heroin) is prepared by mixing formalin solution (37%–40% formaldehyde;1 ml) with concentrated sulphuric acid (9 ml). The solution has to be prepared fresh. It can be used in spot testing.

Trinder reagent

This reagent is used for detecting salicylates which give a blue or purple colour with it. The reagent is prepared by dissolving mercuric chloride (40 g) in water (850 ml), to which concentrated hydrochloric acid (10 ml) and hydrated ferric nitrate (40 g) are added, and the volume made up to 1 litre.

Van Urk–Salkowski reagent

It is prepared by dissolving *p*-dimethylaminobenzaldehyde (1 g) in ethanol (100 ml) to which concentrated hydrochloric acid (10 ml) is added. It can also be used as a spray agent for detecting indole derivatives on TLC plates. The colour ranges from red to blue to violet. Full colour development may take about 10 minutes. For example, tryptamine gives a blue colour, the alkaloid reserpine a green colour, and tryptophan a violet-blue colour.

Zwikker's reagent

To 40 ml of a 10% solution of copper sulphate in water, pyridine (10 ml) is added, followed by dilution with water to produce 100 ml of the reagent. This reagent gives a violet colour with barbiturates.

Ammoniacal silver nitrate

To 20 ml of 0.1M silver nitrate solution (in water), sufficient liquor ammonia is added till the initially formed precipitate completely dissolves. This reagent is useful for detecting the presence of antioxidants in a sample. The range of compounds which respond is quite wide —dihydric and trihydric phenols (catechol, hydroquinone, pyrogallol), flavanoids containing a catechol grouping, adrenaline, dopamine and ascorbic acid. The final colour, however, varies from compound to compound. Hydroquinone shows a play of colours—green changing to yellow and finally brown. Wedelolactone also gives a green colour. Adrenaline gives a reddish brown colour. In the case of ascorbic acid the solution turns black. To perform the test, a small amount of the test sample is dissolved in minimum amount of water, with the addition of ethanol, if necessary. To the resulting solution an equal amount of the reagent is added and any colour developing is noted down. It is then warmed in a water bath and any further changes in colour are noted.

Antimony pentachloride

Antimony pentachloride is dried in a vacuum desiccator over phosphorus pentoxide. It is then melted and chlorine gas is passed into the liquid. (Caution! This experiment should be done only in a fume chamber, under the supervision of a teacher.)

The resulting yellow fuming liquid is diluted with 10 times its volume of chloroform. The solution is filtered and stored in a dark, glass-stoppered bottle and kept in a desiccator. The reagent is useful for the detection of steroids, including cardiac glycosides. The test can be done as follows: A drop of an ethanolic solution of the test sample is spotted on a filter paper. Over this spot a drop of the reagent is added and the paper is dried in a current of warm air. The colour which develops is noted down. For example, cholesterol gives an orange colour which changes to brown. It can also be used as a spray reagent for spotting steroid compounds on TLC plates.

Chromotropic acid (1,8-dihydroxynaphthalene-3,6-disulphonic acid)

Chromotropic acid (20 mg) is dissolved in concentrated sulphuric acid (10 ml). To 1 ml of the reagent, a small amount of the test sample, solid or liquid, is added and the colour developed is noted down. The solution is then added to water (0.5 ml) with cooling. Formaldehyde gives a red colour before dilution. The reagent is specific for this aldehyde, and has been used for the detection of the methlenedioxy group, which is a functional group often found in flavonoids and related compounds. Another example is the alkaloid, piperine. In this case the functional group is subjected to acid-catalysed hydrolysis and the formaldehyde liberated is led into the reagent solution. The reagent cannot be stored for more than two days.

Folin–Ciocalteu (Folin–Denis) reagent

This reagent is useful for the detection as well as quantitative estimation of phenolic compounds. The stock is prepared as follows:

Sodium tungstate (10 g) and sodium molybdate (2.5 g) are dissolved in water (80 ml) in a 250-ml round-bottomed flask. To this solution, orthophosphoric acid (5 ml) in concentrated hydrochloric acid (10 ml) is added and the mixture refluxed for 10 hours. After cooling, lithium sulphate (15 g), water (5 ml) and a drop or two of bromine are added and the mixture allowed to stand for two hours. It is then boiled for about 15 minutes to expel any excess bromine (in a fume chamber), cooled, filtered and diluted to 100 ml with distilled water. The resulting yellow-coloured stock solution should be stored at a low temperature (below 4°C). The shelf-life is about 4 months.

The reagent is added to the test sample and the mixture made alkaline with the addition of 2M sodium hydroxide solution. Phenols give a blue colour.

Anthrone reagent for sugars

The reagent is prepared by dissolving 1 g of anthrone in 100 ml of concentrated sulphuric acid.

To about 0.5 ml of the reagent in a microtube, 0.5 ml of an aqueous solution or suspension of the test substance is added carefully, with the help of a capillary tube, so that two layers are formed. On mixing, a deep blue or bluish green colour is formed if the test substance is a carbohydrate.

Ceric ammonium nitrate reagent for alcohols

The reagent is prepared by dissolving 1 g of ceric ammonium nitrate in 2.5 ml of warm 2N nitric acid. 20 to 25 mg of the test substance is dissolved in 0.2 ml of dioxane. One or two drops of this solution are then added to a microtube containing 0.5 ml of the reagent. The formation of a red colour is a positive test.

Dimedone reagent

5,5-Dimethylcyclohexa-1,3-dione (dimedone; 5 g) is dissolved in 100 ml ethanol to make this reagent, which readily gives crystalline derivatives with aldehydes. A milky suspension is immediately formed when the reagent is added to a small amount of an aldehyde; a drop or two of piperidine may be added to catalyse the reaction.

Fuchsin aldehyde reagent (Schiff's reagent)

This reagent is a 0.1% solution of *p*-rosaniline hydrochloride (fuchsin) decolourised with sulphurous acid. It is prepared by dissolving 100 mg of the dye in 20 ml of warm water and saturating the solution with sulphur dioxide gas until the pink colour disappears. The solution is treated with 100 mg of decolorising charcoal, filtered and diluted to 100 ml with water.

The reagent (2 ml) is taken in a small test tube, and a few crystals or a few drops of the test substance are added and the test tube gently shaken. Within a few minutes (5– 30 minutes, depending on the sample), a red to purple colour develops, if the test sample is an aldehyde. This reagent can also be used as a spraying agent on paper chromatograms and TLC plates.

Spray Reagents for the Detection of Compounds on Paper and Thin Layer Chromatograms

Aniline phthalate

Aniline (0.93 g) and phthalic acid (1.66 g) are dissolved in moist butanol (100 ml; butanol is shaken with distilled water in a separatory funnel and the layers allowed to separate; the butanol layer is separated and used. The developed paper or TLC plate is sprayed with the reagent and heated for 10 minutes at 105°C to detect reducing sugars which appear as dark brown spots (rings).

Anisidine phthalate reagent

This is a 0.1M solution of *p*-anisidine and phthalic acid in 96% ethanol. With this reagent, hexoses give a green colour, whereas pentoses give a red-violet colour. Uronic acids appear as brown spots. This is a very sensitive reagent which can detect microgram quantities of a sugar.

Hydroxylamine-Ferric reagent

This consists of three solutions:

(a) A solution of hydroxylamine hydrochloride (1 g) in water (9 ml);
(b) Aqueous sodium hydroxide (2 g of the alkali in 8 ml of water);
(c) A solution of ferric nitrate nonahydrate (4 g) in water (60 ml) and acetic acid (40 ml).

The developed TLC plates are sprayed with a mixture of equal parts of solutions (a) and (b) and then dried at 110°C for 10 minutes.

The plates are then sprayed with a mixture of (c) (45 ml) and concentrated hydrochloric acid (6 ml). The reagent is useful for detecting esters, sugar acetates and lactones.

Vanillin–Sulphuric acid

This reagent should be prepared fresh by dissolving 0.5 g of vanillin in a 4:1 mixture of sulphuric acid and ethanol (100 ml). After spraying with the reagent, the plates are heated for 5 minutes at 100°C. Different compounds give different colours; if the heating is extended, all the spots appear brown. The reagent is useful for the detection of steroids and terpenes.

Zinc chloride

A 30% methanolic solution of zinc chloride is used. The plates, after spraying with the reagent, are heated for 1 hour at 105°C and then examined under a UV lamp. The reagent is used for detecting steroids.

Alcoholic 2,4-dinitrophenylhydrazine

A 1% solution of the reagent in aldehyde-free ethanol is prepared by warming, after adding a few drops of concentrated sulphuric acid. The reagent is useful for detecting aldehydes and ketones. A 0.4% aqueous solution can also be used. It is prepared by dissolving the reagent (0.4 g) in 2N hydrochloric acid (100 ml).

Alcoholic aluminium chloride

Fresh, dry aluminium chloride (yellow in colour; 5 g) is dissolved in distilled methanol (100 ml). The reagent is very useful for detecting 5-hydroxyflavones and flavonols on paper chromatograms, which form a fluorescent complex with the reagent. After spraying and drying, the developed paper is viewed under a UV lamp when the test compounds appear as bright yellow fluorescent spots or rings. This reagent can also be used as a shift reagent in the UV spectroscopic analysis of flavonoids.

Alcoholic ferric chloride

A 5% solution of neutral ferric chloride in aldehyde-free ethanol is useful for detecting a variety of phenolic compounds on paper chromatograms—including flavonoids and related compounds—on paper chromatograms. Colours ranging from brown to purple to green are seen, depending on the degree and pattern of hydroxylation.

Ninhydrin

Ninhydrin (0.3 g) is dissolved in butanol (100 ml) containing acetic acid (3 ml). The reagent is useful for the detection of amino acids, some of which appear without heating; others may require heating up to 100°C. The colour varies from yellow (proline) to purple (phenylalanine and other amino acids). Alkaloids appear as red spots.

Anisaldehyde–Sulphuric acid

To a solution of anisaldehyde (0.5 ml) in acetic acid (50 ml), concentrated sulphuric acid (1 ml) is added. After spraying with this reagent, the chromatograms are heated to 100°C when colour develops. It is a general reagent and can be used for spotting terpenes, steroids and phenols.

Liebermann–Burchard reagent

Four volumes of acetic anhydride are carefully mixed with 1 volume of concentrated sulphuric acid. This is a widely used reagent for the detection of triterpenes and steroids.

Bromocresol green

To a solution of bromocresol green (0.3 g) in 80% (by volume) methanol (100 ml), 8 drops of 30% sodium hydroxide solution are added. The reagent is used for detecting carboxylic acid on paper as well as thin layer chromatograms. Yellow spots against a green background appear. Buffered bromocresol blue solution can also be used when yellow spots appear against a blue background.

Besides the above, the most commonly used reagents for general viewing of TLC plates are iodine vapours and 10% sulphuric acid. Iodine crystals placed in a suitably covered container serve to visualise spots on a TLC plate. In the case of sulphuric acid, after spraying, the plates have to be heated for the colours to develop.

Diazomethane (*Organic Synthesis*, Collective Volume II, 165–7)

Acetylmethyl urea To a solution of acetamide (29.5 g) in bromine (14 ml) in a 500-ml beaker, a solution of sodium hydroxide (20 g in 80 ml of water) is added in drops with vigorous stirring. The resulting yellow solution is heated on a steam bath until effervescence sets in (about 4 minutes). The mixture is heated for 3 more minutes when crystals start appearing. The beaker is then cooled in an ice bath for 1 hour and then filtered. The solid is pressed dry on the funnel under suction and then dried in a desiccator. The compound melts at 169–70°C. Yield is 26 g. (Organic Synthesis, Coll. Vol., II, p. 462).

Nitrosomethyl urea A mixture of acetylmethyl urea (24.5 g) and concentrated hydrochloric acid (25 ml) is heated, with stirring, on a steam bath for about 10 to 15 minutes when no more solid can dissolve. It is then diluted with an equal volume of water and cooled to 10°C in an ice bath. A cold saturated solution of sodium nitrite (19 g in 27.5 ml of water) is run in with stirring. After several minutes of standing in the ice bath, the crystalline nitrosomethyl urea which separates out is collected on a Buchner funnel under suction and washed with about 5 ml of ice cold water. It is then air dried. Yield: 16–18 g; m.p. 123–24°C.

In a 250-ml beaker cooled in an ice–salt bath, aqueous sodium hydroxide (50%; 30 ml) and diethyl ether (100 ml) are taken. When the temperature is 5°C, nitrosomethyl urea (10.3 g) is added in small quantities with shaking. The diazomethane liberated by the action of alkali on nitrosomethyl urea goes into the ether layer. The yield of diazomethane is 63%–70% of the theoretical, that is, about 2.6–3.0 g. The ethereal diazomethane solution thus prepared is quite suitable for esterification of carboxylic acids and *O*-methylation of phenols. If a dry solution is required the ether extract is dried over potassium hydroxide pellets for about 3 hours, filtered and used.

Purification of dimethyl sulphate

(*Vogel's Textbook of Practical Organic Chemistry*, 5th edition, ELBS with Longman, Harlow, Essex, England, p. 430, 1989).

The commercial reagent may be dried by allowing it to stand over anhydrous potassium carbonate (prepared by igniting potassium carbonate in a nickel dish for a couple of hours), or carefully stirring it with an equal volume of ice-cold water in a large beaker, pouring off the upper water layer and then repeating the process with one-third of its volume of cold, saturated sodium bicarbonate solution. After discarding the upper aqueous layer, the heavy liquid is dried over calcium oxide. The reagent thus purified should be all right for *O*-methylations of phenolic compounds. If further purification by distillation is necessary, it should be done in a fume cupboard and in the presence of the supervising teacher. Pure dimethyl sulphate has a b.p. of 72–73°C at 13 mm pressure.

For a more comprehensive list of spray reagents see the following books.

1. Merck E, *E. Merck Handbook—Dyeing Reagents for Thin Layer and Paper Chromatography*, Darmstadt, Germany, 1980.
2. Stahl E, (Ed.), *Thin Layer Chromatography—A Laboratory Handbook*, 2nd Edition, Springer-Verlag, Berlin, 1969.
3. Wagner H and Bladt S, *Plant Drug Analysis—A Thin Layer Chromatography Atlas*, Springer-Verlag, Berlin, 1984.

APPENDIX 2

Preparation of Reagents for the Detection of Alkaloids

Dragendorff's reagent

Bismuth nitrate [$Bi(NO_3)_3$, H_2O; 8.0 g] is dissolved in 30% (w/v) nitric acid (sufficient amount to dissolve the solid). This solution is mixed with a solution of potassium iodide (27.2 g) in water (50 ml). The mixture is allowed to stand for 24 hours and then filtered. The filtrate is made up to 100 ml with water. Alternately, a stock solution is prepared by mixing a solution of bismuth subnitrate (1.7 g) in water (80 ml) and glacial acetic acid (20 ml) with a 50% (w/v) aqueous solution of potassium iodide (100 ml). The mixture is shaken or stirred till it becomes clear and homogeneous. It is stored in a dark bottle. When testing for alkaloids, the stock solution (100 ml) is mixed with glacial acetic acid (200 ml) and diluted to 1 litre by the addition of distilled water. This solution is stable for 2–5 months when stored in a coloured bottle. It gives an orange-red precipitate with a solution of an alkaloid in 1% sulphuric acid.

Dragendorff's reagent can also be used as a spray reagent for detecting the presence of alkaloids on paper and thin layer chromatograms. The alkaloid can be recovered from the precipitate by treatment with sodium carbonate and subsequent extraction with diethyl ether.

Mayer's reagent

This reagent gives a white or pale yellow precipitate with a solution of an alkaloid. It is prepared by mixing a solution of mercuric chloride (2.72 g) in distilled water (120 ml) with a solution of potassium iodide (10 g) in distilled water (40 ml), and making up the mixture to 200 ml distilled water.

Wagner's reagent

This reagent is prepared by dissolving sublimed iodine (1.27 g) and potassium iodide (2 g) in water (20 ml), and making up the solution to 100 ml with water. It gives a brown precipitate with an acidic solution of an alkaloid.

Ammonium reineckate

Ammonium reineckate is prepared as follows. To a saturated solution of 4% ammonium reineckate, hydroxylamine (0.2 g) is added and the solution acidified by the addition of dilute hydrochloric acid. This reagent gives a pink precipitate with alkaloids.

Index of Compounds

Index of Plants

Index of Reagents